History of the Progressive Party 1912–1916

by A M O S   R.   E.   P I N C H O T

Edited with a biographical introduction

by H E L E N E   M A X W E L L   H O O K E R

NEW YORK UNIVERSITY PRESS
Washington Square, 1958

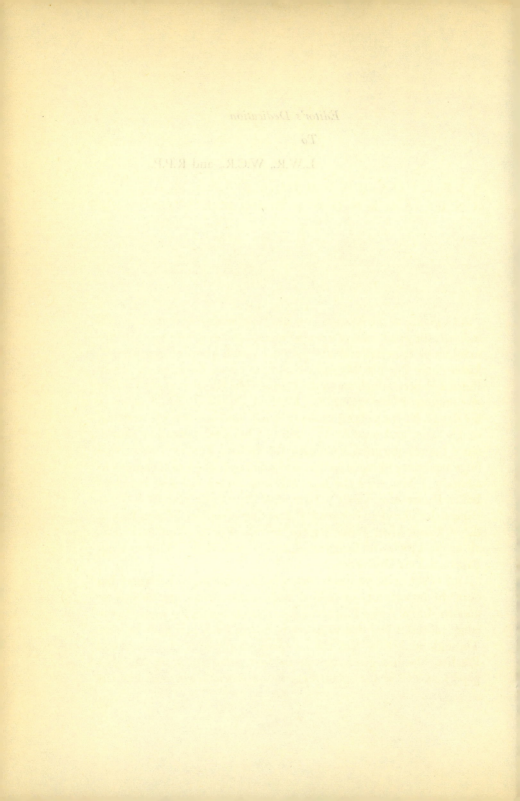

BIBLIOGRAPHICAL NOTE AND ACKNOWLEDGMENTS

As a glance at the footnotes for the Biographical Introduction will indicate, the great bulk of my information comes from two sources—manuscript material and the personal recollections of people who knew Amos Pinchot. My most important source has been the Amos Pinchot Papers, which are in the Manuscripts Division of the Library of Congress, Washington, D.C. Here are deposited carbon copies of his letters, letters to him, drafts of books and articles, memoranda, rough notes, and most of his published material. Second in importance for my purposes have been the Gifford Pinchot Papers, that huge repository of material that is also in the Library of Congress. In addition, I have used the Jane Addams Papers, the Ray Stannard Baker Papers, the Albert J. Beveridge Papers, the Harold L. Ickes Papers, the Theodore Roosevelt Papers, the Woodrow Wilson Papers, the William Allen White Papers, and the Robert Woolley Papers, all at the Library of Congress. I have also used the William Kent Papers at Yale University.

One of the great pleasures connected with editing this *History* has been the opportunity of talking with persons who, in one way or another, knew Amos Pinchot. I have drawn heavily on their knowledge; indeed, I feel that in many ways this book is a joint venture. Throughout I have had the complete cooperation of Mrs. Amos Pinchot. She has given me unqualified access to Amos Pinchot's papers, as well as the opportunity to use Pinchot's personal libraries in New York City and in Milford, Pennsylvania. She has answered my endless questions, and she has asked a number of Pinchot's old friends to talk to me. I am also particularly indebted to Miss Fola La Follette, who for ten years has tirelessly answered my questions and shared with me her unique knowledge of the progressive period and the years when Amos Pinchot was associated with Senator Robert M. La Follette. It is obvious that I have leaned heavily on her knowledge. She has been unfailingly generous to me. Only Mrs. Pinchot and Miss La Follette can know how thoroughly I am in their debt.

Other persons, too, have helped me greatly. Roger Baldwin, Dr. John Haynes Holmes, Dr. Alvin Johnson, Mrs. Agnes De Lima, George Rublee, and Norman Thomas, all of New York City; the late Mrs. William Kent of Kentfield, California, the late Basil Manly, Miss Katherine Brand, George Middleton, Mrs. A. B. Fairbank, and Mrs. Gilbert Roe, all of Washington, D.C., have given me a great deal of information and, as a result, many new insights that I could not have reached through manuscript sources alone. C. A. Horsky of Washington, D.C., answered some questions about trusts that otherwise would have remained forever insoluble to me. One of my particularly informative "living archives" has been Mrs. Margaret De Silver of New York City; she has answered hundreds of questions, she has given me letters of introduction to some of Pinchot's friends, and she has let me use her library.

In all these cases I must stress that while my indebtedness for information is heavy, I am solely responsible for any seeming misinterpretations.

The listing of published sources has posed a troublesome problem. Limitations of space will not allow me to cite the hundreds of books, pamphlets, magazines, and newspapers I have read but not cited. The footnotes contain references to all material specifically cited, but I wish to note my special indebtedness to the work of Professors Link and Mowry. I regret that Professor Richard Hofstadter's *The Age of Reform* (1955) and Professor Link's *Wilson: The New Freedom* (1957) were not available when I wrote the Biographical Introduction. I should like to indicate my special indebtedness to Belle Case La Follette and Fola La Follette's *Robert M. La Follette, June 14, 1855–June 18, 1925* (1953). I have used that informative book far more than my scattered references indicate.

A number of persons have read the Biographical Introduction in whole or in part. Professor William Haller of the Folger Shakespeare Library, Washington, D.C., Jay Leyda of Washington, D.C., Professor Willson Coates of the University of Rochester, Hilda Coates of Rochester, New York, Martin Loftus of the International Monetary Fund, Washington, D.C., Robert Allerton Parker of New York City, Watson Washburn of New York City, Professor Phyllis Bartlett of Queens College, Flushing, New York, and Frances Troy Schwab of Cotuit, Massachusetts, have been generous of their time and their suggestive comments.

The staff of the Manuscripts Division of the Library of Congress have been cooperative far beyond the requirements of professional courtesy. Like everyone who in the past years has read in the Modern Manuscripts section of the Division, I am under heavy obligations to Miss Katherine Brand, formerly chief of that section.

My special thanks go to Peg Snow and Polly Hitchcock, who uncomplainingly typed and retyped the manuscript.

A grant from the Guggenheim Foundation at exactly the right time enabled me to spend an uninterrupted year of reading and necessary interviewing.

Finally, I want to indicate my special gratitude to Laura Wood Roper of Washington, D.C. She cheerfully took time from her own book to read my entire manuscript, to suggest revisions, and to discuss problems. The thanks I here indicate are a small and inadequate token indeed.

For permission to use quotations from unpublished and copyright materials, I am indebted to: Miss Katherine Brand, for the Ray Stannard Baker Papers; the late Mrs. William Kent, for the William Kent Papers; Miss Fola La Follette, for Senator La Follette's *Autobiography;* Mrs. Gifford Pinchot, for the Gifford Pinchot Papers; Harvard University, for the Theodore Roosevelt Letters.

ix

CONTENTS

Section III: Appendixes

Section IV: Notes

Section I

Section 1

EDITORIAL NOTE

Amos Pinchot's *History of the Progressive Party* [1912–1916] is a unique manuscript that forms part of the Amos Pinchot Papers at the Library of Congress in Washington, D.C. Pinchot originally intended to publish his account, but he never completed it. It exists in two drafts. The first five chapters of the manuscript stand in nearly finished form. Typists' dates indicate that these chapters were typed from January 4, 1933, to March 6, 1933. Chapters VI through IX were typed from December 19, 1930, to January 9, 1931. These last three chapters are in somewhat rougher shape than are the preceding five.

The *History of the Progressive Party* grew out of a book that Pinchot projected in the mid-twenties and began to write about 1927. This first book, which Pinchot called *Big Business in America,* was to deal with one of its author's principal intellectual occupations—the interrelations of concentrated wealth and American politics from 1896 to 1932, that is, from the administration of President McKinley to the election of Franklin Delano Roosevelt. The preliminary outlines show that he planned nine chapters, but the actual results fell far short of this design.* He wrote only an introduction, Chapter I ("The Roose-

* The results of Pinchot's labors in connection with these two books are contained in 23 binders, all of them at the Library of Congress. Although at first glance the contents may seem rather a confused jumble, the material consists of outlines, first drafts, revisions of chapters, jottings, and quotations, all (with the possible exception of the quotations) apparently intended to be used in one way or another in his grand study of power. Some of the material, notably the material on oil and steel, he reworked as late as 1934 and 1936.

EDITORIAL NOTE

velt Administration, Steel"), and Chapter II ("The Taft Administration, Coal and Water Power"), which together come to 234 pages.* The *History of the Progressive Party* grew out of this uncompleted earlier work and is dependent on it for its major thesis.† This will explain why, in the present *History,* specifically in Chapter I, Pinchot occasionally refers to points he has made "in an earlier chapter." When they occur, such references are noted in the explanatory editorial notes and are identified as coming from the binder *Steel.*

Big Business in America was to be an economic study. It was to deal with "the problem of concentration of wealth and its control of government, as well as that of monopoly and overproduction." From the first, Pinchot envisaged a distinctly personal approach. In an early note he wrote, "I have tried to trace the process and the general principles employed in acquiring power only in the few instances with which I have been personally thrown in contact." He believed his examples were typical; at the same time he knew that he had no more than skimmed the surface of the subject he was discussing. Much of his material came from government reports and from secondary sources like biographies, histories, and newspapers. From any point of view the result is not successful. Sometimes Pinchot gives personal details that stimulate one's interest, but he never seems in control of his work. The effect is prolix and disorganized; perhaps the subject got out of hand; perhaps he relied too greatly on secondary sources; in any case, such a work requires an enormous amount of synthesis, checking, and verification before hearsay, opinion, and verifiable data can be sifted and fused into what we consider acceptable history.

The more nearly completed *History of the Progressive Party* was intended as a *political* counterpart to *Big Business.* In the *History* Pinchot was on familiar ground; he had a considerable firsthand knowledge of his subject, for he had been a founder of, and an active worker for, the Progressive party and had known many of its intrigues and many of its leaders. More important, his files contained an extensive correspondence with progressives all over the United States. Therefore he went through these files and selected eight boxes of letters to and from the elder La Follette, Colonel Roosevelt, Louis D.

* This much was placed in a binder, misleadingly called *Steel,* where it has since remained.
† See *History,* Chapter I.

4

Brandeis, William Kent, Francis J. Heney, George Record, Norman Hapgood, Harold Ickes, and many other well-known contemporaries. He used his own diaries as well as pertinent articles, speeches, and pamphlets, some of which he had written at the time. His account, he believed, was valuable because he approached the story from an unconventional point of view. "I think it is fair to say," he wrote, "that up till now, no one has given the principals in the 1912 episode their just place in the political and economic setting of their time." He carried his narrative through eight chapters; then in the course of Chapter IX ("Reflections on the Rise and Fall of the Progressive Party"), he faltered and did not finish. Perhaps the lack of satisfactory source material for the year 1916 made the task more difficult than he had anticipated; but, as the Biographical Introduction shows, he became absorbed in matters very different from the political events of 1912–16 and decided not to finish his *History*.

Since the *History* is incomplete, some explanation of editorial procedure is necessary. Chapters I to IV follow Pinchot's revised version, while the last four of necessity follow the text of his earlier draft. Some of the references to the *History* stand within brackets, while others are unbracketed. The unbracketed are Pinchot's own; the bracketed are mine. In places I have supplied words or dates in the text itself; these additions stand within brackets. Titles for Chapters I to V are mine, and I have provided chapter numbers in place of the original "New Chapter" headings. The dates 1912–1916 were not part of the original title of the book. What is now Chapter IV originally consisted of two chapters, the second beginning with "As we look back . . ." (p. 155). In the appendixes I have added material that seemed to me to throw further light on Pinchot's point of view.

Although I probably do not have to explain this point, I have followed the accepted rule that a writer should be allowed to speak for himself, that editorial fussing and correcting frequently amounts to bowdlerizing. Therefore I have retained what some readers may consider occasional infelicities and even barbarities of expression. I have, however, silently corrected misleading or downright ambiguous constructions, such corrections being the accepted prerogatives of an editor; I have also regularized spelling, capitalization, punctuation, errors in tense, and the form of Pinchot's citations. I have capitalized Democratic and Republican, and the word "progressive" when the reference is to the political party; when the movement is indicated, I have left the word in lower case.

The name of Pinchot is well known in the history of the Bull Moose party, but most people think of Gifford, Theodore Roosevelt's friend and lieutenant. Unlike his brother, Amos Pinchot was not a lieutenant. By his own description he was "merely an admiring satellite."* He was also a general handy man. There was another difference between the two Pinchots. Where Gifford Pinchot refused to criticize Theodore Roosevelt openly, Amos differed publicly, finally breaking with the Colonel over trusts and George Perkins. As a Progressive he had belonged to the so-called "radical nucleus" (in less sympathetic quarters sometimes classed with the "lunatic fringe"); when he wrote the *History* he retained his dissident point of view.† That is why, in spite of its unfinished state, the book is a worth-while addition to the moving and often dramatic story of the progressive movement before 1917. That is why this manuscript has been made available to students of modern American political history.

* See Appendix II.

† The reader need not be reminded that Pinchot's account antedates Harold L. Ickes, "Who killed the Progressive Party?" *American Historical Review*, XLVI (1941), 306–37.

BIOGRAPHICAL
INTRODUCTION

On the evening of June 10, 1916, Amos Pinchot walked into the lobby of the Auditorium Hotel in Chicago. Most of the men in that hot and crowded place he knew; some he knew well. He noted that they were "wild-eyed," that they were tearing badges from their coats and throwing them into cuspidors. The word he heard oftenest was "traitor." Pinchot pushed on into the café and joined a group of friends at a table. One of them asked him:*

"How are you on your history?"

"Pretty weak," he replied. "Why?"

"Well, we have run out of adjectives to use on the Colonel, and we are searching history for the names of traitors. Can you help?"

Pinchot had a reputation for invective. Furthermore, he was known for a number of uncomplimentary remarks, public and private, that he had made about the Colonel—Theodore Roosevelt. But this time he rather surprisingly replied that he thought the request was "childish and unjust." Several years later he wrote:

And upon mature reflection, I do still. I do not feel that the great majority of those Progressive delegates who assembled at Chicago in 1916 had a valid right to call Colonel Roosevelt a traitor, or feel grieved at his desertion of the party at the moment when they thought he stood ready to

* This dialogue is cited as Pinchot reported it.
Numbered notes begin on p. 267.

lead it into battle. On the contrary, I think the majority of them . . . got
exactly what was coming to them.[1]

Amos Pinchot had been a founder of the Progressive party in 1912
and an active Roosevelt man in the campaign of that year. His experience had not been happy. Increasingly he had differed with the
Colonel and had left the party sometime before that August afternoon in 1916 when the Colonel, seeking to shift his political course,
had sent the Progressive delegates his "conditional declination."

Pinchot's remark, spoken with seeming dispassion, was the measure of his bitter disillusionment and of the long distance he had
traveled in a short time.

Part I

1873–1912

I

In 1912 Amos Richards Eno Pinchot described the American privileged classes as a small but powerful group who are "well above and
beyond that battle for the crude necessities of life which is the lot of
the average man. . . . They are not obliged to concentrate their
energies upon the task of making a bare living for themselves and
their families."[2]

The description fitted him. His father, James Wallace Pinchot,
had been in the dry-goods business, later becoming the senior partner
in Pinchot and Warren, a New York wall-paper firm. A substantial
businessman and long-time member of the New York Chamber of
Commerce, he was active in numerous educational and philanthropic
causes. He was treasurer of the committee that undertook in 1877 to
raise funds for the Statue of Liberty's long-delayed pedestal.* Something of a connoisseur, he collected paintings, principally of the Hudson River school, and was friendly with artists like Frederick Church,
Jervis McEntee, Eastman Johnson, and with the Irish-American sculp-
tor, Launt Thompson. His literary acquaintances included William
Cullen Bryant, Parke Godwin, and Bayard Taylor, and he was proud
of his long friendship with Edwin Booth. But his interests did not

---

* Other members of the committee included William M. Evarts, Frederic R.
Coudert, Theodore Roosevelt, Sr., and Joseph H. Choate. James Pinchot sub-
scribed $5,000 to the fund.

stop with the arts. He was a pioneer in still another field: American forestry; indeed, his older son described him as "the Father of Forestry in America."[3] He gave some of the money for the Yale Forestry School (the earliest such school in the United States), the Yale Summer School of Forestry, and the Milford (Pa.) Experimental Station (the first Forest Experiment Station in the United States).[4]

Mrs. James Pinchot was born Mary Eno. Her father was Amos Eno, the well-known New York real estate operator and builder. He was responsible for that "visionary project" once known as "Eno's Folly"—the old Fifth Avenue Hotel that he built on some undeveloped pasture land beyond the city limits, at what is now Twenty-third Street, where Fifth Avenue crosses Broadway.[5]

Amos Pinchot, the third and youngest child of James and Mary Pinchot, was born in Paris on December 6, 1873, where his parents were on a pleasure jaunt. He grew up in New York, a boss-controlled city containing over a million inhabitants. Wide open and tolerating almost every form of vice, it was saturated with municipal corruption. The waterfront area was run down and pestilential. In the older part of the city large blocks of slums bred disease. Lawlessness was so general that after dark no woman would willingly venture alone into these districts. Even the new residential sections north of Madison Square were filthy and badly lit, unsafe for casual walking at night. Here the streets were lined with double rows of brownstone houses, each one with a flight of steps leading from the street to the front door. Years later, Edith Wharton recalled as one of the most depressing memories of her youth that "little low-studded rectangular New York . . . hide-bound in its deadly uniformity of mean ugliness."[6]

Ugly it may have been, but there was another side. The fashionable and business center was Union Square, where one could shop at Tiffany's, Brentano's, Gall and Lembke's (the opticians), Arnold Constable's, and other well-known stores. On Broadway, half a block above the Square—indeed, not far from "Eno's Folly"—Huyler's sold that delicious novelty, ice cream sodas. Until 1863 not a store, not a shop, had marred the solidly residential Fifth Avenue, where Henry James's transplanted aristocrat, Lady Barberina, had spent much time behind her ambush of lace and brocade curtains, peeking at the goings-on in the street, where "everything and everyone went by."

One of the most attractive spots in Manhattan was Gramercy Park.

Here, at one time or another, lived Stanford White and Robert Ingersoll and the Barrymores. The Pinchots lived at No. 2, one of those four-storied red brick houses that still face the fenced-in little park. Their neighbors included the Hewitts, the Coopers, the Gerards, and the Minturns. This was not a New York of poverty. In the suffocating summer most of the family friends left for Newport or Bar Harbor, or for their summer places in Connecticut or Massachusetts. Some traveled abroad. In the winter it was a New York of great sociability, of afternoon calls made in broughams with footmen wearing red-topped boots and side whiskers, of skating and driving in Central Park, of supper at Delmonico's, of art exhibits and concerts and dinners.

Here, in a world well ordered and prosperous, Amos Pinchot was brought up with his older brother Gifford and his sister Antoinette. Like many wealthy Americans, his family looked to Europe as a cultural center, and there they frequently traveled. The children were often taken to France and they all spoke French easily. One year Mrs. Pinchot took them West, not because she really wanted to see cowboys and Indians, but because her old friend General William Tecumseh Sherman urged her to see her own country. In summer the family usually went to the Eno home at Simsbury, Connecticut, or to the Pinchot house at Milford, Pennsylvania.

Milford, a small town on the Delaware River, is in Pike County, in the foothills of the Poconos.* In the early nineteenth century great forests still surrounded the town, and the people of Milford—mostly French—made a living from lumbering and trapping. Amos Pinchot's grandfather, Cyril Désiré Constantin Pinchot, came there in 1816 to begin a new life and to find a permanent home. Although he was still in his very early twenties, his life had already been full of adventure. At nineteen he had served as a captain in Napoleon's army and subsequently had taken part in an unsuccessful plot to rescue the deposed Emperor from St. Helena. Expelled from France by the Bourbons, Pinchot fled to England in a fishing boat and a year later arrived in Milford. There he lived for the rest of his life, in time owning a lumber business, land, and the general store—one of those places where one could buy "anything from a silk dress to a plow share."[7]

* One reason for remembering Milford is that Charles Sanders Peirce (1839–1914), the father of pragmatism, retired there to die.

And there his son James was born. James Pinchot owned Milford property and after he moved to New York kept in touch with his home town. He planted trees along many of the streets and gave, in all, five different free libraries. He tore down the general store and built Forest Hall, a stone building that today contains the post office, an auditorium, and a series of small shops. In 1884 he started to build Gray Towers, the Norman manor house that looks across the valley of the Delaware to the Jersey hills. Designed by Richard Morris Hunt, constructed of blocks of stone quarried out of the land on which it stands, it took two years to build. As early as 1870 the Pinchots had begun taking trips abroad, particularly to London and Paris, to buy chests, highboys, beds, and chairs for their new house.

Many people visited them. Edwin Booth, a neighbor at Gramercy Park, stayed at the old house. A special horse was kept in the stable for General Sherman, who often went to Gray Towers, where he liked to ride through the forest and along the Sawkill.*

To both Amos and his older brother Gifford, Milford was always one of the most important spots in the world. It was their home, and no matter where they traveled or how much they moved about, there they always returned.

Amos went to school first in New York City and then to Westminster School at Dobbs Ferry. From Westminster he entered Yale in the class of 1897. This choice was obvious: a great-great-uncle, a great-grandfather, uncles, a cousin, and his brother Gifford had all gone to New Haven. When he grew older he described a Yale education as "a grudgingly performed mechanical ritual,"[8] but in his undergraduate days he enthusiastically fulfilled the rites. In his freshman and sophomore years Amos was treasurer of his class boat committee, and in his last year he was on the Senior Prom Committee. He was a member of the golf club; his social clubs included He Boule, Psi Upsilon, and Skull and Bones. A senior yearbook picture shows him dressed

* Later he used the Pinchot horse when he posed for the Saint-Gaudens statue that now faces the New York Plaza. A Pinchot family story has it that General Sherman was reluctant to pose, but that Mrs. James Pinchot persuaded him. The General agreed to go if Mrs. Pinchot would go with him. She went. Saint-Gaudens was so struck by her beauty that he asked her to pose for the angel leading the General's horse, and she did. (Lloyd Lewis in *Sherman, Fighting Prophet* [New York, 1932, p. 646] indicates that the persuader was Whitelaw Reid.)

in a well-cut tweed suit and wearing a high collar; a pince-nez attached to a cord dominates the face, so that one looks twice before realizing that he was rather long of skull, curly-haired, and handsome.

Occasionally he wrote for the yearbook. His writing was about what one would expect from a young man with a good background and a general education. One of his professors was "Billy" Sumner, who influenced him considerably and whom he later described as one of America's most brilliant teachers and profound scholars. At New Haven he read American and European history and he developed a passion for Shakespeare and Euripides. This passion never left him. All his life he read widely; one of his later notebooks includes material from Bertrand Russell, Tolstoi, Gibbon, Volney, Walt Whitman, and Emerson.[9] Bury and G. M. Trevelyan he read again and again. In the course of his everyday work he read economics, sociology, and history. For relaxation he read westerns. But always, until he died, he returned to Shakespeare (he was particularly fond of the sonnets) and to Euripides.

Shortly after Amos' graduation, Gifford Pinchot, who had just been appointed confidential Forest Agent, left for an inspection tour of the Northwestern Forest Reserves in Idaho, Washington, and Montana. Amos went along, and later Henry Stimson joined them. These weeks of hunting and exploring Amos always remembered as one of the happiest summers of his life.[10]

On his return to New York in the fall of 1897 Amos entered the Columbia University School of Law. At this time the United States was well on its way to the "splendid little war" that was formally declared against Spain in April 1898. Three weeks after the declaration of war Amos enlisted; years later he explained, "I enlisted for service in the Spanish-American war because I felt that Spain was exploiting Cuba."[11] Although his father wanted him to take a commission, he chose to go in as a private in Troop A of the New York Volunteer Cavalry and trained at Camp Alger, Virginia. He went in a private and he came out a private. The war lasted only about three and a half months after Pinchot's enlistment. In this brief term of service, during which he was attached to Army Headquarters in Puerto Rico, he was disciplined for lateness at least once; he fell off a cliff and a horse landed on top of him, permanently injuring his hip; and he got a bad case of typhoid fever.

The war over, he returned to his studies, this time at the New York Law School. In 1900 he was admitted to the bar and soon after was appointed a deputy assistant district attorney in New York City. But apparently Pinchot did not like the everyday practice of law. A year later he left the district attorney's office and thereafter did not bother with cases unless they involved a cause in which he was interested. Instead he managed his mother's estate, as well as his own, Gifford's, and his sister Antoinette's.

He went to balls and operas and was considered a society swell. Generally speaking, Pinchot loved and always did love elegance and the formalities of social life; he built a white stone house at 1021 Park Avenue; he belonged to clubs, including the Racquet and Tennis, the Yale, the University, and the Boone and Crockett, that club of big-game hunters founded by Theodore Roosevelt. Born into the Republican party, as a matter of course he belonged to the Republican Club.

Often he visited Washington, where his mother, father, and Gifford now lived, for in 1898 Gifford had been appointed Chief Forester, later becoming a well-known member of President Roosevelt's "tennis cabinet." The diplomatic and official world came to his mother's home, 1615 Rhode Island Avenue, the large house that a friend later described as the best hotel in the city. Through Gifford, Amos met many Washingtonians; one of them was President Roosevelt, who occasionally invited him to the White House or for a brisk walk through Rock Creek Park with the tennis cabinet.

He was, of course, interested in civic matters; one would be surprised if he had not been, for his father, Gifford, and (as Pinchot said) Theodore Roosevelt all set examples for him to follow. In those early years he usually pursued what he later called "mild civic dissipations" on charitable boards. He was a trustee of the University Settlement, the Association for Improving the Condition of the Poor, and the Orthopedic Hospital, and a manager of the Manhattan State Hospital for the Insane. Such enterprises he considered a necessary part of reform, and he was pleased that he was doing good. He worked hard; "he thought he was a sincere reformer, and took lots of trouble to establish himself in that belief."[12] In 1908 he regarded Republican and Democratic politics and vote getting with some disdain.[13] But, soon after, the meaning of privilege, the function of government, the distribution of wealth, became intensely important matters to him.

13

At the same time he decided that his civic efforts had been trivial—"patching up the butt ends of humanity which privilege and poverty had broken and cast into the gutter"; his "civic dissipations" had been "hypocritical" and "harmful"; he and all those who attempted such reform were working in "petty movements which got nobody anywhere, but merely tickle the conscience of those who like to picture themselves as actively engaged on the side of civic righteousness."[14] The change was not capricious; it resulted from a political controversy that is now almost forgotten.

II

That controversy was the Ballinger-Pinchot case. As every student of the progressive period knows, it centered on the conservation policies of Theodore Roosevelt and William Howard Taft, and Gifford Pinchot was one of the principals.[15] All the Pinchots believed Gifford destined for greatness. Amos believed that the future of American conservation depended on his brother, and that in time he might be elected president of the United States; Gifford's name must be defended and at the same time the conservationists must get their immensely important cause before the American people. Amos threw himself into the fight with such fervor that forty years later Gifford Pinchot recalled:

The man to whom I naturally turned first was my brother. . . . He could not, of course, appear as my formal representative. Nevertheless, his advice and his help were invaluable. . . . He was indispensable, and was especially useful in getting the facts to the public before and after the hearings were over and the verdict rendered.[16]

In these months Amos Pinchot saw and learned many new things. For the first time he began to understand the inner workings of grand politics. "It is easy to write of America—but hard to write of it discerningly, because we have seen it for so short a time," he later wrote in a private notebook. "I came a little into the light, or perhaps we should call it the darkness, when, in the winter of 1909 and 1910, in a great congressional investigation, I saw the inside of the American cup."[17]

What he saw disillusioned yet exhilarated him, filled him with a sense of mission. He emerged from the controversy a dedicated progressive, an enemy of government by special privilege, a passionate devotee of the principles of popular government.[18]

In the Ballinger case he was fascinated by the economic implications that unrolled before him. He saw how powerful groups, notably the Morgan-Guggenheim interests, sought to control public lands for their own gain. Small wonder that civic reform seemed of only limited concern; after 1910 the interrelation of politics and economic forces and their interplay with government became his basic interest. As far as Ballinger was concerned, the question whether he was a good or bad man was negligible. Ballinger was "merely a symptom of the disease which has attacked the Republican Party, if not the country at large, and I believe that it is of the utmost importance to show up this symptom in plain strong colors in order to diagnose very clearly the disease itself."[19] In other words, the controversy was "part of the great political, or rather ethical, contest between the interests," and its value lay in the way it could be used to help the American people regain what they had apparently lost—the controlling voice in government.

Throughout 1910 Pinchot acted as his brother's adviser and liaison officer. He experienced deep disillusion when his old friend Harry Stimson first agreed and then refused to represent Gifford before the congressional committee. On Stimson's advice, Gifford engaged George Wharton Pepper, a choice that Amos later regretted. When Gifford Pinchot went to Porto Maurizio for his crucial conference with Colonel Roosevelt, he delegated his brother to keep in touch with his lawyers. Amos Pinchot's correspondence with Pepper suggests that he was already arriving at his later expressed opinion: "to all intents and purposes, Gifford had no counsel." Pepper and Amos did not always agree on what was important, and after one conference Pinchot wrote somewhat severely:

It seemed to me that your conception of the needs of the situation did not sufficiently embrace the necessity of giving to the country a clear-cut outline of the methods which are being used against the people by members of the Administration who are too sympathetic with the special interests.[20]

Later, probably in an attempt to offset what he considered Pepper's ineptitudes, he retained his old friend and college classmate, Nathan A. Smyth, as Pepper's assistant.

When the two Pinchots won permission from President Taft to present a memorandum "upon the evidence taken at the hearings in the Interior Department held to determine the validity of the thirty-three so-called Cunningham coal entries in Alaska,"[21] Amos Pinchot wrote the brief submitted by counsel.*[22] Submerged in its 127 pages are statements of principle on three problems that were henceforth his lifelong interests—monopoly, the conservation of natural resources (in this case, coal), and the question of how far corporations should be allowed to control natural resources. Within the next year he was acting as a specialist on such matters; for Louis D. Brandeis, who had been working on the general problem, put Pinchot to work drafting a bill that would ensure the development of the resources of Alaska while protecting the territory from exploitation.[23]

In addition to opening new interests, the Ballinger case cemented friendships that lasted for many years. One was with Brandeis, whose carefully reasoned attitude on many industrial and political questions found Pinchot's ready acceptance. In addition, he was impressed by Brandeis' work in bringing social questions into court.† George Rublee,[24] who was associated with Brandeis and who wrote the brief for Louis Glavis, remembers that Amos Pinchot traveled to Boston from New York at considerable inconvenience because he was interested in the brief and wanted to see how Rublee was writing it. The outgrowth of their meetings and conferences was another lifelong friendship; for Rublee found Amos "intelligent and acute, loveable and gallant."[25]

As was natural in the circumstances (for it will be remembered that the Insurgents made the case their own), he saw a great deal of the progressive senators, particularly Dolliver and La Follette. Cummins, Clapp, and Beveridge he also saw and liked. He was friendly, too, with the Insurgent congressmen and was already in active correspondence with a number of the men who were to become prominent in the progressive crusade of 1912.[26]

Of them all, he most admired La Follette. To the end of his life

---

* *The Outlook,* XCVII (January-April 1911), 49, praised the brief in a long editorial that began, "Should a virtual monopoly of the accessible coal land of Alaska now belonging to the people of the United States be granted to a group of thirty-three men?"

† In 1916 he worked actively in support of Brandeis' nomination to the Supreme Court.

Pinchot thought La Follette one of the truly great men of the era. Their social and political philosophies were similar. La Follette epitomized his own definition of the spirit of moral reform when he asserted that "defeat was a matter of no consequence." The Senator's constant fight for the "basic issues," his unique record of social legislation, his battle for popular government, his refusal to compromise on important points for the sake of political expediency, his leadership of the Insurgent forces, all influenced Pinchot. The events of 1912 temporarily separated them, but in the war years they became reconciled and remained friends until La Follette's death.[27]

Many of the letters Pinchot wrote in 1910 and 1911 are worth noting because he was here developing ideas that he held later, in the 1930's; in them we find the key to his subsequent opposition to the New Deal. One of his basic beliefs was that the purpose of government is "the furthering of the interests of the individual."[28] Another was that "the Government should be first, last and always, an instrument for the happiness, health, and material welfare of the people,"[29] and closely related was his attitude toward socialism. A strong individualist, Pinchot did concede that the socialists "have been very sound in just one faith, the faith that Government could be used for the benefit of everybody, and with this end in view could do many things better than anybody else."[30] But he believed that the socialists were sentimental and unrealistic. The individual, he always contended, could do far better than any government. Nevertheless he argued passionately that the government should control natural monopolies and railroads, but in the fields where he advocated these concessions to state socialism, he, like his friend George Record, would tolerate them only as a means of "restoring free industrial competitive conditions in the large fields of industry where he was convinced the government should never enter."[31]

In the summer of 1910 he was principally concerned with firing his sluggish friends with his own zeal. "I wish you would get your active intelligence to work on the political situation today," he wrote to a misguided Democratic friend. "It seems to me it is vitally and almost thrillingly interesting."[32] Like many a convert to a new cause, he reacted to almost everything he heard and saw. Gifford had just rewritten Theodore Roosevelt's Ossawatomie speech, and Amos followed closely the comments and reverberations. He was disturbed by a conversation with Henry Stimson, who told him that he believed the cause of the present unrest could be traced to the unavailability of good homesteads in the West—a doctrine that sounded to Pinchot like something out of Elihu Root,[33] although to us it recalls Frederick Jackson Turner.

As a concrete means of helping the progressives, Pinchot gave money to several campaigns.[34] He thought he would join Gifford in contributing to Stimson's campaign for the governorship, although he hated to help anyone "get elected, even Henry, on a rotten platform, but of course he does not understand."[35] He experienced the pride of co-authorship when Peter Dunne took some of his material in order to convert it into a series of sage remarks by Mr. Dooley. Finally, he wrote his mother that he was much interested in a progressive magazine that might be founded in a few months.[36] This was probably the project that involved buying *Success Magazine,* a design that H. H. McClure quickly discouraged.[37] Pinchot's letters were full not only of plans but of comments on the political scene, revealing the excitement of his discovery that the American people were reawakening politically, that the long overdue revolt against privilege was taking concrete shape:

> The progressives, I believe, are trying to bring about a condition where public servants will be less politicians than they are today, and political ends will be subordinated to the duties of effective administration. . . . What the progressive movement needs today is not loud shouting but men who will take the time to sit down and consider how government will fulfill the real purpose of good for which it was invented.[38]

Such remarks suggest a surprising insularity. He sounds as if he were unfamiliar with the magnificent work the Senate Insurgents had already accomplished during the past three years. He never mentions Middle Western insurgency, apparently not knowing that as early as 1909 some of the progressive members of Congress had been discussing "the formation of a national league to promote progressive legislation."[39] Somewhat naïvely lumping together as a base lot all politicians who did not work for the common good, he found, fortunately, that some might be more amenable to the idea of public welfare than others. This amenable class he viewed with hope: "Whatever the faults of the men who are leaders in the progressive movement,

I think that they have in common the positive advantage of standing for aboveboard methods and no special privilege for any class of citizens." In spite of their drawbacks, he would work with them. "If the Devil himself led a campaign with such an idea in view I should not on account of any feeling that his past career had been a checkered one refrain from doing anything I could to help him along."[40]

This message was too urgent to share with only a few friends. Pinchot must get it into print, for the American people must know what was happening. In September 1910 *McClure's* published his "Two Revolts Against Oligarchy."[41] Here he drew the parallel between the insurgent movements of 1850 and 1910, arguing that the same industrial and political causes that brought about the Civil War produced the later insurgency. "The Insurgents are the true Republicans of today," he asserted, and offered as a cure for the abuses of Stalwart Republicanism the progressivism of Theodore Roosevelt.

The circumstances of publication, in themselves an interesting example of the circulation of political ideas, must have been highly gratifying to a man who was appearing in a national magazine for the first time. He tried to sound deprecatory but he could not disguise his gratification; for although the article reached the editorial offices after the issue had been entirely made up, the editors decided to publish it immediately. This meant that at considerable expense it had to be tacked on to an already completed book. "Two Revolts" got another boost when the Scripps-owned Newspaper Enterprise Association syndicated a large section, so that Pinchot got several million additional readers in parts of the country *McClure's* did not reach.[42] Six months later a doctor in Canton, Illinois, wrote that "Two Revolts" had created so much interest throughout the West that he wanted to distribute ten thousand copies over the country.[43]

Pinchot sent copies to Washington, New York, Boston, and wherever else he thought a sympathetic friend would read it. Reactions were mixed. Insurgents like La Follette and Clapp praised him; Beveridge wrote to him somewhat condescendingly, as from one author to another, assuring him that he had written "a crackerjack."[44] From California Gifford wrote to his mother, "You ought to hear people talk about Amos' article. Men like Governor Pardee* tell me they have read it two or three times, and everyone is agreed that it is

* George C. Pardee, governor of California, 1902–6.

beyond question the article of the month. It has given Amos an important position at one stroke."[45] In contrast, most of his old New York friends thought his position extreme. Perhaps some of them anticipated the complaint of an elderly cousin who, two years later, wrote that she was losing sleep over his unhappy theories of government, his "fatal tendency to put the bottom on the top."[46] Undoubtedly others agreed with J. P. Morgan, who cordially disliked Colonel Roosevelt and sometime later bluntly told Pinchot so.

As he [Morgan] was leaving my house, one day, where he had come to see a relative who was stopping with me, he suddenly turned, with a fierce gleam in his eye, and growled at me, "I don't like your friend Roosevelt; he's no good. You'll find that out and so will Gifford." And he was so shaken by this sudden gust of rage, that he tripped on the steps, missed his footing, and fell down the stoop. Luckily he was unhurt, though considerably ruffled, and, jumping up before I could reach him, he climbed heavily into his car, slammed the door, and disappeared, shouting an address to the chauffeur.[47]

Pinchot, however, seemed unperturbed by the adverse reactions and viewed the results with equanimity. "Not more than half the people in New York who read it seem to think I am sane and even the ones who class me as *non compos* feel more sorrow than anger," he told Gifford.[48]

III

For more than a year some of the progressive senators and representatives in Washington had been discussing the possibilities of a league that would support progressive legislation in the various states.[49] La Follette, an expert in assessing the strength of progressive trends, decided that the time was ready for the formation of a cohesive national organization. Late in December 1910 he drafted a tentative set of principles and a constitution. These he sent to a small group of well-known progressives whose backing would unquestionably guarantee the genuineness of the organization. Nine United States senators, one former senator, six governors, sixteen congressmen, and nineteen private individuals signed the call. The private citizens included Ray Stannard Baker and Louis D. Brandeis of Massachusetts; Charles R. Crane of Illinois; James R. Garfield of Ohio;

William Kent and Francis J. Heney of California; W. S. U'ren of Oregon; Gilbert Roe of New York; William Allen White of Kansas; and Gifford and Amos Pinchot. These names indicated coast-to-coast support. Soon afterward, on January 21, 1911, the National Progressive Republican League was organized at La Follette's home, 1864 Wyoming Avenue, Washington, D.C. One notes that Theodore Roosevelt was urged to join and declined.

The organization of the National Progressive Republican League, its support of La Follette as presidential candidate, the shift of many of its individual members to Roosevelt, and the ensuing formation of the Progressive Republican party are part of Amos Pinchot's *History* and therefore need not be discussed here. Nevertheless, his account should be read against a background of information he does not give.

The new group's first problem was the selection of a progressive candidate for president. It was inconceivable that the League should limit its activities to progressive legislation; an attempt at the presidency was an obvious move, particularly when national feeling against the conservative Republicans was mounting. Roosevelt had already been approached and had firmly declined to consider the nomination. As Pinchot points out, many possibilities were discussed, many names were offered, but of them all, only one name persistently survived. That name was La Follette. No one else was of his stature. Both Pinchots supported him, being certain that Colonel Roosevelt, whom they would have preferred, would not accept the nomination. Senator La Follette was not so sure. Highly suspicious of the purity of Roosevelt's intention to stay in retirement if the progressive chances looked promising, he was also suspicious of some of the Colonel's more ardent supporters, particularly Gifford Pinchot and James Garfield. He emphatically refused to become a stalking horse for another candidate who would remain in the background until the proper moment, when he could take over and ride to victory. As he said with all candor in his *Autobiography,*

[Progressivism] had become my life work, and I felt that I had achieved results of a character too important and substantial to lend myself to any campaign plans which might permit me to be made a mere pawn in the national game. . . . I estimated my own worth to the Progressive cause too highly to consent to being used as a candidate for a time, and then, to serve some ulterior purpose, conveniently broken and cast upon the political scrap heap, *my ability to serve the Progressive cause seriously damaged, and possibly the movement itself diverted* and subordinated to mere personal ambition.[50]

He repeatedly stated that he would oppose such a shift, no matter who the candidate might be. As the requests that he announce his candidacy increased, he stipulated that if he did agree to run, his backers must understand that he was in it to the finish, that he would withdraw for no man. This is essential for an understanding of La Follette's position and must be kept in mind throughout Pinchot's description of the difficulties during the hectic months that preceded the Senator's undoing.

The National Progressive Republican League leaped ahead. Within six weeks state Progressive Leagues had been organized in Minnesota, Michigan, Nebraska, South Dakota, Washington, and Wisconsin. Individual Eastern members included Norman Hapgood of *Collier's,* S. S. McClure of *McClure's,* Howard Brubaker of *Success,* and Lincoln Steffens. From the beginning, when the movement for La Follette's candidacy got under way, Amos Pinchot was one of his most energetic supporters. In the middle of March the Senator asked him to come to Washington for a conference. Pinchot did so, and the two men talked for a long time. "He is anxious to take immediate steps looking to the nomination of a proper Republican candidate for President," Amos told his brother.[51] To Crane he wrote that the Senator wanted to seize "the opportunities of the present situation"; that he had suggested a few progressives get together to raise a fund and draft a statement telling why they had done so. The explanation would be that the Taft administration was not acting in the interests of the people.[52] Pinchot thought this course eminently wise. He immediately got in touch with E. A. Van Valkenburg, editor of the Philadelphia *North American* (whom he later described as having been "the sage counsellor, the wily Ulysses of the Progressive group");[53] together they talked with La Follette and planned immediate action. Pinchot was delighted, for "there has been too much conversation and not enough things done."[54]

In line with getting things done, he talked with Brandeis, who promised to do anything he could in Boston.[55] Pinchot himself pledged $10,000 to the campaign, remarking, "I think it is the best cause that I ever contributed to."[56] His brother and William Kent each contributed $10,000, and Charles R. Crane agreed to give $5,000 a month until the national convention met in Chicago.[57]

Meanwhile the conferences in search of a strong candidate continued. La Follette was repeatedly urged to run and he repeatedly refused. He suggested other men, all of whom were considered and all of whom were turned down. In his *Autobiography* he tells of a "typical meeting," held in Senator Bourne's committee room. Several of the best-known progressive senators and representatives and a group of leading progressives, principally from the Middle West, discussed the presidential possibilities, dismissed each one, and concluded by urging La Follette to run. Many such meetings took place before the Senator, convinced that he would get the support he stipulated, consented.[58] In July the campaign began in earnest;[59] by late August La Follette headquarters had been opened in Washington, D.C., and work was well under way.

Reacting to this new impetus, the progressive organization gained strength with such rapidity that the strategists decided to call a large conference that would demonstrate the extent and vitality of the movement. This conference was held at the La Salle Hotel in Chicago; it began on October 16, 1911, and lasted three days. Present were three hundred progressives from thirty states who, before they adjourned, passed a resolution supporting La Follette's candidacy.[60] Ironically, this impressive demonstration for La Follette did much to undermine Colonel Roosevelt's expressed determination not to be a candidate in 1912. His behind-the-scenes supporters increased their activities, and from this time on the disintegration of La Follette's strength became evident. Many regard the subsequent scuttling of La Follette for Roosevelt as an act of political treachery.

Before the conference Pinchot was active in rounding up New York progressives who wanted to see the Senator nominated.[61] Delighted with the results of his scouting, he described the political situation as "immensely satisfactory." The Western response was strong and matters were picking up in the East. Periodicals like the *Saturday Evening Post* and the *American Magazine* published articles on La Follette, giving him a great deal of favorable attention. "People are beginning to ask whether after all he is not a pretty safe kind of man,"

23

Pinchot reported to Garfield. Pinchot believed in his candidate not only politically but personally. He considered him open-minded, a student, not vindictive, endowed with a remarkable temperament—in short, ideal.[62] If he were elected, Pinchot reasoned, his advisers would include Garfield, Brandeis, and Gifford Pinchot; surely the Senator would listen attentively to their suggestions.

To William Kent, Amos Pinchot sent a glowing report. The Chicago meeting was successful and impressive, "a proof of great progressive strength throughout the country." Everything looked wonderfully promising. George L. Record, Charles R. Crane, and Mark Sullivan agreed that "it is most probable that we will be able to defeat Taft for the renomination, and that La Follette will be the Republican candidate," a heartening possibility because the consensus was that Woodrow Wilson had misjudged his pace and had got off too fast too soon. The prospect of La Follette's election, once remote, now seemed encouragingly closer.[63]

But in spite of the vigorous showing at Chicago, La Follette faced a serious problem. His strength was largely Western and that was not enough. To win the nomination, he must be assured of Eastern support. In November he showed Ray Stannard Baker a telegram from Chester Rowell, chairman of the La Follette organization in California, stating that 400 progressives gathered from all parts of the country had unanimously declared for him. Not deluded by this encouraging show, Baker realistically commented: "His [La Follette's] stock is growing rapidly, but he has little or no following in the East."[64] The situation demanded an educational campaign, particularly in New York. As Amos Pinchot put it, the progressives must show that "La Follette is not a wild man, but a sane and constructive statesman, who wants to aid business by constructive legislation and has no desire to destroy it."[65] Pinchot discussed the general Republican situation with his brother, with Charles R. Crane, Medill McCormick, Rudolph Spreckels, George L. Record, with Senators Beveridge and Clapp, and with Walter Houser, La Follette's campaign manager. They all agreed something could be done, that Taft was steadily losing ground, and that for the first time in years the solid line of the reactionary Republicans seemed to be cracking.

As reports of progressive strength gained force, however, disquieting rumors also reached La Follette's headquarters. Colonel Roosevelt, shrewdly aware of public sentiment, evidently recognized the trend. To some of the experts his frequently stated resolution that he would not try for the nomination seemed to be disappearing like an ice cake in the sun. Late in November Ray Stannard Baker commented on a conference he had attended with La Follette, Gifford Pinchot, Walter Houser, and Gilson Gardner, who had just come back from Oyster Bay. "Will Roosevelt be a candidate! That is the great question."[66] The Wisconsin Senator, too, was perturbed. Sensing the Colonel's shifting attitude, La Follette thought he detected signs that the solid support he had insisted on was dwindling, and he became increasingly suspicious of Gifford Pinchot and James Garfield. As La Follette later described it, he believed that men like Gifford Pinchot were guilty of treachery: while they ostensibly supported him, they were negotiating with Roosevelt behind his back. It is true that he could get hold of nothing explicit, but his conviction grew that the Colonel might decide to stage a *coup*. Other people agreed. "[T.R.] can get the Progressive following from La Follette if he wants it—while La Follette is bearing the heavy brunt and toil of the work of making the Progressive campaign," Baker wrote.[67]

By December 12 the campaign for uninstructed delegates had begun. On or about December 8, Ray Stannard Baker saw Theodore Roosevelt at the *Outlook* office and walked with him to the Long Island train. Baker told Roosevelt that the progressives in Washington, D.C., were in a great state of uncertainty about the Colonel's possible candidacy. Roosevelt evasively replied that he had given encouragement to no one. "But," wrote Baker, "I soon saw that he had got a good deal further toward welcoming the idea than he was two weeks ago, when Gilson Gardner was up here to meet him." Baker, privately reminded of a war horse sniffing "the air of distant battles," pointed out that the first presidential primaries would be held in North Dakota in March; he emphasized that the former President must make up his mind. "I don't see why I should," T.R. replied; but Baker saw clearly that if there were sufficient demand, he would come in.[68]

Meanwhile the cleavage within the progressive ranks widened and the La Follette desertions continued. Pinchot tells us that by mid-December the progressive leaders had turned to the Colonel in such numbers that a few of the Senator's closest advisers met at La Follette's house to discuss the black situation, and that the Senator set about writing a letter offering to withdraw in Roosevelt's favor if the Colonel would assert himself immediately.[69] The La Follette version contradicts this story: the Senator never dreamed of getting out once he had agreed to go in, nor would he write such a letter.[70] A possible explanation of this much-discussed episode is that La Follette frequently liked to hold conferences and discussions before a matter was settled. In case of differences, the arguments were often long and loud. Sometimes La Follette was converted, sometimes the advisers won. At the meetings in December and January the subject of sending the letter was perhaps discussed. Someone may have presented a draft, but the Senator himself had no part in it.[71]

Meanwhile the hostility had increased to such a degree that Amos Pinchot felt he must try to make peace. At least twice he arranged luncheons for Theodore Roosevelt and La Follette, where the matter could be discussed, but each time he failed because the Senator did not wish to appear. Pinchot was in a peculiarly advantageous position as a negotiator; he had entree to Roosevelt, and although La Follette mistrusted Gifford, he liked Amos and believed in his integrity. The Senator had good reason to believe in his support, for Pinchot "arranged for" and "made possible" the highly successful Carnegie Hall meeting of January 22, which La Follette described as one of the best of his long career.[72] Immediately after this meeting, when the antagonism between the two sides was reaching its height, La Follette wrote a touching letter of thanks to Pinchot, affirming his confidence in his loyalty and understanding and assuring him of his friendship, whatever the outcome of the unhappy struggle.

Having failed to bring Roosevelt and La Follette together, Pinchot tried another tactic. Apparently he reasoned that if La Follette would not negotiate in person, he, Amos Pinchot, might deal directly with Roosevelt, urging him to clarify his position.[73] Twice—once at the *Outlook* office and once at the University Club—he talked to the Colonel. He emphasized that La Follette must be treated honorably, for his leadership in the progressive movement had made possible both the fight against Taft and Roosevelt's potential candidacy.[74] Both times he urged T.R. to state publicly that he would not accept the nomination, that he was stepping aside for the Senator. To these representations the Colonel was always urbane and agreeable; he spoke warmly of La Follette, but he refused to indicate his intentions. In later years Pinchot described this behavior as "the hyphenated I-don't-want-it-but-must-not-resist-the-will-of-the-people way that has become so popular among candidates."[75]

Throughout the last part of January the uncertainties increased, the tensions mounted. By this time the two Pinchots and Medill McCormick, three principal backers, were advising La Follette to relinquish his claims, but he refused to consider their advice. After a particularly painful session on January 29 the Pinchots and Gilson Gardner withdrew their support; Amos Pinchot then wrote to the Senator that he regretted T.R.'s attitude toward the nomination, but feared more than he could say that La Follette's decision to stay in would mean that a reactionary would be nominated at Chicago and that the progressives all over the country would be split into factions.[76] He explained his break this way: although he did not think the Senator should be abandoned, he thought that the progressives should pick the more useful man. La Follette was a real progressive; the Colonel was less of a progressive; but this difference was balanced by Roosevelt's great hold upon the American people. Furthermore, even if he was not advanced in his thinking, he was on the people's side. One last consideration topped all the others: La Follette, it now appeared, could not be elected president in 1912, but Theodore Roosevelt did have a chance to win.[77] In other words, expediency should decide the candidate.

Expediency was aided by a heaven-sent accident. On February 2 the Senator came to Philadelphia to speak at the annual dinner of the Periodical Publishers Association. (The story is well known, but the accounts are contradictory.) He arrived late and desperately tired, harassed by the strain of the past months, sick with worry because his youngest child, Mary, was to be operated on the next day, deeply troubled by the evidences of treachery among his own followers. Amos Pinchot, who was there, gives in the *History* his version of how La Follette apparently lost his place in the manuscript, became confused, rambled, and repeated himself for an hour and a half before sinking exhausted into his chair.

No more was needed. When he started to speak, La Follette was one of the leading contenders for the Republican presidential nomination; when he finished, he was out of the running. Quickly the reluctant

27

backers of Battling Bob seized their chance and repudiated their man. Across the country they renounced him. The episode, which they magnified out of all proportion, gave them an opportunity for self-righteous excuses: La Follette's physical condition, they said, made further support impossible; they could and would support only one candidate—Theodore Roosevelt.

IV

With La Follette disposed of, the Roosevelt supporters could turn their attention to the Colonel's political future. He in turn obliged his adherents by yielding to the prearranged importunities of seven progressively inclined governors who begged him to consider the Republican candidacy. Their plea was dated February 10. Two weeks later T.R. publicly yielded to this pressure, and matters began moving with speed. Soon after, Gifford wrote Amos that Senator Dixon of Montana had "agreed to take general charge of the prenomination campaign if $100,000 can be raised to give him the certainty of a fair chance to win out, and he very properly wants the money in hand before he begins."[78]

Although the New York primaries, held in April, showed that only about one third of the voters there had come out for the Colonel, Amos Pinchot nevertheless regarded the returns with considerable satisfaction: the proportion was higher than could have been expected, for the progressives had had to fight under several disadvantages. There had been a great deal of effective talk about how a vote for T.R. would mean abandoning the Republican party. In addition to this bogey of party irregularity, the progressives had to fight the Republican machine, money, and party organization—in other words, the resources of organized political power and wealth. But the New York vote showed that the Colonel's name carried enough magic to counteract these handicaps, at least in part; Pinchot at any rate interpreted this small success as a sign that Taft was slipping. Ebullient, he thought that in the final hours of the Republican convention the Rough Rider might easily become the compromise candidate.[79] In no time he was working as ardently for Roosevelt as he had previously worked for La Follette.

As in most of his public activities, Pinchot worked behind the scenes, for he was essentially a committeeman. His associates soon discovered that he possessed valuable assets: a clear sense of the value of all sorts of opinions and the ability to synthesize them; a well-ordered mind, crammed with useful information that he could organize for others to use in speeches or editorials.[80] While advocates like Gifford Pinchot, former Senator Beveridge, and Hiram Johnson exhorted the voters, Amos Pinchot stayed in New York, made no speeches, but took care of innumerable details.

Men who work in political campaigns can often be compared to lawyers. We have the public pleader who presents the argument, hoping he will convince the court that his client's case is meritorious. We also have the man whose role is less spectacular but equally important. He marshals the case; he assembles the facts, prepares the briefs, negotiates where it is necessary, but assumes no conspicuous role in the courtroom. Similarly in a campaign, oratory and personal appeal are indispensable; but no campaign can be effective without the workers behind the scenes, the men who anticipate and organize the large and small details that must be integrated if all is to go forward smoothly. In such activities lay Pinchot's forte.

In the spring of 1912 he helped raise money, wrote drafts of speeches, worked on the platform, answered press attacks. He tells us that he turned out "boiler plate" and did countless odd jobs. If Colonel Roosevelt thought that a pamphlet should be written, Pinchot often was the writer.[81] The unsigned campaign document *Theodore Roosevelt and William Howard Taft* was his work. Intended primarily for the Roosevelt League of New York State, it was also used by other organizations and sent to other states; again Pinchot himself made sure that it reached personal friends. His own list for distribution in Washington included Ambassador Bryce, Ambassador Jusserand, Chief Justice White, Mr. Justice Holmes, Mr. Justice Hughes, Senator Francis Newlands, Mr. and Mrs. Henry White, Dr. Harvey Wiley, and Dr. William H. Wilmer. He sent one hundred copies to Hiram Johnson for distribution in California. He gave press interviews and furnished material for editorials to friends like Philip Littell of the *Globe* and Norman Hapgood, who wanted to write something on the relative amounts of money spent by the Taft and Roosevelt supporters in the New York primaries.[82] Less pleasant assignments also came his way. Early in April, when Senator La Follette telegraphed to Rudolph Spreckels a denunciation of the two Pinchots and Medill McCormick,

Amos wrote the public reply to Hiram Johnson, explaining why the three men had shifted to Roosevelt.[83]

A magazine article proved more difficult to place than any of his pamphlets and releases. "The President—A Study in Character" was based upon the documents in the recent Alaska hearings and dealt with President Taft's part in the Ballinger case. Amos Pinchot showed it to Roosevelt, who recommended that he "publish it unchanged and 'without any soft pedaling,' remarking that it was weak enough as it was, and fell far short of giving Taft his just deserts."[84] But Amos quickly learned that such an article was suspect if it was written by Gifford Pinchot's brother. Magazine after magazine—even those with progressive leanings—rejected it on the ground that it reflected upon Mr. Taft's integrity. One editor wrote that because of Gifford's quarrel with the administration, he feared the article would be considered retaliatory.[85] Pinchot finally made a personal appeal to the editor of *Pearson's*. As "President Taft—Candidate for Re-election," the disquieting piece appeared in the April issue, in time to take its place in a salvo of antiadministration literature. "Your fine article in *Pearson's*, together with Turner's in *McClure's* and William Allen White's in the *American*, ought to put the finishing touches on the walloping Taft is getting everywhere just now," a friend wrote.[86]

During these days Amos felt very much a part of the inner group. Although never an intimate like Gifford, he saw a great deal of Roosevelt, giving the older man much advice that was good-naturedly received but never followed.[87] Pinchot's attitude toward the Colonel was ambivalent. Like almost everyone else, he recognized his enormous magnetism and personal charm. He saw that T.R.'s "unfailing asset was his ability to take the center of the stage."[88] At the same time he was increasingly troubled by what seemed to him the Colonel's fuzzy-mindedness. He was bothered by Roosevelt's inability (or disinclination) to find the basic economic explanations for social and political conditions; he was troubled by his preference for the superficial view. "Roosevelt was vastly interested in society, just as he was vastly interested in big game shooting and football," he said.[89] Like Bryan, T.R. would in one wide leap often travel from a premise to a general conclusion, frequently with no idea of how he had made the jump. Not only did he make logical leaps without going through the intervening steps, but his conclusions were likely to be "absurd and generally as unsupported by fact as medieval papal bulls."[90] Pinchot believed that the consequences of such lack of "intellectual hardihood" could be exceedingly dangerous. They could lead to downright unreliability of judgment; for the Colonel, shunning the drudgery of systematic thought, refused to be bothered with details that were unattractive to him. Such habits of mind inevitably resulted in compromise or outright expediency, both of which Roosevelt obviously considered natural to politics. An improviser, he charted a contradictory and unpredictable course when important decisions had to be made.[91]

For his part, Amos Pinchot must have irritated the Colonel. Pinchot liked to proceed in an orderly course from one given point to the next. Most of the time he looked for the economic bases of social and political problems, and, except for his temporary defection in 1912, he was convinced that principles, not personalities, must form the basis of a successful political party. He did not believe that victories must be won at any cost. He did not like expediency and he did not like the Colonel's fondness for "balanced statements." Therefore he dogged the Colonel, trying to force him to step forward squarely on the paramount issue, the trust. To Roosevelt, Pinchot must have seemed at first rigid and finally a complete maverick.

As the years passed, however, Pinchot softened his earlier judgment. In 1938 he told Fola La Follette, "You must remember . . . that when I wrote it [the *History*] I was probably in a state of mind where it was hard for me to be just to Colonel Roosevelt, who, on the whole, in accordance with his lights and his nature, acted pretty decently all around, though I was pigheaded with him and tried to insist on his taking a course which was not in accordance with his nature, and probably not the best one anyhow."[92]

Late in May 1912 the two Pinchots went to Chicago to work on the platform that some of the Roosevelt supporters wished to present at the Republican National Convention, only about two weeks away. Both brothers wished to include a strong tariff plank that would benefit the American people instead of the trusts, but the obscurity of the Colonel's position raised doubts as to its inclusion. Pinchot insisted that the tariff question was important because it was another phase in the battle of the people against entrenched privilege. "I don't think," he wrote,

That he [Roosevelt] appreciates the terrible effect of this kind of graft on the country, and it seems to me his friends ought to get around him and get him to take a more positive view of the tariff. It seems pretty clear to me [that] the tariff and a real representative government, with the people instead of the bosses choosing candidates, are the two great issues before the country—issues upon which the average man is fairly well educated and quite ready to fight.[93]

The Republican convention of 1912 was one of the most spectacular conventions in American political history. Amos Pinchot gives it a large place in his *History;* therefore it is not necessary to describe its hatreds, its charges and countercharges, the noisy brawling that finally resulted in the renomination of "the large person in Washington" (as William Kent called Taft) and the bolt of the Roosevelt supporters from the Republican party. To believers like the two Pinchots, the progressives had no choice but to bolt. Yet even in those early days, when the air was full of fervor and moral rectitude and the lines for Armageddon were being formed, Pinchot privately voiced a reservation. "The only thing to worry about now," he wrote to his conservationist friend W. J. McGee, "is the chance that the politicians will butt in and try to make this movement their own." Nevertheless, he was sanguine. "I don't think they can do it, especially if we keep radical enough to stay them off."[94]

Publicly he admitted no doubts. On his return to New York he immediately submitted his resignation to the Republican Club, 29th Assembly District; he explained that at Chicago he had been forced to make a decision: whether to remain a regular Republican, which would mean ignoring the principles on which that party was founded, or to leave the party and reaffirm those basic principles. The issue that forced his decision transcended the matter of who had been nominated for the presidency. It involved "the eternal vital issue of whether the people themselves or the representatives of the great financial interests in the country shall hold the power of government." Taft's renomination, he argued, was achieved partly through fraud. The decisions in the California, Texas, Arizona, and Washington contests were reached because the old guard had refused to recognize those principles of popular government that were everywhere on the rise. With this conspiracy to defraud the American people Pinchot would have no dealings. He would ally himself with the new Progressive party which, under Theodore Roosevelt's leadership, would cut across party lines in the fight for popular government. "A new Progressive Party made up equally of progressive Democrats and Republicans is the one great political necessity of the day. The stand of Roosevelt at Chicago, and the formation of a new non-partisan party under his leadership, has made this necessity a fact."[95] It is important to note that he believed the progressives from the two main parties could successfully unite.

Pinchot foresaw "the liberation of this country from special privilege and boss government." Overlooking his earlier hesitations, he predicted that the movement would be led by a great leader "who believes in the people and the cause." The Progressives, he believed, would throw aside the threadbare and corrupt practices of party politics. Instead of meeting behind closed doors, using the worn machinery of caucuses and private agreement, they would fight in the open. Their leader, their cause, and their methods could produce but one glorious outcome: the Progressives would "bring back to the people of this country confidence in their government, and a greater and more just opportunity to earn a living in a free land."[96]

These inspired convictions lasted about two weeks. Early in July he confided his growing unhappiness, particularly with campaign issues and party leaders in New York State. His questionings are interesting, forecasting as they do the issues that soon split the Progressives nationally. For although the new party included such dedicated souls as the irreproachable Jane Addams, it also contained an embarrassing representation of big-business and old-line politicians whose interest in fighting trusts, curbing monopolies, and ensuring the growth of popular government was highly dubious. Two of these new presbyters were the well-known conservative publisher Frank Munsey and the Morgan partner George Perkins, whose name had already been prominently associated with insurance scandals and the International Harvester Trust. The white samite of Progressivism similarly draped the shoulders of such political bosses as "Bill" Flinn of Pittsburgh and Tim Woodruff of New York. This meeting of unlike minds explains Pinchot's misgivings. He saw that most of the people who actually dominated the New York State movement were not real progressives, that they had not the slightest conception of what the country

33

needed.[97] These old-school bosses, with their questionable tactics and standards, weakened the effectiveness of the group that demanded reform.[98]

Nor did his reservations stop here. Woodrow Wilson's nomination was a great blow. To Medill McCormick Pinchot wrote that the Democrats had wiped out the moral advantage on which the Progressives planned to capitalize. No longer could the Democrats be charged with being as bad as the Republicans, merely another party dominated by the big interests.

I am very much in hopes that the Colonel will not make any personal issue with Wilson, and that he will not try to show in any way that Wilson is insincere, or that under him the Democratic party cannot make a real advance. Our movement is a non-partisan movement, and now we must not declare we are against him because he is in another party. This is a difficult situation and one in which we must look very far ahead and try to find out what is the thing that the country needs most.[99]

Somewhat apprehensive, Pinchot still hoped that the Progressives would fight for principles rather than for a man. He did not want to see the Colonel in a position where he would use any device in order to win, at the expense of the party's stated platform.

As Pinchot diagnosed the situation, he saw one impossible and two possible courses. The impossible choice was to rejoin the Republicans. The two possibilities were: first, that the Progressives should accept Wilson, as Norman Hapgood wanted them to do; second, that they should follow "the Chicago schedule and make our fight," drawing support from the ex-Republicans and those Democrats who would back Roosevelt out of affection. This second possibility would involve tremendous labor, and he wished the Progressives did not have to accept it. But if this line was followed, it must be remembered from the first that this was a fight "for progress and for progress only, dominated and led by progressives and only by progressives." If, having made the choice, they deviated from this line, they would be "wiped off the map and deservedly so. If anyone can claim with any show of justice that we are simply outs trying to become the ins, the whole people will certainly hand us a full portion of lemon salad."[100]

Increasingly fearful that the Progressives would sacrifice their principles, increasingly convinced that the top leadership was shoddy, he found no comfort in the issues on which they planned to make the campaign. There were none. "At Chicago, while fighting Taft, we had the fraud issue; that's gone. We cannot ask the people to vote against Wilson because Taft stole Roosevelt's delegates." High-sounding generalities about boss rule would no longer suffice. The Progressives must now produce concrete proposals. Wilson had come out with a series of specific recommendations like tariff reduction and the initiative and referendum, and if the Progressive candidates were to be worth voting for, they must offer even better remedies than these. Pinchot well knew that the views of "the mad men" like Gifford Pinchot, Francis Heney, Hiram Johnson, and himself were probably not acceptable, but he felt that this group should talk to the Colonel and persuade him that only a strong new platform would justify the new party's existence. But he was pessimistic. Among too many of the Bull Moose leaders the zeal to win at any cost was too great. A course of compromise was therefore almost inevitable.

Zealous though he was, Pinchot knew that by this time he was the last man to submit his program to the party leader. "I am tired of being a Cassandra to the Colonel," he told Hiram Johnson. Furthermore, he was *persona non grata* with the New York organization, for he had been making exceedingly pointed criticisms of the New York Progressive party, and his barbed remarks had not endeared him to the "practical men." In spite of numerous reservations he chose to support the Progressive party to the end, although the prospect gave him no comfort. Morosely, he reviewed the situation.

Possibly a constructive, radical program or program of any kind is impracticable at this stage of the game. Perhaps no remedy can be at this moment thought out. We have painted the average man as strung up by his thumbs upon the gallows erected by special privilege. Perhaps it is not up to us to suggest a way to cut him down; perhaps the only thing to do is to get a fairly decent line of public servants, and then let nature take its course. But I feel that our inability to blaze the trail beforehand puts us in the position of the man who says, "Follow me—I don't know where I'm going, but come along just the same."[101]

His disillusionment and uncertainty did not abate, but Pinchot had the questionable consolation of knowing that others shared his depression. Soon he wrote to Norman Hapgood,

Confidentially, I do not feel quite so good over the Bull Moose as I did, and I have had letters from several Progressive leaders who do not feel happy. They don't see that we have any real issue to fight on, and there isn't, I fear, much probability that our platform will furnish one.[102]

Meanwhile he and Gifford went to Chicago for a platform conference; in spite of differences with George Perkins, this meeting temporarily raised his spirits.* He returned to New York much pleased, professing to believe that in spite of itself the new party would succeed.

V

The summer moved on and the Pinchots were in the middle of the campaign. Amos worked as he had in the spring, taking care of jobs that, although unspectacular, were necessary and sometimes difficult.

His most ambitious effort was a pamphlet, "What's the Matter with America: The Meaning of the Progressive Movement and the Rise of the New Party"; it is a more elaborate restatement of the thesis of "Two Revolts Against Oligarchy." Contending that both the progressive movement and the Progressive party were part of that long conflict between old and new ideas that forms the see-saw of human history, he tried to show that new (or progressive) ideas are closely connected with the willingness to tolerate the spirit of free inquiry. These ideas came to America from England, France, and the Netherlands, where they had originated in the sixteenth and seventeenth centuries. John Knox, Sir Francis Drake, Benvenuto Cellini, Dürer, Holbein, Titian, Leonardo, Spenser, Shakespeare, Bacon, Milton, Bunyan, Dryden, Pascal, Descartes, Locke—these are only a few of the progressives who appear before Pinchot gets to the American Revolutionary and Civil wars! The catalogue is overwhelming. Sometimes one fumbles for his basis of inclusion, and the astonishing list amuses rather than convinces the reader. But Pinchot saw in the lives of all these men one common denominator: that devotion to the spirit of free inquiry which must be present if progress (and therefore progressive thought) is to take place. "What's the Matter with America"

* Chester Rowell later recalled that at this meeting Gifford Pinchot and George Perkins wrangled with such acrimony that Colonel Roosevelt put the two men in separate rooms and then, in order to keep the peace, "ran back and forth himself as messenger." (Chester H. Rowell to William Allen White, November 29(?), 1919. William Allen White Papers.)

states certain ideas that guided Pinchot and his "radical" associates during these years; in addition, its fundamentally nonpartisan approach shows why these same men soon felt that Woodrow Wilson had stolen their thunder and was effectively undermining the new party's reason for existence.

Pinchot did not flatter himself that he had written a best seller, but he hoped he had demonstrated that "our whole trouble today is economic and not political, and that the purpose of our country from the beginning has been to destroy economic privilege."[103] Neither George Perkins nor Frank Munsey would approve; of that he was reasonably certain.[104] His pamphlet was probably too highbrow for the average reader, but if it were circulated among Progressive editors and if they used it,[105] perhaps an occasional individual might be convinced by his argument.[106] That it was somewhat "radical," he did not deny; but if one remembered that the Progressive party claimed to be the champion of the people against the trusts, perhaps it was not radical enough.[107]

Part II

1912–1914

I

The events of the 1912 campaign and of the following year rapidly established Pinchot as one of the most articulate members of what he called the "radical nucleus." In his *History* Pinchot tells how even before the elections he began to suspect that many of the Bull Moose leaders were motivated by self-interest rather than by a true belief in progressive principles. He saw the members of the new party splitting into conservative and liberal factions. The ensuing course of compromise, trading, and expediency he condemned as a betrayal, and he determined to fight for those basic principles by which he and his friends of the radical nucleus tested themselves and called themselves Progressives.

No discussion of the radical nucleus can be complete without mention of three elements: a complex of emotions, a man, and a philosophy.

The emotions were distrust and bitterness, and increasingly they colored the feeling between the conservative and radical wings. The conservatives distrusted the radicals, calling them impractical, un-sound, unrealistic, followers of chimeras, and therefore dangerous. As we have seen, the radicals (or more accurately, perhaps, many of the radicals) distrusted the conservatives, regarding them as men who neither knew nor cared about the true progressive movement (i.e., the movement that emphasized popular government) but rather as converts of dubious value, because they were in the game for their own ends. The radicals mistrusted the "practical" approach, the con-cern with getting votes and winning elections before a solid ground-work had been laid, the willingness to compromise for immediate gain. As they saw it, conservative domination would surely harm the party. That is the reason why Pinchot and his friends constituted themselves a voice of opposition.

Radicals like Amos Pinchot contended that the *ultimate* goals of the new party transcended considerations of *immediate* gain, that for life and strength the Progressives must reach down into the center (or grass roots) of American life. In June 1916, after the disastrous Progressive convention, William Allen White (himself no radical) summed up the radical dream: these men had wanted to build a group that would "draw into it the radical thought of the American middle class citizens—the men of vision and ideals. . . ." These men had wanted to "present intelligently and in their most attractive form the advanced ideas of the world's soundest thinkers . . . looking forward to the acceptance of these ideas."[108] By what specific means this party of middle-class radical thought had intended to put across its pro-gram, White did not say. Indeed, one of the criticisms that one can make of the Progressives is that although they talked about the need for specific moral and political reforms, too many of them were hazy as to the explicit means by which they planned to achieve their end. Here they often straddled. As Pinchot later conceded, "We were al-ways inclined to claim a kind of monopoly of conscience and general honesty of intention." He thought that part of the explanation of failure lay in the leadership.

We took the cue from our distinguished leader, who, in his political re-lations, has always acted toward the cardinal virtues like a hostile army that carefully corrals all of the food, fuel, fodder and other munitions necessary to carry on warfare, in the territory in which it is operating.[109]

Actually, the difficulty was more fundamental than this. The Progressives were vague about their specific program because they could not agree on specific reforms. Many of them generalized about "invisible government," "money power," "monopoly," and such favorite terms, and there dropped the matter. Even the members of the radical nucleus did not agree among themselves as to the proper course. Some thought that they were united by a particular attitude of mind. A few —a very few—like Amos Pinchot demanded a concrete program with specific economic reforms. Pinchot argued that the Progressives could justify their existence only if they tried to work for something not found in the goals of the Democratic and Republican parties—the establishment of "real democracy and economic justice." If the expressed goals were sufficiently enlightened, all the liberal voters in the country would rally to the new party.

The second obstacle, the man, was George Walbridge Perkins. At first he was merely a cloud as big as a man; finally he covered the landscape. Amos Pinchot came to believe that the curse of the Progressive party lay in the domination of money power, a domination that existed with the Progressives as surely as it existed with the Republicans and Democrats. The symbol of Progressive money power was Perkins; indeed, some of his detractors said that he owned the party. Financial oligarchy, big business, questionable business connections, Wall Street—these were some of the forces his name conjured up. As chairman of the National Executive Board of the Progressive party, as the man who increasingly controlled Progressive publicity, as a founder of the party, and as Colonel Roosevelt's good friend, he was in a position of great power. From the first both the Pinchots and a number of their friends mistrusted him, and as the years passed Amos Pinchot became increasingly certain that the Colonel had been the Chairman's innocent dupe.[110] Perkins, his opponents claimed, was a conniver: witness the episode of the missing trust plank,[111] his persistent playing down of the Sherman law in the 1912 campaign, and his increasing assumption of power, which became so pervasive that within a short time the people's party had become no more than "Perkins and a push button."[112]

Actually, Pinchot had opposed Perkins since the days of the Ballinger case. Later, in 1912, he had differed with him about Progressive matters at the convention; during the fall months he had tried to outflank him by getting liberal Progressives to speak in the campaign. At that time he had bluntly told the Executive Chairman that the Progressives must make clear their opposition to legalized monopoly. In addition, Pinchot opposed Perkins' prominent place in the Progressive "campaign of public education," in which the Morgan partner was to outline the party's policy on trusts and their control.[113]

But here again Perkins was only the symbol of a far deeper problem, the clash of two opposing philosophies. *In ideas, not in George Perkins, lay the impossibility of reconciliation.* Historians like to point out that in the new party the philosophies of Hamilton and Jefferson met head on. The differences showed most clearly in relation to the recognition and treatment of business and its corporate growth. Theodore Roosevelt (who once described Jefferson as his "pet aversion") was an exponent of the Hamiltonian point of view. He and Perkins believed that the growth of trusts was inevitable, that since it was, the solution lay in their regulation. As Professor Mowry has observed, "Perkins and Roosevelt stood together as exponents of a new paternalism which took sharp issue with historic individualism."[114]

Pinchot and his group were the historic individualists. Like La Follette and Brandeis, the Pinchot group opposed the growth of large combinations. They stood in opposition to the view expressed by J. P. Morgan when he testified before the Pujo Committee: "I like a little competition, but I like combination better. . . . Without control you cannot do a thing." They contended that the growth and maintenance of the capitalistic system depended on competition; therefore, if competition was to be encouraged, combination must be forbidden. For Pinchot the fight centered on the matter of big versus little business, of monopoly versus free competition. He believed that competition could not flourish without the essential condition of the "even chance"; to achieve this end, large concerns must be fractured into relatively smaller units. In other words, Pinchot wanted business to be regulated in the direction of smallness.

At this point, and perhaps because he recognized that the modern trend was toward monopoly, he made an important distinction. Two kinds of monopoly existed: one he abhorred and would destroy; the other he would allow. The intolerable kind was private monopoly, which he considered "legalized graft," the means by which the few exploit the many, the source of the great wealth of the few and the great poverty of the many. Following the lead of George Record, he declared that private monopoly was "created . . . by a monopoly group controlling transportation, raw material, or some other essential industrial factor to which all producers in a given field must have access, in order to do business."[115] The money trust, privately owned railroads, the land monopolies, patent privileges, and the tariff, all these resulted from this kind of combination and control. Such monopoly bred special privilege, which in turn bred poverty and wars. Since regulation by commission had proved unsuccessful, only one solution remained: abolition.

However, Pinchot and his group would tolerate one necessary and important exception: natural monopoly. In this category came public utilities, for they were "established by franchise and recognized by the law,"[116] railroads, telephone and telegraph companies, public service corporations, and other businesses where competition served no purpose. They must, however, be owned and operated by the people; they must not be privately owned.[117]

Pinchot's position on natural monopolies frequently led people to assume that his solution for industrial ills was either socialism or government in industry. Actually, he disapproved of both, although he sought to make a compromise.

I do not believe that either the city, state or federal government should go into industrial production. Industrial production should be conducted by private concerns. I believe in competition in industry. I do not hold with either monopolists or socialists, for both advance the elimination of competition in industry. In order to have competitive industry which spells efficiency, we must make transportation and the raw materials, which are the basis of industry, accessible to all on even terms. That is why I advocate government ownership of railroads and government ownership of natural resources, with a leasing system such as is now in practice with regard to water power on federal property.[118]

This position placed him in direct conflict with the conservative wing of his party. Which view would dominate? The answer, Pinchot believed, would determine life or death for the Bull Moose.

When Pinchot thought of private monopoly, he immediately thought of the corporation that he termed pivotal in America: the United States Steel Corporation.

41

Upon the steel company . . . hangs, to a large extent, the question of the recognition of labor's right to organize, collective bargaining, etc. The big fight between monopoly and the people will be with this bunch. They are more powerful, more brainy, more resourceful, and more hypocritical than any other corporation, and, of course, they have vastly more influence in high places and with the press. We have got to have it out with this crowd. It is the biggest game in the world.[119]

And when he thought of steel he thought of George Perkins, a Morgan partner and a director of the United States Steel Corporation.

II

During the pre-election months of 1912 many of the radicals were particularly disturbed by the Colonel's increasingly open reliance on Perkins and Munsey. In the spring T.R. had seemed (or so they thought) to agree with the radical group, to accept their recommendations for uncompromising curbs on trusts and monopolies. But with the election nearing, he leaned increasingly on the "practical men," spoke softly and equivocally, and apparently had put away his big stick. To be sure, his straddling was no novelty. As early as 1910, when Roosevelt was creating consternation in both wings of the Republican party by his alternately progressive and conservative remarks, Pinchot had written to James Garfield that T.R. must not "combine the roles of a moral reformer and a moral delinquent." But in 1912 forthrightness was needed. Perkins' apparent propaganda against the Sherman Act, and the extraordinary Progressive party pamphlets justifying the trusts and praising George Perkins, suggested that the party was bound on a devious course and that Colonel Roosevelt was tolerating that indirection.

Progressives were not alone in opposing this course. Pinchot's files indicate that a number of persons who were by inclination Progressives but who were registered as Republicans had decided to vote for Wilson because they did not trust Roosevelt on either past or present performances. "Is he a worthy leader of so devoted an army?" asked one reader of "What's the Matter with America?" He added that since he neither trusted T.R.'s sincerity nor believed that he would bring about the great changes Pinchot had shown were needed, he would vote for the Democrats.[120]

Meanwhile, forgetting his former resolutions, Pinchot again tried to convert the Colonel, but in vain. Soon he was writing to former Senator Beveridge, "We are having difficulty here from two well meaning people, Munsey and Perkins. Our papers are framing the Progressive party up as the protector of tariff and the trusts."[121] On the same day he wrote to Louis Brandeis, who had recently come out for Wilson, confiding his regret at the activities of Perkins and Munsey:

Munsey is painting us, as he has no right to do, as the party of protection, while Perkins is giving people an opportunity to assume that we are the defenders of the trusts. This makes me pretty sick, for I feel that the great majority of the people who have gone in with us are right-thinking and unselfish.[122]

Solely as a means of propagandizing the new party in New York, Pinchot ran for Congress from the 18th Congressional District.[123] A friend, Lindon Bates, who had been in the Assembly for two years, was running for the nomination from the 17th District, and the two men campaigned together. Pinchot produced an impressive array of endorsements. Progressives all over the country, including William Allen White, George Norris, Theodore Roosevelt, Hiram Johnson, Francis Heney, and Senator Bristow, recommended him to the voters of the 18th District. Several, among them Heney, personally campaigned for him. One of Pinchot's disadvantages, however, was lack of public service. All he could point to was his work in the Ballinger case. "My sole claim to gratitude from the people of New York City," he told Hiram Johnson, "is that I wrote a brief which to some extent helped to prevent a larceny of some coal about three or four thousand miles away—and I admit that is rather a far cry."[124]

The 18th District was overwhelmingly Democratic, and from the first Pinchot knew that he stood no chance. But he leaped at the opportunity to educate, to tell people about the new party that was opposed to entrenched privilege, trusts, and monopolies. In almost every speech he discussed the tariff, describing the present Republican schedules as "graft-schedules." He attacked standpatters, saying,

I feel that the danger to this country—to all classes alike—consists in trying to meet new and serious situations with old weapons. The plain indian [sic] who tried to stop a locomotive with a bow and arrow was not more of a fool than the man who tries to fight a great modern political machine with the rusty, archaic weapons forged a century ago by our fore-fathers.[125]

He and Bates canvassed the two districts assiduously. "We walk about the streets of the 17th and 18th Congressional Districts, borrow a chair from a saloon, gather a few citizens around us by force of lung power and preach the gospel. It is extraordinary how the people seem to lis-ten."[126] In spite of the drawbacks, he was not ineffective. When the returns were counted in November, Pinchot was second in the poll-ing.[127]

The outcome of the 1912 national elections needs no analysis here. The Munsey-Perkins alliance and the attempts of the Progressive party to be all things to both monopolists and workers gave Woodrow Wilson a superb opportunity. With devastating good humor he re-viewed the Colonel's presidential record on industrial control and ended by showing that the Roosevelt plan to make everybody richer and happier (except, of course, the bad trusts) could not succeed. The campaign was spectacular, highlighted by an attempt to assassinate Colonel Roosevelt. Shortly after, thanks to the Republican split, the Democrats won their first national election since Grover Cleveland's second term. Although Wilson received a bare plurality of popular votes, his electoral vote carried all states except six for Roosevelt and two for Taft.

Pinchot regarded the entire campaign with misgivings. Two weeks after the defeat, he wrote a full analysis of the situation to Harold Ickes. What he said is worth summarizing, for it is an admirable statement of many of the problems that were bothering Progressives who did not cleave to the conservative line.

The party, he said, was in a bad state; it was falling more and more into the hands of Perkins and Munsey. Perkins, who had be-come the party mouthpiece, was hard-working, full of ability, and "acquisitive of power." Munsey was "an honest, straightforward re-actionary" who believed that the poor did not work long enough hours and that they were overpaid. What could happen with this leadership? In addition, Pinchot questioned the Progressive program: "Popular government" was not sufficiently substantial, because popu-lar government was not a fundamental question; it was remedial —a means, not an end. The social and industrial program of which the Progressives were so proud was "merely a palliative, and no party can nourish itself on palliatives alone." Therefore, the one big issue must be the trust question. The entire program of social and industrial justice would be a fraud otherwise; although the program of shorter hours, increased wages, pensions, and safety devices might improve working conditions, it would also increase the cost of living; "our industrial justice program helps the workman as a wage earner, but not at all as a consumer, and it does not help other classes than the working classes at all, or very little." The trusts would foist increased costs of production on the public, and in the end the public would be worse off than ever.

Here both Gifford and Amos Pinchot agreed: if the trust question was the important question, George Perkins must be blocked; the election returns justified some kind of action. In this connection several facts, frequently overlooked, should be stressed. In the opening round of the postelection fight, neither of the Pinchot brothers wished to drive Perkins off the Executive Committee. On the contrary, they were willing that he should remain as *head* of the Executive Committee, provided this position did not entitle him to speak for the Progressive party in what might be interpreted as an increasingly official manner. As Gifford Pinchot told Theodore Roosevelt, "There is a notable difference between being in an army and being at the head of an army. In order to stand by a man it is not necessary to put him in charge."[128] Supporting the Pinchots were prominent Eastern radicals like George Record and Bainbridge Colby; Middle Westerners like Harold Ickes, Raymond Robins, Medill McCormick, and Charles Merriam; Westerners like Ben Lindsey, Hiram Johnson, and Francis Heney; and John Parker of Louisiana. Beveridge, who can scarcely be called a radical, moved in and out of this group. The Pinchots stressed that their protest against Perkins represented far more than the dissidence of a mere handful; "we are fighting for those who have not been able to help themselves, and against those who have helped themselves too freely," Gifford told his former chief.[129]

Amos Pinchot tells us that by the time the December 1912 meeting was held in Chicago, his outspoken attitude on the trust question and the missing plank had cost him the favor of the Progressive chiefs. The meeting was acrimonious, with Colonel Roosevelt energetically defending both Perkins and Munsey. The episode of the missing trust plank was angrily discussed, and finally, after Amos Pinchot had re-peatedly insisted, it was restored to the platform. Subsequently, the two Pinchots and the Colonel exchanged a series of letters,[130] but no one was satisfied. By the first of January 1913, Gifford wanted to drop the entire matter.* He had not changed his mind about Perkins, and neither had the Colonel. But in order to ease Progressive tensions and almost certainly to ease his personal relations with T.R., Gifford sug-gested that he and the Colonel close their correspondence on this touchy subject.[131]

Amos, however, refused to modify his position. Instead he began to plan new ways of outflanking Perkins. Early in January 1913 John A. Kingsbury wrote to Jane Addams, reporting a meeting at Pinchot's house. The group, which included George Record and Dean Kirch-wey of Columbia University, met to discuss the Colonel's alliance with the conservatives. Quick and decisive action was imperative, they all agreed. What should they do to save the party from the control of those conservatives in Progressive skins who controlled their chief? The discussion was long and thorough; finally they came to two de-cisions. First, they must formulate a clear-cut set of minimum de-mands that could be presented at the next convention, for without such a program they could not hope to get anywhere with Colonel Roosevelt or with the rank and file. Second, they must appeal to Miss Addams for support. "As the men at Mr. Pinchot's house said last Saturday evening," wrote Kingsbury, "the Colonel has become suspi-cious of the whole social worker crowd except Jane Addams, and he is afraid of her, and we must depend on her to save the situation." With Miss Addams to keep the Rough Rider in check, and with a set of principles on which a fairly large group of Progressives could agree, the future of the party seemed more assured. Spirits rose, and the host sounded the note of jubilation on which the evening ended. When this program is achieved, said Amos Pinchot, "we ought to set sail for Roosevelt, and we will take him aboard our craft."[132]

* At this time Gifford was a member of the Progressive party's Legislative Reference Committee. On January 29, 1913, he and Francis J. Heney sent a joint telegram to Jane Addams; they requested her to come to a committee meeting in which they wanted "to put forth program of essentials in such positive form that it will be difficult for any individual whatever to commit our party to any wrong policy on any subject covered by us." (Jane Addams Papers.)

Apparently Pinchot was willing to try anything, even propagandizing Perkins. A few days later he gave a dinner party for George Perkins, George Record, Joseph Cotten, and a few others. Perkins and Record got into "a long argument conducted on parallel tracks, so that their minds never once met; Perkins retreated sidewise, so that it was impossible for Record to reach him." Perkins, on his side, talked a great deal about "the splendid work of the Steel Trust and human uplift." From a proselytizing standpoint the evening was not satisfactory, and Pinchot was discouraged. He did not think the radical nucleus would get far with George Perkins.[133]

III

During the next months Amos Pinchot watched the gyrations of the Progressive leaders. Despairingly he noted the old adherence to the old course, the eagerness to placate conflicting interests, and an uncritical acceptance of Perkinsism. Although Gifford was milder in his publicly expressed opinions, in private he too deplored Perkins' prominence. But Gifford's long friendship and loyalty to Colonel Roosevelt prevailed, and he again refused to make public his opposition. In addition to Perkinsism, the Pinchots were disturbed by persistent rumors of the imminent "amalgamation" of the Progressives and Republicans. Strong denials came from Progressive headquarters, but the rumors continued.[134]

Meanwhile Amos Pinchot's ideas about political action had changed. For him the goal of the new party was still to "make it easier for the average man to make a living and raise a family," but he no longer believed that the guarantee of the better life lay in the election of honest men. During his first exhilarated months in the Progressive party, he had, as in earlier days, insisted that good government must be the result of the disinterested "service to society" of honest men; but after November 1912 he had lost much of his faith in the effectiveness of such well-intentioned officeholders, unless they would support concrete reform. "There ought to be a law against electing honest men to office unless they are pledged to a platform embodying specific measures." The honest man was merely window dressing, "the ideal tool of the big grafters." Concerned with a "creditable administration," he fussed with trivia, with surface reforms, while underneath the entrenched graft remained untouched. Therefore, the honest man defeats the ends for which he is elected; he "is harder to get rid of than the crook; and all that our big gas, electric and traction grafters want is to keep men in office who will leave the big grafts alone and get the public excited about vice, police protection and little meticulous accounts."[135] Such conditions endanger our democracy.

This shift in emphasis explains much of Pinchot's political strategy after the elections of November 1912. It explains why he decided to pursue a course that made him increasingly unpopular with many Progressives, and it also explains why he persistently attempted to clarify the grounds of division in the Progressive party. In December 1913 he wrote to Gilson Gardner,

During the last few months, I have been trying at odd times to find how we could draw simply and sharply a line which would divide simply and sharply the friends of real democracy from those who treat the subject of democracy as a stage property, or as a kind of inspiring Victrola music to which they may perform the political tango or the hesitation waltz.[136]

In this letter Amos confided a plan which he and Gifford supported. The radical nucleus wanted a strong platform, and he was now working on it. This new document was to be kept secret until the convention; there, at the proper time, it was to be presented. Amos was not altogether clear as to what would happen. Presumably he and Gifford thought that the delegates, caught by surprise, would spontaneously demonstrate in favor of the new platform, thereby bringing about "a sharp re-alignment on issues." This strategy would bring the party together again, and in that way "we may be able to keep certain of our leaders from coaxing the party back into the Republican fold or to the amalgamated What-is-it that is already the blessed vision of some of them and the nightmare of others."[137]

As part of their efforts to save the Bull Moose they would advocate public ownership of water power, forests, coal, oil, and all other sources of energy; they would back municipal ownership of public utilities; and they would oppose the tariff. Finally, they would recommend breaking up the ownership of large segments of land. Pinchot was much pleased with these four propositions. They were vital to the growth of true democracy in this country, and, taken together, they presented a real economic program. He reflected with pleasure that the Progressive sheep would quickly separate from the Progressive goats; the general attack should therefore be made under the slogan "Abolition of Private Monopoly." The prospects of success he viewed optimistically; the showdown would "soon and suddenly shake out the Perkinses and I think would place T.R. in a position where he would choose to come over with us, rather than play with the Philocrats and Republicans."[138] Matters were lined up for 1914.

IV

Nineteen-fourteen was Amos Pinchot's climactic year in the Progressive party. Determined to force the Perkins issue, he made an almost singlehanded attempt and was beaten. For about two weeks he was front-page news; today that episode is almost forgotten. In his chapter "The Decay of the Progressive Party," Pinchot gives a generalized account, but his story is slight, telescoped, and unsatisfactory. However, the Perkins-Pinchot quarrel—or better, the Pinchot rebellion—is worth describing here; for its outcome left the Perkins faction in command; it made public the behind-the-scenes friction that had been building up for two years; and it left Pinchot in political limbo.

Nineteen-fourteen was also a year of reckoning for the Bull Moose. The 1914 elections, the first to be held since President Wilson's victory in 1912, would show whether the American people supported the New Freedom, or whether the loyalty and dedication (and the 4,126,020 votes) of Armageddon still held. Since 1911 skeptics had been saying that a third party could not compete successfully with the well-organized Democratic and Republican machinery, that the progressive elements of the two established parties would not leave them to join the newest group. Nineteen-fourteen would be the first real test of the new party's competitive strength and its command of a support more enduring than the fervent emotionalism of 1912. Intent on election, Progressives in different states—Gifford Pinchot in Pennsylvania, Francis J. Heney and Hiram Johnson in California, E. P. Costigan in Colorado, Victor Murdock in Kansas (to name a few)—announced they would file for state and senatorial office.

Amos Pinchot was deeply concerned with the Pennsylvania elections, where Gifford was opposing Boies Penrose. From the Progressive point of view the situation there was disquieting, for in the state primaries the party had shown an ominous loss of strength. While the

Progressives had *lost* 396,644 votes in eighteen months, the Republicans had *gained* 55,565. The returns also showed that Penrose controlled 55 out of the 67 counties—all this in spite of the fact that, as the *Evening Post* put it, "If there is a state in the Union in which the Progressives have a genuine issue, it is Pennsylvania. Boies Penrose, of course, gives them the issue."[139] Amos believed that Gifford was the best candidate that the Progressives could find anywhere in the country. Characteristically he wanted his brother to stress economic issues, to demand the abolition of monopoly, which, to his mind, riddled people's lives with its complicated, interlocking evils. He wanted Gifford to advocate a government-owned coal mine and coal road and a change in patent laws. These three points might sound innocuous, but they were dynamite; for government ownership of railroads and natural monopolies and the abolition of patent privileges hit directly at three of the basic strengths of monopoly. Therefore, in advocating this program Gifford would be defying both Penrose the Stalwart Republican and Perkins the Progressive.[140]

As Amos Pinchot looked around the country, he felt little but discouragement. In the first place, the 1912 Progressive platform (he was fond of describing it as a jumble of *isms* that included everything from the higher catechism to how to make a birchbark canoe) was now almost useless as a call to arms, for the President had appropriated the very weapons his opponents should have used. While the Progressives had prattled about the need for reforms, Mr. Wilson had legislated impressive changes.

Then, instead of recognizing that Wilson's strategy was effective, and at the same time advocating measures that would show up the weakening compromises in the Democratic program, the Progressives presented no countermeasures. Relying on the inspirational effects of noise rather than on suggestions for action, they moved in a kind of camp meeting atmosphere, quavering or shouting semireligious cant. Understandably they were getting a reputation for insincerity. Pinchot thought that if they were to regain the ground so needlessly lost, they must work from a new psychological basis. "We have no fighting ground as things stand," he said.[141] He therefore proposed to create new fighting grounds on state and national levels.

There was no mystery about the target of the national attack: George Perkins. On this point Pinchot mistakenly believed he would have strong backing. How he reached his conclusion we do not know, but he was convinced (as he had been in 1913) that the rank and file would support him, that Colonel Roosevelt, impressed by this array of strength, would leave the conservatives and join the radicals. Perkins would then resign, after which he and his strongest supporters would leave the Progressive party. Amos estimated that his own sizable support would include his "nucleus," Westerners like Francis Heney and Hiram Johnson of California, "the Illinois crowd, *the bulk of the National Committee,** the Colorado Progressives, the Jerseyites, Mat Hale's people in Massachusetts; and all Roosevelt's real friends will be profoundly glad to have the atmosphere cleared." Just who Roosevelt's "real friends" were, Pinchot did not say. That he anticipated the support of most of the National Committee indicates that he did not accurately assess the attitudes of many of the men with whom he had worked during the past two years. His general position shows that he did not correctly understand where the sympathies of many of the Progressives lay.

He had, however, some plausible reasons for his miscalculations. Party leaders like Dixon and Poindexter believed that someone other than Perkins should be executive chairman. Pinchot himself had talked and written to a number of men in the Middle West, West, Far West, and East, and their remarks were to him a gauge of rank-and-file sentiment, a confirmation of his belief that opposition to the Executive Chairman was running strong. In addition, he was undoubtedly swayed by a number of letters written both to him and to Gifford, letters saying that Perkins should go and that Gifford should take his place.

He knew that if his revolution succeeded, many conservative Progressives would leave the party, but he believed that this loss would actually be a gain; then the progressively inclined Democrats and Republicans who had refused to vote the Bull Moose ticket because they mistrusted Perkins would not stay aloof. For every vote lost, three or four would be gained.

Meanwhile, he had some small reason to feel encouraged about his insistence on the antimonopoly program. On January 20 Gifford, who was getting under way for his senatorial campaign in Pennsylvania, wrote in his diary that he had seen Senator Clapp, who unreservedly

* Italics mine.

endorsed the plan apparently put forward by Amos, that the federal government buy Pennsylvania coal lands and also, if necessary, a railroad in order "to break [the] anthracite trust." On the next day Gifford wrote that Victor Murdock had advised him "to put some vitriol in every speech. . . . Wilson's Message on Trusts making Amos' program abs. essential. It puts the Dems in our hands. It will be taken generally as the first backward step."[142] But almost immediately Gifford turned cautious. Van Valkenburg had warned that though in principle he did not oppose Amos' coal plan (that same plan which Clapp had already approved), he did oppose it on political grounds,[143] and Gifford agreed that at this moment political considerations should take precedence over principle. Amos, on the other hand, refused to compromise. To him Perkins was a worse evil than Ballinger. Apparently he had begun in earnest to frame his attack on the evangelist of trusts, for on March 30 Gifford, apparently in some consternation, wrote,

Tried to get Amos by phone. No use. Letter from O[verton] W. P[rice], who says that Amos is sure we are wrong and he is right in attacking Perkins. I am most anxious he should not ruin the party by such a break just before election, and I don't believe he will.[144]

The very next night Amos went to Philadelphia. He spent the greater part of April 1 conferring with Gifford, A. Nevin Dietrich (the chairman of the Pennsylvania State Committee), Van Valkenburg, Raymond Robins, and Dean Lewis. Specifically they discussed a plan for trust legislation and, of course, the Perkins matter. Concerning the trust plan, Amos objected that the bill gave too much power to the proposed trust commission, thereby providing no solution, for "no commission can be really effective." Gifford again summed up their difference of opinion: "A. very strongly anxious to drive Perkins out now. I am opposed, believing it wiser to wait until after election. But he has got to get out before 1916."[145]

Meantime, determined to force action, Amos decided on two steps. Knowing that Van Valkenburg was angry with Perkins for his favorable stand on monopolies, he proposed to write two articles for the Philadelphia *North American*. One was to deal specifically with Perkins, the other with the general problem of trusts. Then, at the urging of George Record, he decided to try for the senatorial nomination in the New York State primaries. His reason in 1914 was largely the same as his reason for campaigning for Congress in 1912. He never deluded himself that he might win; he dreaded the time and energy his fruitless attempt would consume, but once again he saw a chance of educating the New York voter. This time he would advocate a truly radical platform defending labor unions and collective bargaining; by denouncing the Steel Trust specifically, he could dramatize the iniquities of monopoly and special privilege.[146] Such a program might do more than educate; it might perhaps force the New York State Progressive bosses to choose a less conservative candidate than they might if they remained free from attack. Conceivably they might adopt a truly Progressive platform, rather than an innocuous compromise.

The reaction to these proposals was immediate. Although Perkins was regarded with disfavor, few wanted to attack him publicly. Van Valkenburg conceded that Amos' position was correct but he refused to publish the denunciation.[147] Gifford also thought it should be withheld; soon after, he discouraged the New York primaries plan, candidly admitting that Amos' campaign in New York would hurt his own senatorial chances in Pennsylvania.[148] A. Nevin Dietrich asserted that if Amos ran in New York, he would help no one; his stand on Perkins would be immediately dragged into the Pennsylvania campaign, and this issue would only embarrass Gifford. Dietrich said flatly that at all costs he wanted to avoid the question of Perkinsism, even though he thought the Progressive party would be in much better shape were Perkins at the other end of the world.[149] Van Valkenburg, Clapp, and Murdock opposed Amos' candidacy on the ground that it might well split and destroy the party. Finally, Pinchot's mother, virtually on her deathbed, objected, presumably because Gifford's chances would be seriously affected. Mrs. Pinchot's request clinched the matter, and Amos decided not to run. His letters show that he took the defeat hard. To Gilson Gardner he confided that he might even drop the whole trust matter.

I am heartily sick of it, of course, but yet I do have a certain feeling of affection for the Progressive Party that makes me hate to see it destroyed by the Steel Trust crowd. It is rather a pitiful business. I certainly am feeling down in the mouth.[150]

Although he had been persuaded not to make an open quarrel, he was still determined to fight Perkins. Yet the problem of how to protest remained. Perhaps he remembered that early in April former Governor Stubbs had come to see Gifford and had read Amos' attack. While supporting Amos' position, the Governor advised against publishing it, suggesting instead that Perkins could be driven out through the National Committee. Nothing in Pinchot's correspondence at this time indicates that he doubted his earlier prediction that he would be supported by "the bulk of the National Committee." In any event, he changed his articles into a seven-thousand-word "Confidential Letter" to Senator Joseph Dixon, deciding to send a copy to him, to Colonel Roosevelt, and to each member of the National Committee.

Meantime it was public knowledge that on May 26 the Colonel was going to Washington for an important conference with Progressive leaders prior to his departure for Spain, where his son Kermit was to be married. It could hardly have been by accident that on May 22 Pinchot sent the long-planned attack. With it he enclosed a letter emphasizing the confidential nature of his material: it was not to be published and "The substance of the letter has been collected with care."[151] The letter reviewed Perkins' record as chairman of the National Executive Committee, cited his position on private monopoly, his antilabor stand, his pamphleteering, and ended by calling for a clarification of issues.

To talk against monopoly, to place the words, "Social and Industrial Justice" upon our banner, and then to hand this banner to a man who has been monopoly's ardent supporter and one of the most distinguished opponents of social and industrial justice that our generation has produced, is, in my opinion, a handicap to the party and a fraud on the public. . . . Our party cannot exist as a party of balanced phrases and equivocations. It cannot stand on the one hand with the people and on the other hand with the forces that oppress the people. It cannot shout for industrial justice in one breath and tolerate monopoly exploitation in the next. There is little room to-day in American politics for parties, or individuals, who attempt to be all things to all men. Our party must take sides in the struggle between democracy and privilege—and we must make it as clear as sunlight which side we have taken.[152]

Pinchot sent this letter to the Colonel, to the members of the National Committee, and to a number of well-known Progressives who were his personal friends. The response was immediate and disappointing. Of course, the radical nucleus, that fiery handful, declared immediately and enthusiastically for Pinchot. But the larger number of Progressives were either outspokenly hostile or, as Pinchot put it, "guarded." Beveridge wrote angrily to Gifford; he was "dumbfounded" and "astounded" by the attack, which was "unjustifiable" and "utterly stupid" (and which took an "unnecessary fling" at Beveridge). The letter, he continued, was a godsend to the enemy, who more than anything else wanted a rift in the party. Clearly he thought that Amos Pinchot had created that rift; everyone he had talked to was bitter at what Amos had brought about.*[153] Other Progressives, like Medill McCormick and Raymond Robins of Chicago and Meyer Lissner of Los Angeles, took a middle position, saying that they supported Pinchot's idea, although they did not go along with the plan for its execution. But the general point of view was expressed by a Minneapolis lawyer who reported the consensus of a meeting of the Minneapolis Progressive party: many of the members agreed with Pinchot, but they did not think a family row would help.[154]

Pinchot quickly realized that his anticipated support was nonexistent. "The responses that I have had from my letter to Senator Dixon have, I confess, been immensely discouraging," he told Herbert Knox Smith. Much depressed, he saw that the Perkins view on trusts would prevail, that the National Committee would not act as he had hoped. And he was right. The members of the committee did not protest against Perkins. Instead, they protested against Amos Pinchot. They told Pinchot exactly what they thought of his letter—with carbons to George Perkins. "My correspondence with members of the National Committee and prominent Progressives has been such that a kind word is particularly appreciated at this date," Amos wryly remarked.[155]

Thus far the quarrel had been contained within the party, but news of it soon leaked out. Pinchot never located the source of information, but by June 9 the newspapers had all the data they needed. On that

* Gifford Pinchot replied, "My brother is right. I am in hearty agreement that the Progressive Party should be free from the burden of Perkins' chairmanship." (GP to Albert J. Beveridge, June 24, 1914. Albert J. Beveridge Papers, Box 277.)

day Amos wrote to Gifford, saying that the *American* and the *Evening Post* contained articles about his letter, that they were about to report the efforts to force Perkins' resignation. Newspapermen wanted interviews, but he refused to see them. The next day he wired Gifford, reporting that someone had given the press a gnarled version of his letter; that it contained false charges and statements more harmful than those in the original; that it was now impossible to try to stop the publicity. His only course was to release the correct text. On June 11 several of the New York metropolitan newspapers carried the story, with liberal quotations from the letter itself. (Significantly, the two Progressive newspapers did not mention the episode.) The *Evening Post* announced that the letter had "hit the party's leadership straight between the eyes."* In the absence of Colonel Roosevelt, who was still in Spain, the Progressive leadership was coldly uncommunicative, but the *Post* predicted that the general feeling was that the Colonel owed Perkins too much to break with him.[156]

Other newspapers carried the story. The New York *World* honored the set-to by a cartoon by Rollin Kirby ("For We Stand at Armageddon and We Battle for the Lord"); The *Times* loftily remarked, "While Amos Pinchot is not important in himself, he may give the Bull Moose considerable trouble"; The *World* asserted that Pinchot "belongs with Woodrow Wilson and the Democrats, not with Theodore Roosevelt and the regulated monopolists."[157]

When reporters asked George Perkins for his opinions, he remarked "imperturbably," "I don't think Mr. Pinchot's letter will either help or hurt him. I don't think anything will happen as a result of the letter. I don't think it will change either his relations or mine to the Progressive party. . . . I don't question Mr. Pinchot's sincerity."[158] But Colonel Roosevelt, who would not comment until he returned from Spain, was not so bland. When reporters asked him for his opinion, he exploded, "As for reading George Perkins out of the

* The *Post* (June 11, 1914) observed: "That Amos Pinchot, although rejecting Mr. Perkins, is still faithful to the Roosevelt tradition is shown by the fact that his letter is seven thousand words long."
Perkins received attention from still another source. The Live and Let Live League of New York requested that President Wilson allow them to hold a mass meeting in front of the old Treasury "to protest against the efforts of George Perkins to chloroform the Progressive Party to insure success to the Republican Party in 1916" (New York *Evening Post,* June 10, 1914).

party, when that is done they will have to read me out, too."*[159]

Of course, the New York Progressives did neither. After T.R. defended Perkins, the New York Progressive leaders came out crushingly against Pinchot, and his mail brought an increased number of condemnatory letters.

On June 12, the day after the newspapers carried the story of the letter to Dixon, a group of reporters cornered Pinchot in Washington. What would he now do, they asked. If Perkins stayed, would he bolt? Pinchot replied, "Nothing can drive me from the Progressive Party." Reporting this firm sentiment, the *World* speculated that nothing would come of the fracas but words: "Pinchot can keep on battling for the Lord and Perkins can keep on signing the checks."

But the *World* was mistaken. It is true that Pinchot was not driven from the Progressive party. It is more correct to say that he faded from it, but he did not do much more battling for the Lord. During the 1914 campaign he worked hard for Gifford (who was defeated), and he sent money West, where friends were running for Progressive nominations. To Costigan of Colorado he sent $1,000. To Heney of California he sent $350. He still hoped to organize the radical nucleus over the entire country, but by this time he was willing to wait until after the elections. Basically, however, he felt that the party leadership lacked courage, agreeing with George Record that "The Progressive Party is dead."[160]

The November elections supported that charge. Nineteen-fourteen was indeed a year of reckoning for the Bull Moose. Of all the leading Progressive candidates in the country, only Hiram Johnson was elected.† To Pinchot these results demonstrated without question that a new party could not exist by merely advocating "superficial reform," that such an approach only gave the enemy the chance it needed.

---

* Roosevelt told William Allen White that he believed the Eastern section of the party would have been destroyed if the idea had got around that the Progressive leadership supported Pinchot and Record rather than George Perkins. (Theodore Roosevelt to William Allen White, July 6, 1914. See also Theodore Roosevelt to Meyer Lissner, December 11, 1914.)

† The following figures, based on the national vote for representatives, are significant. In the entire country the Democrats received 5,929,887 votes; the Republicans, 5,781,563; the Progressives, 952,481. "Poor showing of latter due to combining with other parties on candidates, notably in Pennsylvania" (Robert Woolley Papers, Box 5).

If the Progressive Party had only realized this and had fought for things which people could really believe in and care about, we would have been licked just as badly at the polls, but we would have had something left to continue fighting for. In other words, the party would not have gone out of commission.[161]

In summing up, two questions present themselves. The first concerns the effectiveness of Pinchot's rebellion. Professor Mowry believes, "The episode served to bring the latent hostility to Perkins within the party to the surface. . . . Never again was Perkins fully trusted by a large group in the party."[162] But a careful reading of Pinchot's correspondence suggests otherwise. It is true that Pinchot forced the showdown; but it is also true that Perkins won the vote of confidence. Pinchot wanted Perkins to leave the party, but in effect, Pinchot left. Almost from first to last his plans miscarried.

The other question centers on whether the open letter offered the opposition, as Beveridge claimed, its God-given chance. Here again, the answer is probably no. The troubles in the Progressive party went beyond bickerings as to who should be executive chairman or how he should function. A perspicacious analysis of the matter is contained in a confidential letter written by David Hinshaw to William Allen White; this letter was written on November 7, 1914—in other words, immediately after the election.

My own opinion is that we are doomed as a party. We somehow have failed to connect—we caught but could not hold the imagination of the middle class voter,—and he was the very man we appealed to,—and we went a mile high over the head of the working man. At Friday's meeting great contempt was generally expressed for the working man because his political morals and standards were swept aside so easily by what they termed "The Belly Issue"—and there were just thirteen millionaires in the room—only two of the crowd who were not comfortably fixed. And yet these men were trying to put over plans and direct the work and establish the issues for a party whose strength must come from those who know want. . . .[163]

Pinchot was probably correct when he told E. W. Scripps that in any event the Progressive party would probably have lost in 1914, but if they had got rid of Perkins they would have had "something left to continue fighting for." But one wonders how deeply and how long people would have cared about the issue of Perkinsism. For Pinchot overlooked one basic question that applied directly to practical politics: how far or how effectively could the Progressives have fought in view of the gains created by the Democratic reforms and the additional crisis of a world war?

Part III

1915–1919

Once—the date and occasion are not known—Colonel Edward House was talking to Pinchot's sister. They mentioned her brother Amos, and the Texas Colonel remarked, "He is always right, at the wrong time." If Colonel House really believed that Pinchot was always right, he belonged to an exceedingly small circle that probably included few members beyond himself and the select group of angels he invoked in his confidential moments. Many people believed that Pinchot was more often wrong than right, while others impatiently dismissed him as a supporter of lost causes. A glance at some of his nonpolitical activities during these years shows why: he spoke a great deal for labor, civil liberties, and against war. He was closely connected with that well-known radical literary magazine, *The Masses;* finally, after World War I, he took part in another unsuccessful attempt to organize a third party. A consistent principle underlies these apparently diverse concerns: here again he stood for the rights of the individual and in opposition to economic monopoly and its concomitant, war.

I

As we have already seen, as early as 1910 Pinchot began to write articles, and he enjoyed seeing his work distributed in news releases, political pamphlets, and magazine articles. He liked to go through statistics and complicated tables of railroad rates or electric light schedules, or to investigate alleged gains and losses of corporations. (In other circumstances, he might well have become a college professor and have written learned books and articles on socioeconomics.) Having assembled his material, he understandably wanted to get it published, so that others could read what he had discovered and be warned. And, of course, when people sent him fan mail he enjoyed the evidences of his moderate successes. As he became increasingly interested in economics, "especially the relation of industrial monopoly to the social and political control of society," he became increasingly convinced that capitalism could be saved only by some kind of reconstruction—a belief he shared with many persons, including Wilson, La Follette, and Brandeis. He determined to write about these beliefs in language that ordinary people would understand. He became, in short, a publicist, not so much of the type described by Mr. Lippmann as "the kind of writer . . . who gives to political and social thinking the form in which it can be assimilated by educated people,"[164] as one concerned with communicating his ideas to *interested* people. Never a popular writer, he was still not without his readers. Max Eastman says that whenever he wanted, Pinchot could call up the *Times* and get a double column in a good spot.[165] From time to time his columns appeared in *Collier's, Pearson's, Harper's Weekly, The New Republic, The Nation,* and *The Freeman;* a great deal of what he wanted to say, however, appeared in magazines and newspapers like the *Anthracite Labor News,* the *Locomotive & Enginemen's Magazine, La Follette's Magazine, The Masses,* the Socialist party's *New York Call,* or in labor newspapers.

Pinchot's writing was characterized by intense personal conviction. Whether he was discussing water rights or monopolies or George Perkins or armed intervention, he was forthright, factual, yet emotional; his articles often left the impression that though the author knew he was arguing on behalf of unpopular ideas, he was convinced they must in time prevail. This note of certainty, of passionate partisanship, probably made many readers take a strong Sir-I-take-my-pen-in-hand position and send him their detailed objections to his articles. Some resented his wayward prejudices. Others, exasperated by his reformer's concern with social conditions, sounded as though they had taken their text from Mark Twain's aphorism: "Whom God sees fit to starve, let not man presumptuously rescue to his own undoing." His critics variously and sometimes anonymously suggested that he was unrealistic, incurably romantic, a donkey, a menace, a maverick, an anarchist, a wild-eyed Wobbly, a penny-farthing socialist, a pacifist, a slacker, a lunatic, a "liberal fanatic," a radical, a hopeless reactionary, and a traitor to his class.* Pinchot vigorously denied that he was mad, remark-

* This list is taken at random from Pinchot's correspondence.

ing, "I know that anyone who puts forward anything locally unaccepted must expect to be considered a crank. Of course, I do not like that feature of it but it is a part of the game."[166]

II

And he was quite right when he denied that he was a revolutionary. By his own definition he was a liberal reformer;* he wanted reform because he wanted to maintain the status quo. In 1914 any thinking man or woman could recall the Russian revolution of 1905—and its causes. Pinchot liked to point out that for years England and Germany had recognized the need of social measures to benefit their working classes. He approvingly quoted Disraeli's remark: "The social question of today is only a zephyr which rustles the leaves, but will soon become a hurricane." In the United States, he believed, a "reckless and thoughtless commercialism" had gained such control over the lives of average men and women that concessions on the English and German plan were immediately necessary. Otherwise we would have revolution.

What I am trying, in a humble way, to help do, is to prevent violence, disorder, and misery by getting people to see the justice of the average man's demand for a better economic position in this country, and the utter futility of denying or ignoring this demand.[167]

* "Liberalism might be defined as the impulse that leads us to take part in the upward evolution of society, but we can take no part in this evolution unless we can see society in terms of the clash of the antagonistic forces and consciously identify ourselves with one of them." (Amos Pinchot, "Liberalism," speech given at the Civic Club, January 1923.)

In 1933 Pinchot wrote, "If the chances are ten to one, and I think they are, that we're going on for a good long time under the present order of things, shaping and adapting it, we hope, to the needs of the time, the sensible, though less exciting thing to do is not to chase off into the sky and try to rope some legendary Pegasus, whatever the intellectual delights of such a pursuit may be, but to take the horse we already have in the stable, and, tough as the job may be, make him into a fairly serviceable animal. For the present, at all events, he's the only horse we've got.

"And that, as I see it, is precisely what justifies the existence of the American liberal—the poor, despised liberal, who lacks both the dignified but glacial immobility of the conservative and the dramatic appeal of his light-footed brother of the left wing." ("The American Liberal and His Program," *The Churchman*, CXLVII, April 1, 1933, p. 14.)

Like numerous other progressive-minded persons, Pinchot was trying to batter a small hole in the walls of the hermetically sealed house in which lived the old unseeing, unhearing order of reactionaries. He might wish to improve the drainage or the stairways or the ventilation, but he wanted to preserve the house. To him this was the justification of social justice: to maintain what we have.

Nor did Pinchot suggest that social justice carried with it any idea of leveling classes. "Let us not try," he proposed, "to level men, but rather let us level opportunity and then we will have what is better than equality, *for equality is unnatural*."[168]

In this connection his position on labor is worth noting, for one does not find many Progressives taking a strong stand on the matter. It is true that the Progressive platform of 1912 stated, "We favor the organization of workers, men and women, as a means of protecting their interest and promoting their progress," but among the majority of Progressives such talk was largely lip-service, perhaps because there was no great mass opinion about labor. To Pinchot, however, the question fitted in with the larger problem, the battle against privilege, monopoly, and the problem of who should control our means of distribution—all matters that bore directly on the growing unrest in the United States. In 1912 he had supported the eight-hour day, old-age pensions, minimum wage laws, and other protective laws, but he regarded them only as palliatives, subordinate to the principal issues. In a speech given in 1913 he said:

While it is true that the Steel Corporation, like many other great corporations, overworks its employees and fails to pay them a living wage; while it is true that, through its peculiar attitude toward labor organizations, its espionage, its pensions and bonuses, its scientific blacklisting and its policy of employing illiterate and comparatively helpless immigrants, for whom it advertises in the newspapers, it has established a practically unparalleled industrial peonage in its plants; nevertheless, the chief and particular indictment against the Steel Corporation is found elsewhere. It is in the fact that it uses an immense financial power and retains a resourceful and ever active publicity machine to convince the public that overworking and underpaying men and denying them the ordinary rights of freedom are the necessary and humane accompaniments of economic progress.[169]

Between 1912 and 1916 Pinchot observed or spoke at almost every major strike in the East, South, or West. He spoke in New Jersey, West Virginia, Colorado; he spoke at Paterson, the site of "that memorable strike that was the testing ground for where you stood on the question of labor,"[170] and in the steel strikes "in the steel towns along the Allegheny, the Ohio and the Monongahela rivers."

Pinchot saw in the labor troubles of these years a war that would not subside until the wage earner was granted the right of collective bargaining and a guarantee of "fair wages under fair conditions." But fair wages were not enough. The worker must also have a continuity of employment. The United States was no longer a democracy; it was an oligarchy based on control by money power. Our system of production was run on an antisocial basis; the instruments of wealth, if not of existence, were organized for control and exploitation by a few. And what would break such privilege? Not reform movements, for reform movements were superficial and therefore wasteful of effort. Nor could we depend on the church, for it, too, tends to support privilege. Nor could we depend on employers, for "the gentlemen who are rooting for truffles in the field of American industry have understood so little the meaning of the labor movement . . . because they understand so little the meaning of democracy, which is but another word for life itself." The solution lay in the labor movement.

Industrial slavery could best be fought by unionization. "If I belonged to the labor class," Pinchot wrote,

I would spend whatever spare time I had strengthening my union and forcing its recognition by my employers. For I would be well aware that only through recognition of the union is it possible to break the system of so-called benevolent absolutism, by which our great corporations are taking away every right from labor, except the right to work at a wage hardly large enough to supply physical efficiency.[171]

About a year later he became a member of the National Defense Council,[172] which was organized in order to defend unorganized workers whose arrests, particularly in strikes, were open to question. On the whole, however, he encouraged rather than directly participated in labor activities.

63

III

Pinchot made many speeches during his lifetime, but he was never an effective speaker. His friend John Haynes Holmes recalled that although he knew exactly what he wanted to say, "he lacked the extrovert command of the orator, and he had no sweep and power."[173] His audiences saw a well-dressed, slender man, who, in spite of a peculiar habit of stooping, hunched forward, gave the effect of greater height than his six feet one. He was handsome, with graying, light brown, curly hair brushed straight back, and a mustache that he twisted slightly at the ends. In private conversation, his deep, well-modulated voice, his clear diction, his composure, all joined to give an effect of dignity and order, a combination of the "suave" with "virile humor."[174] But before large audiences, Pinchot was usually not effective. The political orators he most admired were Wilson, Brandeis, Borah, La Follette, and George Record. He thought them remarkable speakers, but he never achieved their skill, probably because he could not completely throw off the restraints imposed by his fundamental shyness, and also because he read nearsightedly from a manuscript. For him public speaking was a public duty, and he never really enjoyed his platform appearances. The conviction and the sense of dedication that burned within, he usually did not communicate to his hearers, and he never succeeded in overcoming two of the amateur's greatest disabilities: a falling inflection and the habit of letting his materials—notes, statistics, extracts—raise a barrier between him and his audience. Occasionally he did shake off these restraints. Then, briefly, he flashed into life. The hesitancy disappeared, the faltering note vanished; his voice became warm, rasping, forceful, and his hearers were convinced that "he could turn in and give those damn rascals hell." In 1916, a friend, Charles Hallinan, heard him at a peace rally and wrote a description of the "sea change" he had witnessed. With delight he watched Pinchot become "cool, clever, thrusting, sophisticated," the personification of the "cool, well-bred, New York lawyer—probably one of those smart corporation lawyers—who by the grace of God landed on the side of the people." His hearers, Hallinan thought, probably said to each other, "I'll bet you he's a sarcastic fellow," and even Hallinan muttered to himself, "Well, I'll be damned —he's in his stride already." But then, to his dismay, the falling inflection returned, the hesitation reappeared, and Pinchot lost the ability to project. Once again he became involved in a hand-to-hand struggle with citations. They seemed to absorb his full attention; he was swamped by the sheets of paper before him. Instead of communicating his statistics, he grappled with them; entangled with his notes, he moved farther and farther from his audience. The match dwindled; his hearers lost interest, "and if at any time you had wandered off into the wings still talking, I swear to you, Pinchot, you wouldn't have been missed!"[175]

IV

Another interest was the radical monthly, *The Masses,* which had been founded in 1911. The roster of American periodicals includes nothing quite like this phenomenon. Edited by a socialist, supported by liberals and radicals of many hues, it consistently published the work of some of the best artists and writers of the day, none of whom were paid for their contributions. It was run on a shoestring, cost ten cents, and looked like a smooth paper magazine. The tempestuous life of *The Masses* was marked by an almost uninterrupted series of threatened libel suits and financial and legal difficulties until, in 1917, its mailing privileges were taken away during the wave of censorship that swept this country.[176] In spite of these enormous difficulties, it was always distinguished. Shortly before its demise one contributor wrote, "I believe that *The Masses,* next to the masses of Organized Labor, the Preamble of the I.W.W., the Panama Canal, Jess Willard and the Woolworth Tower is the biggest thing that America has produced so far."[177]

That it survived so long was due to the efforts of its editor, Max Eastman, and a small group that included Floyd Dell, John Reed, John and Dolly Sloan, and Art Young. Its principal lifesaver—or lifegiver—was Eastman. Between writing and editing, he managed to raise one subsidy after another. Here Pinchot helped most. When the first subsidy, which had been extracted with skillful effort from Mrs. O. H. P. Belmont, was nearly exhausted, and the editors were frantically wondering what miracle they could next invoke, the telephone rang and Amos Pinchot said, "I called up to tell you fellows you're getting out a swell magazine." That afternoon Eastman and Reed were in his office. Eastman says they left "charmed with his sagacious humor and richer by two thousand dollars."[178]

Pinchot was interested in *The Masses* for several reasons. First, it gave creative American artists a chance to express themselves. Second, although he opposed socialism he believed in free speech and wanted to fight censorship where he thought it unjust. His files show that he contributed money regularly, which is perhaps one reason why John Reed sometimes called him "Maecenas." Moreover, he harried friends like Mabel Dodge, Charles R. Crane, and William Kent for additional aid, often, of course, without success. He also gave his personal backing and encouragement, and he advised the editors in their frequent legal crises.

In 1913 Max Eastman and Art Young were indicted for criminal libel because they had charged the Associated Press with bias in its presentation of labor news. La Follette's law partner, Gilbert Roe, agreed to defend them without charge, and the man who put up $2,000 bail—which he sent with his congratulations—was Amos Pinchot. Shortly after, a protest meeting jammed Cooper Union. Outside there was plenty of excitement. The police arrested a member of the I.W.W. and carted him off, while hundreds of men and women unsuccessfully sought admission to the hall. There was plenty of excitement inside, too. The aisles were jammed, and the audience cheered the speakers, among whom were Amos Pinchot, John Haynes Holmes, Lincoln Steffens, Norman Hapgood, and Joseph Cannon of the Western Federation of Miners. At the high point of the evening Pinchot, who was introduced as "a rebel in a good many directions," unequivocally associated himself with Eastman and Young, and backed their accusation. "I am perfectly willing," he declared, "to stand behind the charge made by Eastman and Young that the Associated Press does color and distort the news, that it is not impartial, and that it is a monopolistic corporation, not only in constraint of trade but in constraint of truth."[179] The next day the *New York Times* editorially implied that he was "a Socialist champion of freedom of the press" and reminded him that he should "understand that this is not an Associated Press suit; it is a government suit, an action brought by the people to punish the lawless." Perhaps the *Times* would have spoken even more sharply had it known that Pinchot was the man who arranged for Gilbert Roe to take the case, and that he was helping to raise defense funds.

An immediate consequence of this speech was a call from the A.P.'s

Washington attorney, a Yale friend, who informed Pinchot that if he did not retract, he would be the defendant in a $150,000 libel suit. Pinchot retorted, "They can go to hell, and let's have dinner at the Century Club and talk it over." At dinner he explained to the attorney that the A.P. automatically played up the side of the employers and played down the fact that the strikers were not fanatics but human beings who in many instances were paid starvation wages. "You know that as well as I do," he continued, and pointed out that if the A.P. pressed its charges, it would be beaten. The threatened suit never materialized, and after two years the criminal indictment against Eastman and Young was dropped and the bail returned.[180]

Again, Pinchot helped raise funds when *The Masses* was thrown off the New York subway stands on charges of blaspheming the Divinity. In 1914, when it looked as though the magazine must quit for lack of money, he helped ensure its continuation for another year by contributing $1,500 and by persuading Samuel Untermeyer and E. W. Scripps to do the same. He advanced money for outstanding bills, and in 1917–1918 was treasurer of *The Masses* Defense Committee. It is easy to see why Eastman describes Pinchot as a man who "came inside my problem and shared the hazard and the humor of it."[181]

Occasionally Pinchot wrote a piece, sometimes on labor, sometimes on unemployment or against the war. He asked friends for similar contributions. In 1914, he wrote to George Bernard Shaw, requesting an article (which did not materialize) and describing the growth of the magazine and some of the problems it had encountered.

My wife has sent to Mrs. Shaw a few copies of *The Masses,* a paper edited by Max Eastman. We are struggling to make *The Masses* a success, because it is the only magazine where the artists and writers can say what they want. Most of the stuff in *The Masses* is done by the best men we have, but it is principally stuff that could not appear elsewhere. None of the articles or pictures are paid for, except the editorials by Eastman, who gets a small salary for running the paper.

We have been going a little over a year, starting from nothing, and have now a circulation of about fourteen thousand, growing slowly. A few of us will contribute enough to pay the deficit, which I hope will taper off soon.

We are not popular among the best people, and I regret to say that the library committees of the clubs to which I have the great honor of belonging have yielded to the entreaties of the elderly members and banished *The Masses* from the files. This is a pity, for heretofore a number of old gentlemen at the University Club got their exercises by walking up and down the library, tearing *The Masses* up and throwing it on the floor. It is hard to keep printing a paper in the face of such a bar to circulation.

If you feel like writing something for us, it would give us a great boost. . . .[182]

V

As the 1916 elections approached, Pinchot was again dejected. The Progressive party was certainly doomed;[183] Charles Evans Hughes was an impossible candidate—"a wooden man, honest . . . but quite ignorant as to the great social and economic problems that are actually before us";[184] and although Woodrow Wilson surely knew the distinction between privilege and democracy, he had virtually ignored those three fundamental matters, "economics, distribution of wealth, government ownership."[185] However, Pinchot admired the President for his peace stand; furthermore, on domestic issues he belonged with the progressive element in the Democratic party (that very element he had once hoped to capture for the Bull Moose). Therefore, in spite of reservations and in spite of vigorous pro-Hughes pressures from his family and friends, he decided to campaign for the "subversive economic ideas of Woodrow Wilson." Professor Link has pointed out that the support of "the advanced wing of the progressive movement" was one of the important elements that contributed to Wilson's victory.[186] As chairman of the Wilson Volunteers of New York State, Pinchot took a small but active part in this undertaking.

In concept the Wilson Volunteers illustrated Pinchot's belief that in important matters liberals could and should cut across party lines and work together. The Volunteers included Rabbi Stephen Wise, who called himself "a disgusted Republican"; Timothy Healey, who never before had supported a Democrat for president; Norman Hapgood, Walter Lippmann, and Frederic C. Howe. As Pinchot told the President, "We are a lot of uncatalogued people, in a way; most of us are independents, a few of us are personal friends of yours, and a few of us are Democrats." Performing "possibly the greatest whirlwind tour that has ever been made in New York State,"[187] the Volunteers campaigned on the issue of privilege versus democracy. They rode in automobiles "from the Battery to Buffalo and back, covered 1,400 miles, spoke in 108 cities, towns, and villages." Pinchot, Frederic C. Howe, and Dr. A. J. McKelway were called "the Three Musketeers of the Volunteer expedition." In Syracuse Pinchot became "an unheralded Athos, or Porthos or Aramis" because he was reported to have knocked down (a story later denied) a man who shouted, "To hell with the President."[188]

The journey "from the Battery to Buffalo and back" ended whatever flimsy pretenses of friendship still existed between Pinchot and Theodore Roosevelt. Increasingly the Colonel had indicated his distaste for "some of the men who nominally stayed with us, like Amos Pinchot," men who had tried to turn the party "into an aid to the I.W.W., or a kind of parlor anarchist association."[189] On his side, Pinchot had grown increasingly certain that "the oyster man" had been relieved at his defection in 1914. The Perkins quarrel had been bad enough. Subsequently the two men had differed over intervention in Mexico, a matter on which Roosevelt was vehement. As was to be expected, when Pinchot campaigned with the Wilson Volunteers, he attacked the Colonel on the two points where he considered him particularly vulnerable—his false progressivism and his demands for war. Before a group of factory workers he charged that T.R. had become "the bell hop of Wall Street." Just before the election he made another bitter assault, asserting that the Colonel (he later named him "Colonel-Sit-by-the-Fire")* had once been a "little navy man and a pacifist." At these taunts "The Only Patriotic American" threw off his mask of restraint. In an abrupt and formal note (the salutation was merely "Sir") he suggested that Pinchot was either a villain or insane, and he ended, "When I spoke of the Progressive Party as having a lunatic fringe, I specifically had you in mind."†[190]

* George Perkins, who occasionally sent Colonel Roosevelt bits by or about Pinchot, forwarded this reference and with it his own sentiments of shocked surprise. (George W. Perkins to Theodore Roosevelt [n.d.], Theodore Roosevelt Papers.)

† On November 11, 1916, Amos Pinchot sent his warm congratulations to President Wilson. He wrote, "I note with chagrin that according to the Vocal One, the center of population of soft citizens has moved west. We must now adjust ourselves to the idea, that every man who rides a bucking horse or wears

VI

Whether or not Pinchot foresaw the outbreak of the European war is not clear, but he later implied that by 1913, at least, he had known it was inevitable. By 1916 he had become increasingly apprehensive of the rising militarist sentiment in the United States. He specifically denied that he was a pacifist, but his feelings were mixed. Pro-Ally in his sympathies, he agreed with La Follette that Germany was the principal aggressor, that this country had every legal excuse for fighting. As he said to the Senator, "I feel as you do that a German victory would be the most horrible disaster to mankind." Furthermore, he conceded that "even if we had not gone in when we did, we would have had to later on; not, indeed, on account of the issues spoken of when we declared war, but of larger ones [i.e., commercial involvements]."[191] He would always support a war of self-defense, but he would not support our participation in any foreign conflict that could bring about only the destruction of economic progress and civil rights and the hard-won gains of the past six years. Oppressed by hopelessness and futility, he wrote, "I feel as if the militarist game was in some way bolstering up the system of economic absolutism that menaces the country."[192]

It is impossible to convey the contempt and abuse that befell the antimilitarists in World War I. To advocate anything that suggested pacifism required great moral courage and the strength to live in "a solitude of despised ideas."* Even so, Pinchot believed that his work on at least two committees had been effective. The first was the American Union Against Militarism, where he served first as vice-chairman and then as chairman. He opposed intervention in Mexico, particularly at the time of the Carrizal incident. Later, when the American Civil Liberties Union grew out of the renamed Union Against Militarism, he became concerned with civil rights. Shortly after this country entered World War I he organized and served as chairman of a pay-as-you-go committee that advocated an 80 per cent profits tax as

---

a Stetson hat has been deceiving us. Whereas we thought him something of a rugged American, the election proves that he is only a whited mollycoddle. . . .

"It is hard for me to get used to the idea of your victory and Mr. Hughes' defeat, for I have hardly ever been on the winning side."

* The words are George Eliot's, and they were written in another context; nevertheless they are applicable here.

a means of financing the war. Although he and his fellow committee members were bitterly criticized for their activities, he felt that final results were

attended with considerable success. It [the committee] enlisted the co-operation of some 4,500,000 people, furnished Congress with information on taxable profits and the English system of war taxes, which formed a basis for its debates on these subjects. It laid, I think, a broad foundation of public opinion that was of service in the legislative sessions of 1917 and 1918.[193]

While emphasizing his antisocialist convictions, he supported Morris Hillquit for mayor of New York City because he approved of his war position; to the distaste of many of his old friends, he presided at Hill-quit's Madison Square Garden meeting. He was also a member of the group that went to Washington to protest the denial of mailing privileges to Socialist newspapers.

He never forgot some of the things that happened to him in those days, although he did not undergo the kind of opprobrium that La Follette endured. His anonymous mail increased; he was publicly described as "a menace" who with "his pacifists [had] been en-deavoring for the last year to arouse class hatred";[194] he lost old friends, among them Henry Stimson;[195] and after the war a Senate committee, investigating the effects of German propaganda in this country, heard that Amos Pinchot had been active in pacifist and radical organizations—"movements which did not help the United States when this country was fighting the Central Powers."[196]

Pinchot's antimilitarist activity was not as irrelevant to his political philosophy as may appear at first glance. The one was in fact a corol-lary of the other. He hated war, especially imperialistic wars. Wars encouraged privileges and destroyed civil rights and economic prog-ress; no nation ever emerged stronger or better for the struggle. Mo-nopoly was inimical to peace, for monopoly needed war in order to stay strong. Instead of fighting the wars of other nations, Americans should deal with the problems raised by privilege at home. Through the development of popular government, the suppression of monop-oly, the restoration and maintenance of free competition at home, and the maintenance of peace lay the way to a stronger and greater Amer-ica.

Part IV

1919–1944

I

In 1919 a Middle Western newspaper reported that Amos Pinchot was currently known as "the underdog fancier." He had got this name because of his "propensity to leap into any fray in which he thinks the deal is not four-square."[197] The latest "fray" was the Committee of 48, his last stand in the progressive movement. For two years he was associated with it, heart and soul. The Committee is the least-known of his third party attempts, but it is, in some ways, the most ambitious effort—in scope if not in achievement. Pinchot was a founder and leader, and, as William Hard said, he and George Record were the "intellectual combatants of the movement—its philosophers and gladiators."[198]

The Committee of 48 was organized in December 1918. It was so named because it was to be represented in every state in the Union. The idea and the name were conceived by Pinchot's old friend J. A. H. Hopkins, a former treasurer of the Progressive party. Closely associated with Hopkins were James Blauvelt of New Jersey, Gilson Gardner of Washington, D.C., Allen McCurdy of New York, and, of course, Record and Pinchot. Pinchot later claimed that this group was immediately responsible for the ideas and the program that gave the Committee its original vitality.[199]

In the beginning there were no third party intentions. Rather, the purpose was to back the best man and the best measures, regardless of politics. In short, the Committee of 48 was to be independent in the truest sense of the word.

Contributions and workers were to be voluntary. Consequently, money was always short, the Committee was always in debt, and the workers were erratic.* In spite of these amateurish and often disorganized conditions, the response to the Committee was hearteningly enthusiastic. This enthusiasm was further bolstered by the organizational meetings, where Socialists, Populists, single-taxers, La Follette Progressives, dissident Democrats, labor men, and former Bull

---

* According to John Haynes Holmes, Hopkins was the hardest worker, and Pinchot was the runner-up.

72

Moosers appeared. As these meetings, which were exploratory, continued, the executive committee organized plans for a national conference, to be held in St. Louis in November 1919. Out of this conference grew a conviction that a third party, a fusion party of labor, agrarian, and white-collar groups* with an estimated beginning membership of 250,000, would create a formidable coalition.[200] The choice of an effective candidate was now more than ever a serious matter.

Pinchot, of course, was very much in the center of the planning and organization. For him, though, 1920 was not the year in which to try to win elections but the strategic time when the great new party was to be formed. Certain that the conservatives would control the country in 1920, he believed that the liberals might win in 1924. The liberal candidate, therefore, must recognize that in 1920 he would function as a guide, an educator, a man with a program that liberals could follow during the years of conservative domination. A number of presidential possibilities, including Pinchot and Record, were considered, but increasingly one man seemed to fit the specifications of the liberal guide, leader, educator, the strong rock: Robert M. La Follette.[201]

The national convention was set for July 1920. It was to be held in Chicago, where at the same time the Labor convention and a number of smaller conventions, representing groups that would come under the aegis of the Committee of 48, were to be held. Representing the Forty-eighters were 900 delegates from 43 states. La Follette sentiment was strong. (The Senator had already indicated that he would

* About ten days before the St. Louis Conference, an important event took place: the National Labor Party was formed in Chicago. To observers, the implications seemed clear: the New Labor Party, three or four farmers' organizations, at least two "semi-radical 'parties,'" the Non-Partisan League of America, and the Committee of 48 would combine (*New York Times*, November 25, 1919). In addition, two points should be remembered. First the Forty-eighters regarded their 1919 conference as enormously significant, because it was "the first widespread attempt, following the war, of men and women from all walks of life to form a serious opposition to the two old parties" (*Social Progress*, pp. 316–17). Second, remote as the struggle for a third party may seem to the present-day reader, in 1920 its possible repercussions were considerable. As David Lawrence pointed out, if Senator La Follette carried the states of Wisconsin, Minnesota, and North Dakota, he *might* carry sufficient electoral votes so that the Democratic Cox would be elected (Chicago *Daily News*, July 12, 1920).

not accept the nomination unless it were unanimous, but a number of the delegates thought this point a technicality.) Pinchot and Record, who were reported to have written the platform (they were indeed influential members of the platform committee) and who had taken a leading part in the negotiations with Senator La Follette, were much in evidence and generally regarded as among the top leaders. But even before the convention began, trouble was apparent, and the Labor delegates threatened to bolt the proposed united front of labor, agrarian, and white-collar groups. Quickly matters moved to disaster, and in four days the hoped-for fusion movement had all but blown up over the basic matter of a platform. For their part, Record and Pinchot refused to budge from their "individualistic" platform; they balked at the Labor demands for a nationalization of mines, endorsement of the Plumb plan for controlling railroads, and a capital levy tax.[202] On the other side, the Labor people, who were considered preponderantly left wing, refused to budge from their position. Record and Pinchot proved unsuccessful as negotiators. In desperation, a conciliation committee was named. It, too, deadlocked. Meanwhile fights had broken out within the groups themselves. A factional fight, aimed at breaking the power of Sam Gompers, drove the Labor men to increased fury.[203] In the Committee of 48 a regional fight, Eastern conservatives against Western radicals, tore to pieces the white-collar hopes of fusion. The Western "radicals" wanted to affiliate with the Labor group, the Eastern "conservatives" wanted to hold off and negotiate and, in the absence of satisfactory negotiations, to plan an orderly program of procedure. By the fourth day the Pinchot-Hopkins group saw their hopes defeated, their dreams reduced to chaos. They lost control of their own membership, who wanted to amalgamate; they heard the Labor delegates denounce them as "Eastern intellectuals," "plutes," and "shyster lawyers";[204] they lost every move in the conferences, where compromise had been talked of but never realized, as the skillful Labor negotiators outmaneuvered the Forty-eighter attempts to block the "left wing" points in the platform. Subsequently, the majority of the Forty-eighters, ignoring Pinchot's pleas, "Do not become a class party," bolted to Carmen's Hall, to amalgamate with a Labor party that in effect swallowed them up.[205] La Follette, aware of all the nuances in this internal strife, refused the nomination, and in his place, and against the objections of the Forty-eighters, Parley

Christensen was nominated. One may summarize the disaster by saying that the would-be united front moved from fusion to confusion, from confusion to the virtual destruction of the Committee of 48 as a potential political force. Through the conventions of 1920, labor and the farmers reached an agreement and a working basis, but the liberal, white-collar, independent voter was once again left in limbo.

Why did the Committee of 48 fail? Some of the answers to this question are fairly obvious. First, its founders were naïve. Their organizational work was poor. In their negotiations they were no match for the more skilled Labor men, who consistently outsmarted them. Second, they overestimated their importance—that is, Labor's need for them. The Forty-eighters were dedicated to the idea of a strong united front in which labor, the farmer, and the intellectual could freely participate. Only they realized too late that in this mixture they were nonsoluble, that they were really not important to Labor, and that Labor probably did not want them. Third, they were deplorably sloppy. They did not plan carefully. Pinchot's correspondence shows that early in 1920 the Forty-eighters knew that the Labor men were beset by factional struggles but, apparently because they were amateurs at the game of founding a political party, they did not sufficiently prepare for the consequences. Their generalship lacked point. Unlike La Follette, who had carefully explored the situation, they did not take into account the directions and results that could come from the maneuverings of well-organized minority groups. The Forty-eighters were dealing with men who would not give way on their program, a program that seemed perilously close to socialism; yet they could not force through a compromise program. Fourth, the floor leaders of the Committee of 48 were not astute. Throughout the convention they behaved like amateurs. As Gilson Gardner said, the leaders of the Committee simply did not control the basic mechanics that were a necessity for success.[206]

Thus, for all practical purposes, ended Amos Pinchot's dream of a third party. Save for token support of La Follette in 1924 and a brief campaign for George Record in that year, he appeared no more for the Progressives. And thus ended his dream of the regeneration of the progressive movement in postwar America. Disillusioned, he commented, "We have dashed the liberal movement to pieces on the rock of political ambition and selfishness."[207] In short, he decided that the way to political reform could not be reached by third parties, and he withdrew from politics.

II

Probably because he had to occupy himself, he began *Big Business in America,* his account of American sociopolitical history since 1896. Although he had long planned the book, he had trouble in writing it, as the many uncompleted attempts show. Nevertheless, he read, and he wrote sketches, memoranda, and finally chapters first for the economic study and then for the political counterpart that became the *History of the Progressive Party.** "The changes which industrialization and concentration of power have brought about in the United States" became his account of the development of plutocracy in America.

In this presentation Pinchot cited four men who had stimulated his approach. The first was John Fiske. In his essay "Alexander Hamilton and the Federalist Party," Fiske remarked that many of Hamilton's colleagues feared that his practice of strengthening the alliance between government and the financial interests would in time change this country from a democracy to a plutocracy, and that we were already seeing the fruition of this policy.[208] One does not need to look far to find that this remark was congenial, if not stimulating, to Amos Pinchot.

The second was William Graham Sumner. Here it is tempting to argue for a pervasive influence, wiser to stick to the acknowledged indebtedness. Specifically, Pinchot drew from Sumner his belief in the necessity of the "equal chance" and the need for monopoly to control necessary phases of production. Sumner's definition of plutocracy and of the plutocrat, his distinction between democracy and liberty, his prediction that "the social war of the twentieth century" would be the conflict between democracy and plutocracy, all strike the note that Pinchot emphasized in connection with the Progressive party.†[209]

The third was Lord Bryce. Pinchot, who had known him personally and had closely read his books, did not consider Bryce profound. With

* For an account of the two versions, see Editorial Note.

† Anyone who is interested can find some suggestive similarities between Pinchot and his old teacher in Sumner's *Earth-Hunger and Other Essays,* ed. by Albert Galloway Keller, 1913.

76

his estimate that American plutocracy was on the wane, Pinchot did not agree. Bryce's love of America, coupled with a perhaps naïve belief in the force of the progressive movement, had misled him. Furthermore, Bryce was ignorant of the formative influences of economics, and he had almost never looked behind the scenes in order "to inspect the wires by which the puppets of the play were moved."[210] Nevertheless, he was stimulating, and in *Modern Democracies* he had made a useful point. "In his appraisal of the influence of concentrated wealth upon the agencies that form public opinion, Bryce comes close to the marrow of a problem that has fascination on account of the paradox it presents."[211] Politically America is a democracy in which the will of the people is supposed to control the government. But— and here the paradox intervenes—the public cannot make its will operate effectively in its own interest.

The reason is that in matters of great moment our newspapers and magazines, our films, our schools, our bought politicians, and our hired lecturers so distort and pervert the truth that the public is unable to distinguish between fact and misinformation. Great wealth, which wields these instruments for its own purposes, does not rely on bluntly ordering and tyrannizing; rather, its power depends on subtle persuasion.

The fourth, and in some ways the most influential, was Henry Demarest Lloyd, "one of the most remarkable as well as erudite writers on the effect of massed economic power on society." Pinchot knew his articles, particularly "The Story of a Great Monopoly." He knew, of course, *Wealth Against Commonwealth,* which it seemed to him combined an astonishing mastery of facts and figures with a delightful style, lively and readable. Lloyd's exposition was brilliant; he made the abstract concrete, the complex simple, bringing it within easy grasp of the man to whom economics was an abstruse subject, a mass of figures and trends. Had the conditions of the 1890's been slightly different, had Lloyd's book reached minds "ripe for progress, instead of social atavism,"[212] *Wealth Against Commonwealth* might easily have achieved immortality. Lloyd traced the evidences of combination in the rise to power of a specific monopoly, showing how Standard Oil reached its pinnacle through combination with railroad interests. Pinchot accepted Lloyd's thesis and tried to give it a wider application. The throttling effect of monopoly on competition, the close relations between monopoly and plutocracy, and the relation of plutocracy to government, he presented in simple, nontechnical language. In Pinchot's philosophy Henry Demarest Lloyd's influence is basic. "We must either regulate, or own, or destroy"[213] might have been written by Pinchot himself.

Fiske, Sumner, Bryce, and Lloyd admittedly helped form basic concepts in Pinchot's *History*. Still other influences, not cited but of great importance, must be mentioned; for many of Pinchot's ideas are his responses and reactions to persons he knew. The influence of Gifford Pinchot cannot be overestimated, even though the two brothers did not always agree, particularly after 1914. La Follette was another notable force in his thinking. Although the two men sometimes differed, although in 1924 Pinchot felt unduly bitter about the Senator, their differences were temporary. To the last Pinchot acknowledged La Follette's greatness. In his progressive philosophy, in his championship of "the basic issues," Pinchot stands close to the man to whom he once wrote, "In talking to you . . . I feel like a sign painter giving Leonardo advice."[214] Brandeis, especially the Brandeis of *Other People's Money,* cannot be overlooked. But perhaps most important was George L. Record, "one of the most extraordinary minds this country has known." According to Pinchot, the two men first met at the Republican convention of 1912, and they remained close friends until Record's death in 1933.[215] They agreed on almost all points. Pinchot admired the power and practicality of Record's mind, and in him he saw reflected many of his own aims and beliefs, perhaps some of his frustrations. Of this old friend he wrote:

In a sense, he belonged to the golden age of American politics, which formed its tradition in the first decades of the republic, to the time when men cared passionately for ideas and believed in their power and practical bearing upon a nation's life. . . . he was one of the few men I ever knew who spent his life saying and doing precisely what he believed. He was a devoted friend, and I think the only great man I have ever known.[216]

Books also influenced him. He read and reread *The Federalist*. He knew well the writings of Jefferson, of whom he said, "[His] profound and general knowledge continues to reserve for him the title of 'the most considerable American.' "[217] Lincoln he admired. Woodrow

Wilson's *The New Freedom* paralleled much of his own thinking, as his marked copy indicates.

In the years since 1933, when Amos Pinchot put aside his unfinished book, a considerable amount of new material about the Progressives has been made generally available. Letters, autobiographies, reminiscences, biographies, histories, and learned articles are now of easy access. The Progressive leaders have been described; the progressive philosophies, so often contradictory, have been analyzed. In some ways the present-day reader of the *History* is better informed than was its author. He himself seemed to recognize this possibility, for he wrote, "It is doubtful whether a fair account of crucial happenings, where the elements of conflict and misunderstanding are strong, can be written until many years after they took place."[218]

Acknowledging these differences in outlook and knowledge, one may ask what are the strengths and weaknesses of Pinchot's account. The great strength is, of course, the author's firsthand knowledge and experience. He tells a story rich in personal reminiscence, anecdote, and characterization, a story unified by a consistent viewpoint; almost from the first "a Cassandra to the Colonel," he did not, like some of the Colonel's other chroniclers, arrive at his conclusions by hindsight. At his best he writes with vigor. Part of this vigor comes from his bias. In this connection, the reader should not accept uncritically his account of the support and subsequent repudiation of Senator La Follette in 1912. One must remember the hero worship that Gifford inspired in his younger brother. Older and politically more knowing than Amos, Gifford took the lead. Although Amos quickly regretted the switch to the Colonel, his account, written years later, still seeks to justify his brother's course and, by inference, the wisdom of his action. Amos' emphasis on La Follette's precarious health should be read with this qualification in mind.

In the first sentence of the *History* Pinchot implies that his account will be the most impartial yet given. But in the nature of things his book could not be impartial; his very method prevented it. He wrote out of his personal experience, his own memories, his own letter files. He used almost no other primary sources, he did not balance his own with other people's reminiscences. He did not use the La Follette Papers when he described the desertion of the Senator. He did not use the Theodore Roosevelt Papers, the Beveridge Papers, the Johnson

Papers, or the collections of other men with whom he had stood at Armageddon. If he needed a manuscript reference, he occasionally turned to Gifford, but that is about as far afield as he went. Again, his assumption that the steel interests were out to control the Progressive party is fundamental to his narrative. First presented only as a dark suspicion, this hypothesis soon assumes the importance of a proved fact, which it is not. In short, Pinchot's *History* justifies his own point of view, and no matter how absorbing the story, how filled with firsthand detail, the dice are loaded. Indeed, this personal note and this strong partisanship give the book much interest, but they do not make it impartial.

That the book was never finished is its obvious weakness, and still another is an evident unhappiness with analysis. In the final chapter, he intended to evaluate. Instead, he did not pull his facts together; he did not relate facts and theory as he had planned; the chapter falls apart, and the story fizzles to a close. Elsewhere I have suggested that the difficulty may have been an insufficiency of firsthand knowledge.[219] As I have also indicated, Pinchot's views on the effectiveness of third parties had changed just before he began to write his account, with the result that he was possibly not altogether sure of the points he wished to make.* As a result, he was clearly most at ease when he wrote anecdotally, least happy when he started to analyze and to draw his final conclusions.

III

From 1925 to 1933 Pinchot worked hard on his books, first on *Big Business in America;* then, apparently after 1930, on the *History of the Progressive Party*. Meanwhile, although not much interested in politics, he did, in 1928, support Alfred E. Smith for president. Four years later some of his old optimism returned. Franklin D. Roosevelt was somewhat less liberal than he would have liked ("I long ago gave up hope of being able to vote for a presidential candidate cut precisely to my pattern," he told David K. Niles),[220] but he campaigned for him with high hopes.

Pinchot's political disillusionment was commensurate with his first soaring faith in Franklin Roosevelt. He began by thinking him "by all

* In addition, the reader should not forget that the *History* was written *before* President Franklin Roosevelt's New Deal.

odds the best man nominated by either party since Woodrow Wilson."[221] He ended by regarding him as a traitor. In this change of attitude he was not alone, of course, for after 1932 former Bull Moosers had three possible choices: like Harold Ickes and Francis Heney, they could become registered Democrats and strong supporters of the New Deal; like Gifford Pinchot, they could support F.D.R. while not voting for him; or, like Amos Pinchot and George Record, they could repudiate their first allegiance and die fighting Franklin Roosevelt and his administrations.

Amos Pinchot broke with President Roosevelt in 1933. The immediate cause was the New Deal monetary policy, which he called "reflation"; he was, moreover, distrustful of the President's program of managed economy, which he described as "pure regimentation." He agreed with George Record, who predicted that instead of strengthening competition, this experiment would strengthen the trend toward monopoly. It would entrench the trusts, already enormously powerful; it would also give great power to the larger manufacturers, who would take advantage of the managed economy to combine and thus squeeze out their smaller rivals. The New Deal program was not designed to give every man an equal chance; on the contrary, it would secure new and stronger devices for economic inequality.[222] Pinchot called himself an Anti-New-Deal Progressive who opposed regulation. He felt increasingly that though Roosevelt's advisers promised economic aid, they did nothing about the real problems, problems that Pinchot outlined to Brandeis in much the same words he had used twenty years before: "I think," he wrote, "we ought to get back to fighting privilege and monopoly and restoring equality of economic opportunity by every possible means." No administration, he continued, had struggled with this enormous and elusive point; but he was confident that if the question were met, economic difficulties would be solved. Many of our present difficulties could be met by "divorcing the monopolistic industries from the particular things which give them their power, as for instance the pipe lines in the case of the oil companies."[223]

That the New Deal had achieved some good things that should be carried on and that undoubtedly would be retained in a liberal Republican administration, he conceded; but he opposed its recovery program, which had done nothing to help the rank and file. "The

New Deal policies have not only not helped recovery, but on the whole have held it back and needlessly prolonged unemployment."[224] And he regarded with loathing the New Deal method of coping with unemployment. Inherently, he said, it "carries a greater threat to labor than any economic or political force that has confronted labor at any time in America's history."[225] He believed that, partly because of a fondness for experimenting in socialist reforms, but principally because of an inordinate lust for power, the New Dealers deliberately set labor and management against each other, and that in the long run labor would be the loser.

Pinchot agreed that the President "has preached social justice and quickened the country's interest in social problems, even though he has not shed light on them." He admitted that measures like the Social Security Law, the C.C.C., and the S.E.C. were much needed, and that since 1932 other constructive measures had been put through. But Franklin Roosevelt's achievements could not counterbalance the national havoc he had brought about; although a brilliant and unusually flexible politician, he was a "facile, shallow-minded President with little principle and great ambitions." How could one trust or believe in a man who had "no compass to guide him, except a consuming desire for power and a will to control not merely all three branches of government but every phase of economic life"?[226] Cleverly, the President had assumed dictatorial powers. Instead of the reforms they so desperately needed, the American people had been given the New Deal, "an economic and political failure . . . a betrayer [sic] of American progress."[227]

The key to Pinchot's abhorrence of the New Deal lay in the tremendous expansion of government in Washington—in other words, statism. In the vast and growing federal bureaucracy he saw the creation of a great force hostile to the public welfare. This force was political centralization. Pinchot had always believed that the state should be no more than arbiter. In 1910 he had asserted that the end of government was *the furthering of the interests of the individual.** From 1910 until his death he never changed this belief. Government, he held, should maintain free enterprise in all things, including industry and politics; government, the servant of the people, should regulate when necessary, principally to maintain justice and security.

* Italics mine.

But, unalterably, it is the individual who counts. Any government that seeks to centralize power in the hands of a single man or group, that attempts to regulate intensively the economic life of a nation, brings with its program disaster to the nation. Here he was completely consistent with what he had always believed: his conviction that power should rise from the bottom to the top is good progressive doctrine with its emphasis on grass roots.

As he watched the growing centralization of power in Washington, he became convinced that his life's work had been misspent, that his long fight for public ownership of natural monopolies, transportation, and utilities had been wrong. Instead of strengthening free enterprise as he had thought, these doctrines had undermined the power of the individual, had strengthened the power of the state. Unrolling before him, he saw an extension of federal power in contrast with which mere plutocracy was puny. The New Deal, with its political centralization, represented for him the most sinister means yet known of controlling modern society. In these developments he saw the betrayal of everything he had believed in and fought for. While fighting for economic opportunity he had at the last backed men who had built a privileged political caste. His long fight against economic monopoly had ended with the establishment of a political monopoly. His fight for popular government had helped establish a dictatorship.

This loss of political faith was one of the deep blows of his life. Pinchot accordingly determined to take part in a last fight, this one against a far more powerful opponent than any he had previously engaged: Franklin Roosevelt and his New Deal. This new crusade made his work on the interrelations of wealth and politics from 1896 to 1932 seem parochial. It is therefore easy to see why he never completed his manuscripts but instead went back to his old vocation of publicist. Radio speeches, pamphlets, and a large collection of open letters addressed to senators and congressmen and to public men he knew or had known—among them Henry Stimson, Harold Ickes, Hiram Johnson, and the President himself—were the result.

Not only did he oppose the New Deal's domestic program; he also opposed Mr. Roosevelt's candidacy for a third term, because he saw in this move a further device for perpetuating a political dictatorship. Active in the Committee on Constitutional Government, he was subsequently proud of his fight against the court-packing bill and President Roosevelt's government reorganization plans.

In 1936 Pinchot became a founder and a national committeeman of the America First Committee, which was organized to oppose America's involvement in a second world war. His opposition to the Roosevelt foreign policy was based on his long-cherished belief that Americans should support the traditional foreign policy of Washington and Adams. In contrast, he insisted, the Roosevelt program was a job of "war salesmanship" that must inevitably take us into war.

Without war there would be no "great international emergency" to take the people's minds off their domestic troubles, and to serve Mr. Roosevelt as an excuse for breaking an anti-third term tradition and expanding the already immense powers of the President to the point of dictatorship. Without war there would be no way to hide the tragic breakdown of an administration which, in eight years and by the expenditure of sixty billions, has failed to lift the depression, or re-employ ten million idle job-seeking men and women.[228]

IV

Pinchot knew that whatever he said and wrote would probably have no effect on our eventual entry into the war. Melancholy and ill in his last years,[229] he increasingly believed that he had lived and fought in vain.

He died on February 18, 1944.

In his autobiography, Max Eastman writes of Pinchot as "a prince—a subtle thing to be in America, and not easily defined. It requires hereditary wealth, but many who have that do not attain the princely bearing or prerogative."[230] These are graceful words and the description is apt, but a number of Pinchot's former associates have felt that the emphasis is misplaced. Men and women who worked with him say that his characteristic quality was a deep belief in the rights of man, a belief so deep that he did not hesitate to support reforms that were opposed to his personal advantage. Many a reformer is like Disraeli's ducal republican, St. Aldegonde, who believed that all ranks should be leveled except the ducal, all wealth done away with except land. The progressive movement contained many St. Aldegondes, but Amos Pinchot was not one of them.

His point of view was not unique. Like many a capitalist reformer, he was a conservative. He hated privilege, but he wanted to maintain the status quo. He supported capitalism, but he believed that if it were to survive it must be reformed. His emphasis on reform as therapy often led people to assume he was more radical than he really was.

Pinchot held no offices, advised no presidents, undertook no missions, and was almost always on the losing side. He spoke for labor when it was not fashionable to do so. He opposed two wars and was called a traitor. He paid more than lip service to civil rights. In future years some of the causes he worked for will be remembered; some will be forgotten; others will interest only the specialist. But beneath his interests a basic principle runs. It justifies the fighter for minorities, the idealist who is not popular, and it is best described by Lord Acton: "Ideals in politics are never realized, but the pursuit of them determines history."

Section II

A M O S R. E. P I N C H O T

History of the Progressive Party 1912–1916

CHAPTER I

Political Undercurrents—1912

The causes of the rise of the Progressive party and of the passing from the stage of politics of its leader, Theodore Roosevelt, have, I think, never been fully and impartially related. They have been described by friends and partisans of Mr. Roosevelt, Mr. Taft, and of Senator La Follette, while Roosevelt and La Follette have touched on them in their writings, the latter in his *Autobiography*.[1] Claude Bowers in his life of Beveridge[2] has told the story accurately and understandingly, but too briefly and only as a chapter in the Indiana Senator's life. Herbert Duffy's biography of Taft[3] is a eulogy of his hero, a man without a flaw or with the single one of an overgentle and unsuspicious nature. The vivacious letters of Colonel Archie Butt[4] to his sister are written frankly as a defense of his worshiped chief. Charnwood's monograph on Roosevelt[5] rates as a rather banal prose poem about a character that fortunately never lived. Bishop[6] is fair and accurate and replete with facts, but writes from the outside, as one little versed in the hidden game of politics, a comprehension of which can alone give facts their significance.

Mark Sullivan, erstwhile journalistic tribune of the people, seems in the fourth volume of *Our Times*[7] to have reconciled himself to the humbler but more comfortable role of boswelling for the rich and great, and especially for the old guard Republican hierarchy which he once so thoroughly detested. This inconstant nymph of newspaperdom, who now since the Democratic victory of '32 must again

Notes begin on p. 276.

adjust his allegiance, if he is to retain his standing of *persona grata* to whoever occupies the White House, writes of the events of 1911 and 1912 in a vein of gossipy cynicism, praising his former enemies whom he now invests with the romantic atmosphere of an Arthurian legend, ridiculing his former friends, and dishing up fact and rumor with impartiality. It is to be regretted that he indulges so often in assertions of a kind to make Münchausen himself writhe for the poverty of his inventive genius. While in his earlier phase, men like Roosevelt and Brandeis and the Insurgent senators of the period kindled Sullivan's enthusiasm, today he turns to such heroes as Taft, Cannon, and Aldrich. He dismisses Brandeis' great part in the Pinchot-Ballinger controversy[8] in a few lines, leaving the reader to conclude that the administration was the victim of a political cabal. And at the same time he ignores the really important fact that Brandeis and Gifford Pinchot laid bare and checked the Morgan-Guggenheim syndicate's conspiracy to rob the government through the device of fraudulent entries on the only important steam coal deposit on the Pacific, which should have been held as a reserve for the navy.

A fair instance of the factual qualities of *Our Times* is his statement that Brandeis,[9] in order to show that Taft had antedated a public document, namely, Attorney-General Wickersham's[10] brief, put on the stand and elicited (the inference being, improperly) the necessary testimony from Wickersham's own secretary. Reference to the record would have told Sullivan that Brandeis established the antedating not through the evidence of any person, but by finding in the document itself references to events which happened after its alleged date. It is true that a secretary of a cabinet officer was put on the stand, but to prove an entirely different matter, to wit, the existence of a memorandum which Taft withheld from the Senate. The secretary, however, was not Wickersham's but Ballinger's. Referring to this memorandum, Sullivan says it contained over a million words.[11] It contained less than [50,000] words, which he also might have ascertained from the printed record.

Another instance of Sullivan's irresponsibility is the description of my brother at the time of the Alaska coal scandal,[12] which in Sullivan's eyes reflects no discredit on the part of the conservationists for locking up natural resources in the government's backyard.

Now, as a matter of fact, my brother was then, as now, an unusually practical person, though ahead of his time in his vision of what the country needed. A remarkably cheerful and healthy-minded man, he had no ideas such as Sullivan attributes to him—and much less acted on them. A first-rate athlete, devoted to outdoor sports like riding, shooting, fishing, tennis, and mountain-climbing, he, like many men who live in the open and tax their physical endurance, has always been very careful, even fussy, about providing himself with an excellent and comfortable bed, whether at home or in the field. He never had a valet in his life, or a wooden pillow, or to my knowledge slept on the floor, except on a trip we made up the Columbia River on a little stern-wheel flat-bottom steamer, where to Gifford's disgust we had to spread our blankets on the deck, since there were no staterooms.

A little farther on, Sullivan tells how Gifford, in order to influence Roosevelt's mind before he returned to the United States in the summer of 1910, hastened to meet him on the White Nile.[13] My brother met him in Spain,[14] not Africa. Sullivan is apparently confusing Gifford with Gilson Gardner,[15] who did meet Roosevelt on the Nile—not, however, the White Nile.

Sullivan's pictures of La Follette, Roosevelt, Dolliver,[16] and Taft are on the whole, though not so farfetched as that of my brother, good gossip and journalism but bad history. If his narrative of things with which I am not familiar is set down with no more fidelity than his account of matters of which I have personal knowledge, *Our Times,* whatever its defects, should in the future prove a rich storehouse for the creation of myths. But such, I suppose, is the cloth from which a good deal of our history is woven.

So, on the whole, I think it is fair to say that till now no one has given the principals in the 1912 episode their just place in the political and economic setting of their time. Nor have historians traced the currents that swirled through the country in those troubled days. It is doubtful whether a fair account of crucial happenings, where the elements of conflict and misunderstanding are strong, can be written until many years after they took place. I have tried to tell the story of the Progressive party, not so much on account of its personal interest, which to those who took part in it is keen, and indeed still poignantly keen, as for the reason that it sheds a revealing light upon the less visible influences that shape politics now, precisely as they did then. We should realize that, though politics suffers constant changes in its external aspects and minor issues, the underlying forces that govern it vary much less than one would suppose. In other words, the best means of establishing a critique of the confused, half seen, politico-economic tangles of today is to examine a preceding period, in which time has brought to the surface causative elements whose first tendency is to sink.

As has been said,[17] a fair idea of politics from McKinley's death to the summer of 1916 can be gained only when one holds in mind the fact that the United States Steel Corporation, or perhaps more accurately speaking, the Morgan interests, through their spokesman and chief political agent, Judge Gary,[18] directed at least one act of the drama from a prompter's box that was usually but not always properly hidden. The Taft administration, owing to the public outcry against the trusts which followed the congressional investigations of the steel industry in 1908 and 1911—the latter inspired by Louis D. Brandeis and conducted by the so-called Stanley Committee of the House of Representatives, for which Brandeis acted as counsel—had, from the point of view of the Morgans, gone decidedly bad.[19] Attorney-General Wickersham, who had been installed as head of the Department of Justice largely because as a steel trust lawyer he was presumably a safe man, had failed to stand out against the wreckful siege of battering days, and to Gary's astonishment had indicted the Steel Corporation as a conspiracy in restraint of trade under the Sherman law. And this unexpected shaft aimed at the heart of the Morgan metal monopoly had ruined Gary's confidence in the Republican party. What Morgan himself thought of the Wickersham-Taft performance has not been recorded. Morgan was a man of few words, and little given to putting his opinions in writing. But we at least have his statement, quoted in the Tarbell biography of Gary, that he had long stood in dread of precisely such a move on the part of the government; and, as Miss Tarbell points out, had expressed his fears forcibly to his board of directors a short time after the trust was thrown together.[20]

By indicting the Steel Corporation and thus failing to carry on Roosevelt's traditional attitude toward good trusts, Taft at once alienated Roosevelt and lost the support of the country's strongest politico-economic interest. As we shall see, this indictment was also to seal his party's fate in the 1912 election, and at the same time to bring to an end his career in the executive branch of the government. Taft had begun his administration dutifully enough by acknowledging his debt to Roosevelt. In his inaugural he had said that he would be untrue to himself and the platform if he did not "make the maintenance and enforcement" of the Roosevelt policies an important feature of his administration. He had been harshly criticized in the campaign of 1908 on the ground that he was a mere figurehead for Roosevelt. Cartoons pictured him sweating on a treadmill of Roosevelt policies kept in motion by the Roosevelt machine. Whether or not he was reconciled to this by the thought that Roosevelt had, in effect, appointed him to the presidency, he had borne it in public with characteristic good nature.[21] Once president, however, it was not unnatural that he found difficulty in settling down to so humble a role. In addition to an impulse to assert his independence before the country, a personal urge to free himself from the grip of a stronger will may account for his willingness to proceed against the best of Roosevelt's good trusts, and for his hostility to conservation and other Roosevelt policies, as well as for his prompt discharge of all but two of the members of Roosevelt's cabinet.

As the 1912 presidential election drew near, the Morgan interests (and by this I mean especially the Steel Corporation, the largest and most successful industrial merger that has ever been launched) found themselves, politically speaking, in an extremely unsatisfactory position. Like other industro-financial powers of the kind, the Steel Corporation had been consistently Republican, and had helped Roosevelt in the defeat of Parker, coming to his rescue in the fall of 1904, when consternation gripped the Republican machine at the prospect of Parker's carrying the state of New York. It had entrenched itself strongly in the Roosevelt cabinet, shaped Roosevelt's economic thinking and the pro-trust policy of the industrial sections of his messages to Congress. It had spread, through the mouth of the President himself, Morgan's own pet distinction between good and bad trusts, which is still erroneously attributed to Roosevelt instead of Morgan. Through Gary and Perkins,[22] it had made Roosevelt a sincere believer in the soundness of the giant merger system, and gained from him extravagant praise of the captains of industry and finance who were engineering these mergers. It had softened the President's heart to such an extent that he publicly defended the lavish salaries which these men were voting to themselves through docile boards of directors. It had wheedled Roosevelt into giving his indirect and innocent sanction to monopoly and various practices which we now regard as unsound and antisocial, but which were then on trial under the leadership of the Steel Corporation and the International Harvester Company, also a Morgan promotion. And, what was perhaps equally important, it had prevented the publication of the findings of the investigation of the Steel Corporation by Mr. H. K. Smith;[23] and finally, had consolidated Morgan's monopoly power by getting the President's permission to buy its potential competitor, the Tennessee Coal and Iron Company, paying less than fifty million dollars in bonds for a concern whose mineral deposits alone were worth just under a billion, according to John Moody.

Most of these remarkable moves were made, unknown to the public, through the quiet and tactful intervention of the Gary-Perkins-Garfield group and the Morgan contingent in Roosevelt's entourage. But now, with the Republican party under Taft out of hand and plunged in economic heresy, the Morgan interests saw that they could look with almost as little satisfaction to the possibility of a Democratic administration in 1912. The surge of Northern capital toward the South had not yet taken place, and below Mason's and Dixon's line the agricultural interests were still rampantly anti-Wall Street. Both branches of Congress swarmed with Southern Democrats who would gladly play to their farm-bred constituents by abetting a steel or harvester trust prosecution. Brandeis and Augustus Stanley,[24] chairman of the committee that had investigated the Steel Corporation in 1911 and 1912, were the two men who had dug more pitfalls in the path of the Steel Corporation's glorious advance than anyone else. Both were Southerners; both, as it happened, Kentuckians, and men of unusual intellectual force. Again, from the Steel Trust's point of view, democracy in the midwest section of the country held as little hope as in the South. It still smelled of populism and free silver; Bryan was again repeating his famous dictum to the effect that, if the government did not take over the railroads, the railroads would assuredly take over the government. And government ownership of the Morgan ore hauling roads would mean the end of the transportation differential that, as we have seen, upheld the trust's monopoly power and price-fixing

POLITICAL UNDERCURRENTS—1912

power, and consequently the trust's vast profits which, according to Farquhar McRae,[25] the statistician, amounted to 40 per cent of the cost of production.

In the East, a Democratic governor, New Jersey's rising star in the political firmament, was being groomed for the presidency under the tutelage of a clear-thinking, immensely able young lawyer, George L. Record,[26] who knew both business and politics from the inside as well as any man of his time. Record was especially familiar with the technique of the Morgan steel merger, having been retained by independent companies to form a rival merger, a step which he finally advised his clients not to take on account of the impossibility of standing up against the Morgan transportation and raw material privileges.

From Record, Woodrow Wilson was fast gaining an understanding of the philosophy and technique of monopoly, as can be seen from his 1912 speeches, afterward published in book form under the title of *The New Freedom.*[27]

As Gary and Morgan well knew, it was not beyond probability that, in case of Taft's renomination, the Democrats would elect a president who would press the indictment brought by Wickersham; and if opportunity arose, fill vacancies in the Supreme Court with men of the Brandeis or Stanley stamp, who would scout the doctrine of the good and bad trust and, like Supreme Court Justice Harlan, declare in effect that the only good monopoly was a dead one.

This, then, was the situation that confronted Morgan and his advisers as Taft's term of office neared its close and election day approached: a *volte-face* in the historic economic policy of the Republican party, which had hitherto favored big business in all its forms and deplored the Sherman law; a Republican party that had put its revised policy in practice by harrying the Steel Corporation despite Wickersham's promise (as alleged by Gary) to leave it alone; a Democratic party honeycombed with Bryans, Brandeises, Stanleys, and Wilsons, and predominantly agricultural, and which would certainly not extend the hand of friendship to the new and hugely lucrative Morgan promotions.

It was not strange, therefore, that Gary and Perkins, respectively heads of the Steel and Harvester companies, should have begun casting round for a way out of their dilemma, or that the plan that recommended itself was to sidetrack Taft and nominate a Republican, namely Roosevelt, who would bring the party back to sound views. Failing this, there remained the alternative of starting a third party which, though it probably could not win, would at least shelve Taft and rebuke his party for its backsliding.

As to the possibility of electing Roosevelt on a third party ticket, this was not so remote as one might at first have supposed. The activities of the insurgents in Congress, and the havoc wrought by the Payne-Aldrich tariff bill and the Pinchot-Ballinger controversy over the Alaska coal fields, had weakened the Republicans, precisely as similar factors—the oil scandals and the Hawley-Smoot bill—have weakened them more recently in the Coolidge and Hoover regimes.

In addition, the Democratic party lacked coherence and was credited with a talent for pre-election blundering on whose existence many people still insist, despite its adroit tactics in the 1932 campaign. Outside of the Solid South, warring elements—Tammany in the East and the insurgents in the West—hated each other as much as they did the Republicans. As it turned out, but for the accident of Bryan's desertion of Champ Clark in the Baltimore convention and his unexpected attack on Tammany, which forced the choice of Wilson (who showed himself not only a candidate with an invulnerable record but a matchless campaigner), Roosevelt and the Bull Moose ticket might have won by a neck in 1912, especially as Taft proved so weak as to capture but two states, Utah and Vermont, with but eight electoral votes between them.

William Howard Taft

What, if any, steps were actually taken by Judge Gary toward bringing about the formation of the Progressive party is a question which I have never heard answered. I have always been inclined to think that, as Roosevelt's admirer and secret adviser and Perkins' mentor, Gary played a considerable part in the genesis of the third party. That his mind was busy with the subject in the summer of 1911 is hinted by the fact that he told Mr. Leo Everett, a New York lawyer with whom he was talking politics on the deck of an Atlantic liner, that he thought a new party probable in 1912, since, in his opinion, the time was ripe for a party with a liberal and intelligent attitude toward industrial combination. He expressed indignation at the course of the Republican party, and cynicism as to the economic trend of the Democrats. It is possible that Gary foresaw that, for all his unpopularity, Taft would be able to force his renomination through the power of patronage, however friendless he might find himself in the election. In which unhappy case, the Steel Corporation, barring a third party, would have to endure the slings and arrows either of a Republican administration which had indicted it, or a Democratic one which would no doubt prosecute it with the utmost pleasure. Whether the Morgan interests and the Judge were active agents in the new party movement or were merely, so to speak, bought into the party when it became a going concern, is of little consequence except as the answer might serve to divulge the workings of the game of *haute politique*

Notes begin on p. 280.

which the industrial and financial powers constantly carry on, out of range of the public's gaze.

We shall see, however, that when the Chicago convention of 1912 got under way, and the Republican officeholders' machine had unseated as many Roosevelt delegates as were necessary to ensure the choice of Taft, it was Judge Gary's two lieutenants, Frank Munsey[1] and George Perkins, who came forward as the accoucheurs of the third party child, which may or may not have been conceived in Gary's brain. And later on, whether solely with their own money or Gary's assistance, these two men bore nearly the whole financial burden of the campaign. After the November 1912 defeat it was again Perkins who took up the work of reassembling the shattered hosts of Armageddon, with the hope that in 1916 they might combat the subversive economic ideas of Wilson, which have already been alluded to in a footnote.[2]

Let us now turn to the better-known, and more purely political, events which led to the repudiation of Taft's leadership by the more liberal Republicans; to the attempted nomination of La Follette; to the fading of La Follette as Roosevelt returned to the political scene; to the Colonel's failure to take the nomination from his former friend and appointee, Taft; and his formation, and finally his abandonment, of the Progressive or Bull Moose party.

As has often been said, Roosevelt, like Napoleon, had a quality, amounting almost to genius, of understanding other people's points of view and of gaining in a surprisingly short time a first-rate working knowledge of almost any new problem. Though not a man of Napoleonic mind, he had at least a broad and vigorous intelligence, and he was accessible to anyone who had anything of importance to say, no matter whence he came or what might be his philosophy or previous asseverations. Whether on account of this accessibility, or because of his early experiences in the West, which left their indelible impression, Roosevelt, though he began his career in the White House as a New York politician who had fitted without visible discomfort into Tom Platt's machine, had soon formed alliances, though not friendships, with some of the strongest men in the left wing of Congress, recruited chiefly from the Western and Middle Western states. This despite the fact that his two most intimate friends and advisers remained Elihu Root[3] and Henry Cabot Lodge.[4]

98

The Insurgents from 1901 to 1908 closely corresponded to the Farm Bloc of today, and it was in cooperation with this relatively radical bloc that [Roosevelt] succeeded in putting upon the statute books a great deal of liberal legislation, meanwhile popularizing various projected measures which he was unable to translate into law before leaving the White House. And it was chiefly because he believed Taft would carry on these liberal, so-called Roosevelt policies, whether achieved or only planned, that in 1908 he handed the presidency to his late Secretary of War.

Immediately after his nomination, Taft had reassured Roosevelt on the score of his liberalism by publishing an article in *Collier's Weekly* on "My Conception of the Presidency," in which he dealt specifically with the Roosevelt program. "The policies which he (Roosevelt) inaugurated," wrote Taft, "must be continued and developed. They are right, and they are the policies of the people."[5] As we have seen, he followed this up in his inaugural with a vigorous restatement of the same promise.

Unfortunately, Taft's native point of view was not liberalism. On the contrary, it was conservatism, the conservatism of a rich Middle West family, for years engaged in successful investment and industrial promotion. And when he found himself liberated from the pressure of vote getting and safely lodged in power, he quite naturally returned to the principles current in his home environment. This was the more to be expected because his political friends were, for the most part, conservatives from both East and West, who liked good living, agreeable society, and above all the privileges of power, which they had come to regard almost as vested rights. Taft was himself an extraordinarily agreeable man, who shone in the setting of the leisure and gayety to be found at Washington only among the richer groups, who, comparatively immune from the pressure which changing conditions exert on people of less economic security, are satisfied with the status quo, and are generally a decade behind the times in their political thinking. At the beginning of the nineteenth century, as now, for reasons which need not be enlarged on here, our richer propertied class was one from which contributions in political thought or economics were exceedingly rare. Indeed, unlike their European prototypes, little is expected of rich Americans except that they should be really good at the business of accumulating money. And the means of

99

accumulation was generally regarded as none of the public's business.

While president, Mr. Roosevelt used to wake up every morning with the fresh hope that by appointing commissions of gentlemanly, well-intentioned men—preferably graduates of universities—who would do exactly what he told them, he could bring about the millennium within a reasonable space of time. His commissions, like Hoover's, were mainly fact-finding bodies, their members serving without pay; but nevertheless they required appropriations for carrying on their inquiries and printing their reports. Some of these commissions, notably the Country Life Commission and the Conservation Commission, had done work of immense potential usefulness; they had gathered data on farm problems and on the protection and development of our natural wealth which should have been the basis of large economies and improvements. Taft, on the other hand, had not the slightest use for commissions. Their reports bored him, and threatened the little leisure he had left from his irksome official duties. Equally negative on the subjects of country life and conservation, the new President, to Roosevelt's keen disappointment, let most of the commissions die violent deaths at the hands of their old guard foes representing the Tory manufacturing sections which had no farm problems and no enthusiasm for the conservation policy and its leading exponent, Gifford Pinchot, chief of the Forest Service. Conservation, which sprang into life in Roosevelt's administration, was already changing the government's time-honored custom of handing the public domain for a song to the railroads, oil, coal, and power companies, and the Eastern syndicates which, exploiting the wealth of the West, had come to believe they had a vested right in it.

As to the federal income tax, one of Roosevelt's pet measures, Taft was supposed to have sidetracked it upon the advice of Senator Nelson W. Aldrich of Rhode Island,[6] an ancient foe of Roosevelt's, whose influence began to be felt at the White House the moment Taft entered its door. According to Senator Beveridge of Indiana,[7] Taft was worse than lukewarm to the child labor bill also, a measure promoted by the Insurgents. Taft also involved himself in a sharp controversy with Dr. Harvey Wiley,[8] the apostle of pure-food laws, resulting in the latter's resignation. Though the President seems to have been less to blame for these events than his advisers, Aldrich of Rhode Island, Crane of Massachusetts,[9] Kane of New Jersey,[10] Penrose of

Pennsylvania,[11] and Representative Cannon of Illinois,[12] the latter Speaker of the House and an archenemy of the Insurgents, he was charged with them by the entire Roosevelt following.

In a previous chapter,[13] we have spoken of Taft's action in dropping Garfield and the other members of Roosevelt's cabinet; his selection of Ballinger to fill Garfield's place; and his controversy with Gifford Pinchot over the coal claim of the Morgan-Guggenheim syndicate, including the dismissal of Pinchot as well as of the Assistant Forester, Overton W. Price,[14] and of Louis R. Glavis, the young special agent in the Interior Department who had exposed the fraudulent character of the syndicate's coal claims.

Meantime, the Insurgents were rapidly gaining power under the leadership of five men of more than ordinary vigor and sagacity— Senators La Follette of Wisconsin, Cummins[15] and Dolliver of Iowa, Beveridge of Indiana, and Bristow[16] of Kansas. An event which aggravated this bloc's hostility to Taft was his alleged support of a bill, said to have been drawn by his Attorney-General, which, as the Insurgents charged, virtually annulled the more important sections of the Dolliver-Hepburn railroad rate bill, cutting down the power of the Interstate Commerce Commission and permitting the roads to pool earnings and own a majority of the stock of competitors. At a crisis in the fight over this bill, Taft made the unpardonable blunder of trying to force the Insurgents into line by depriving them of patronage in their respective states. It was in September 1910 that the President, through his secretary, further enraged the willful senators by offering to restore their patronage if they would withdraw their opposition to the measure.

An acrimonious debate on the tariff, ending with the passage of the famous or infamous Payne-Aldrich bill, which gave the manufacturers protection but ignored the farmers, also increased the friction between the White House and the liberals. Like the Hawley-Smoot bill, the Payne-Aldrich bill seems to have been drawn narrowly in the interests of the industrialists; and Taft further reduced his standing with the left wing, first, by defending the bill itself, and second, by taking the stump in the ensuing congressional election in behalf of conservative leaders who had steered it through.

Finally came the Canadian reciprocity bill which, perhaps more than anything else, inflamed the Insurgents in both Houses, since its purpose was obviously to keep high duties on commodities which the farmers had to buy, and to place on the free list, or subject to negligible imposts, whatever they raised and marketed in competition with the farmers in other countries.

It is of course unfair to hold Taft solely responsible for the record of Congress during his term in office. He was not a strong enough man to control his own cabinet, much less the acts of Congress. Nevertheless, the Insurgents and Roosevelt, and a large part of the public, did hold him responsible—and with at least a color of right, since the White House seemed consistently to throw its weight on the side of almost every chauvinistic measure. In retrospect and in justice to Taft, we must always keep in mind that the progressivism which Roosevelt, the liberals, and much of the country expected of him was never a part of himself, but an attitude imposed upon him by pressure from without and by the fact that he had made his bid for the presidency as Roosevelt's protégé, nominated in place of Roosevelt only in deference to the unwritten law against three consecutive terms.

Taft was unquestionably a man of good, though not firm, intentions. But as president he found himself in a situation where he could not at the same moment do what was natural and what was expected of him. Lacking in grasp of the problems of the people, perhaps because, backed by the wealth of his [half-] brother Charles,[17] who devotedly fostered his ambitions, he had never experienced such fiscal anxieties as are part of the common lot, he was nevertheless a pleasant and kindly man. Yet, when driven to the wall, as in the Ballinger case, or stung by the blows of his shrewd antagonists in the Senate, he would lose his head and thrash around with the panicky and impotent violence of a wounded whale.

Up to his election in [1908], Taft had never been elected to office. For twenty-eight years he had held appointive positions, and the effect of so long a feeding at the public crib had not been of a beneficial nature. For one thing, like so many men who hold power through sanction of influential friends and backers, he had grown extremely wary of antagonizing the powers that be.

When out of law school but a few months, he was given the post of Assistant Prosecuting Attorney in Hamilton County, Ohio. The next year he was appointed Collector of Internal Revenue for Ohio by

President Arthur. President Harrison made him Solicitor General of the United States, and then set him on the Federal Circuit Court bench. At the instance of General Corbin and Elihu Root, President McKinley chose him to head the Philippine Commission. In 1902, President Roosevelt offered him the vacancy on the United States Supreme Court bench left by the death of Judge [Shiras]. Though Root strongly urged Taft to accept this honor, he declined in order to go on with his excellent work in the Philippines, of which he had become the much and deservedly loved governor.

Meantime, Mr. Root had gone into the Roosevelt cabinet as Secretary of War, and when in 1903 he announced his intention of resigning, Roosevelt appointed Taft as his successor. Taft's last appointive office was at the hands of President Harding, who installed him as Chief Justice of the Supreme Court in 1921, a poor appointment, as Taft was easily influenced and possessed neither a judicial nor an objective mind.

The first time I had the pleasure of meeting Mr. Taft was at a reunion of a college society in New Haven during Roosevelt's second term. He struck me then, as indeed he did everyone, as an amazingly charming person, genial, yet not of the back-slapping sort. One can hardly describe his appearance better than by saying he resembled the plump and mustachioed Jack of Hearts to be found in an old-fashioned pack of playing cards. His smile was delightful, his hearty laugh infectious and overwhelming, his voice pleasant, well pitched and modulated.

However, despite his appearance, his admirable manners, easy good nature, and an indisposition to hard work which gained on him as his years advanced, he could, if his *amour propre* were touched, fly, as I have said, into quite violent tantrums. His public statements, at the time when Brandeis convicted him of antedating an official document which he [had] transmitted to the Senate in order to justify his dismissal of Louis R. Glavis in September 19[09], and his blasts against critical editors showed an unthinking and voluminous rage that had something attractive about it, like the anger of a child who, holding nothing back, protests against real or fancied injustice with uncontrolled passion. Taft's was a sort of self-bailing rage that did not last long and that, when the storm was over, left him as serene and smiling as ever. Yet he never forgot, and harbored grudges longer than the general run of politicians.

So much for William Howard Taft, one of the most attractive and helpless of presidents, and a chief justice who, of all that have held that exalted place, was perhaps the least fitted for his high responsibilities. In contrast to his many wobblings, however, his seemingly reckless and determined action in indicting the Steel Corporation may be credited to him as an exploit of real quality, since it inescapably drew the fire of interests of enormous political potency. Whether he took this action as a defiance of Roosevelt, or in deference to his own convictions, or as a sop to the public opinion aroused by the Stanley-Brandeis investigation of the steel industry, it required courage, as its natural consequence was to jeopardize his chance for a second term.

CHAPTER III

Political Grooming

Of La Follette's effort to capture the Republican nomination, and Roosevelt's belated entry into the presidential race, little has been written that can be relied on. Through La Follette's autobiography runs such an intense bitterness against Roosevelt and the men whom he considered responsible for the breakdown of his campaign that La Follette cannot be regarded as an impartial historian. Both he and Roosevelt stood too near the scene to view it clearly, even if their vision had not been clouded by personal feeling and misunderstanding.[1] . . . It is only by trying to let the facts carry the story that justice can be done to three men who, sorely tried by misunderstandings, disappointments, overstrain, acted as most men do in such cases, that is to say, exaggerated the faults and discounted the decencies of their rivals.

When Roosevelt returned from Europe in [1910] after sixteen months of wandering (he left the United States on March 23, 1909, and got back on July 19, 1910), he was a profoundly changed man. For the first time in his career, his political judgment, that had stood by him from assemblyman to police commissioner, police commissioner to governor, governor to vice-president, and vice-president to the White House, deserted him; and he never regained it. What caused this alteration is a matter of much speculation. One element undoubtedly is that he had not kept in close [enough] touch with affairs at home to estimate accurately the country's swing toward

Notes begin on p. 282.

liberalism.[2] Congress and the people in general had moved ahead, largely owing to a progressive movement in which he had himself been a moving power. But he remained much where he had been before his departure. And from this moment on, until the end of his political activities in 1916, he took one inconsistent position after another, while a pitched battle for the possession of his power and influence, often affording amusing interludes, was carried on between his conservative and his liberal friends, who were equally trying to lead him on paths which he did not want to follow.

Unluckily for him, his chief informant during his trip abroad was his most intimate friend, Henry Cabot Lodge, with whom there had for years gone on a rather one-sided correspondence, consisting of long letters from Lodge and short replies from Roosevelt, the former conveying a picture of American affairs as seen through the eyes of a devoted and somewhat servile admirer, whose political ideals were those of the traditional New England high-tariff machine politician. From the liberal point of view, Lodge's influence on Roosevelt could hardly have been wise. For, in attacking Roosevelt's mind, he based his strategy on affectionate flattery, emphasizing on all occasions the dangerous radicalism of the progressive Insurgents in Congress, and at the same time extolling the virtues of Reed Smoot,[3] Nelson W. Aldrich, and Boies Penrose, and the leaders of the old guard, who had descended upon the unresisting Taft the moment Roosevelt had turned his back on Washington. As Senator Dolliver of Iowa then said, Taft in the White House was "an amiable man completely surrounded by men who know exactly what they want."

The Lodge correspondence is of historical importance because it casts almost as much light on the causes of the downfall of Theodore Roosevelt in 1912 as Seymour's *Intimate Papers of Colonel House* sheds on the passing of Woodrow Wilson, eight years later. Lodge played a part similar to that of House but one of less intellectual independence—that of the comforting, affectionate adviser. But, unlike House, in order to keep his influence, Lodge interprets all things to the honor and glory of his chief, never, as far as one can see, giving him the benefit of objective or fearless criticism. Beginning at the end of March 1909, that is, as soon as Roosevelt left America, Lodge bombards Roosevelt with a series of letters in which he describes what is taking place at Washington. Paraphrasing and quoting here and there, the burden of the letters runs as follows:

The American people are reading the accounts of your trip with enthrallment, as though they were reading an exciting serial story.

Harriman is attacking you.

Prosperity is soon expected.

The Taft administration (for which Lodge well knows Roosevelt feels responsible) is moving along quietly. Taft has a good cabinet.

Taft has done well by offering ex-President Eliot of Harvard the ambassadorship to Great Britain, but Eliot has declined.

Lodge is working tremendously hard on the tariff bill. He has been at it all week in committee, evenings too.

The country is on the edge of marked improvement in business. Aldrich is a man of force. Besides Aldrich and himself, the hard work on the Finance Committee is being done by Smoot and Penrose. "Great joy and comfort to me to have Root in the Senate."

The Insurgents are exceedingly troublesome.

We have had to meet a body of insurgents in our own party, headed by La Follette, Bristow and Cummins, while Beveridge, who has not discussed a single tariff question, has been talking incessantly on every point of procedure that came up.

Nevertheless, "we have won on every vote by a comfortable margin."

"The one thing that surprises me about Taft is that he does not know more about politics."

Wickersham doing extremely well as Attorney-General. George Meyer[4] the same as Postmaster-General. The cabinet is a good one.

Taft is all right on the tariff. "I think his influence has been salutary in a high degree, and his action has strengthened the party with the country."

Root and he think that any suggestion that Roosevelt should come home and run for mayor of New York should not be considered for a moment.

Lodge views the progressive movement of the West with alarm.

The states west of the Mississippi, beginning with Minnesota and running down to Kansas, are in bad condition. The radicalism of La Follette and Cummins seems to be rampant in that direction and I fear that we shall have trouble there. I am told that Taft was coldly received in that region, but he was outspoken and firm on the tariff. . . .

Lodge frowns on the suggestion that Roosevelt should go into the Senate.

But I feel at the same time that your position is unique and that somehow or other even the Senate might impair it. . . . If you live, it is my belief that you are going to have great influence, and that influence is too important to the country to be treated lightly. I know that you are not melancholy when you say that your day is past. . . .

Lodge frowns on attacks on corporations. "The exposure of the misdoings of a corporation . . . always hurts other corporations and brings on general distress in the public mind."

Discusses decision of Circuit Court against Standard Oil. Disclosures about American Sugar Company. "Talked with Root in New York, also saw Morgan who said he was very much disappointed in Taft."

As Lodge predicted in his last letter, Taft has removed Pinchot. "No president could possibly have tolerated such a letter as Pinchot sent to Dolliver. . . ."

Lodge is aware that various friends of Roosevelt who are disgusted with Taft, including Gilson Gardner, chief political correspondent of the Scripps newspapers, are planning to meet Roosevelt somewhere in Europe or Africa in order to post him on the turn of events.

You will be met at Khartoum by eight or ten newspaper correspondents. Some of them will be very hostile to Taft and will try to rouse your antagonism against him by what they say. They will all try to get you to say things. I think it is of first importance that you should say absolutely nothing about American politics before you get home. You cannot form any accurate judgment until you do get home, for the simple reason that you have been away from home so long that there is a mass of facts which you cannot master until you are on the ground and can review the whole situation here.

. . . There is a constantly growing thought of you and your return to the Presidency, and I do not want your name made use of, on the one side to help men who are a little out of the administration and the party organization and who are using your name for their own purpose. On the other hand, I do not want to have you used by some of the friends of the administration against men who are genuinely for you and also against the feelings of the masses of the people. I do not want your name to be used by anybody, and it is for this reason that I want to keep you aloof and apart, for you occupy an absolutely unique position, one not only of great dignity but enormous importance to the country.

From Rome, on April 6, 1910, Roosevelt writes:

Now, Cabot, it seems to me that you have changed ground. In your previous letters you have said most strongly that you wished me to keep out of politics. . . . In this letter you seem to think that I ought so to help . . . You can be sure that if I had the slightest idea of being a candidate I should not have come home until after the Congressional elections. I entirely agree with you that under no circumstances should I accept either the Governorship or the Senatorship. As for what you say about the American people looking to me for leadership, it is unfortunately preposterous and makes me more uncomfortable than ever.

From Porto Maurizio, on April 11, 1910, Roosevelt writes Lodge. He has seen his friend Gardner in Africa, and Gifford Pinchot in Spain.[5] It is clear that Lodge's high estimate of the services of the old guard senators does not impress him much. He has seen his friends and read his letters from the progressives, and is now, for the time being, back on the liberal track.

. . . The Presidency of the United States, the success of the Republican Party, above all the welfare of the country—matters like these cannot possibly be considered from any standpoint but that of the broadest public interest. I am sincere when I say that I am not yet sure whether Taft could with wisdom have followed any course save the one he did. . . . There is only a little harsh criticism either of my sincerity or of his, but there is a very widespread feeling that, quite unintentionally, I have deceived them, and that however much they may still believe in my professions when I say what I myself will do, they do not intend again to accept any statements of mine as to what anyone else will do.

The trouble, as it looks to me, is that much of what has been called leadership in the Republican Party consists of leadership which has no following. . . . The trouble is that the Cannon-Aldrich type of leadership down at bottom represents not more than, say, ten percent of the rank and file of the party's voting strength. This ten percent, or whatever it may be, includes the bulk of the big business men. . . . All this makes a body of exceedingly influential people, but if the great mass—the ninety percent of the party—the men who stand for it as their fathers stood for it in the days of Lincoln, get convinced that the ten percent are not leading them right, a revolt is sure to ensue. If politicians of sufficient ability lead that revolt, as in the Western States, they get control of the organization. . . .

P.S. I could send you a number of very significant letters which I have received, but it is not worth while. Infinitely more important is the fact that I myself cannot help feeling that even though there has been a certain adherence to the objects of the policies which I deemed essential to the National welfare, these objects have been pursued by the present Administration in a spirit and with methods which have rendered the effort almost nugatory. I don't think that under the Taft-Aldrich-Cannon regime there has been a real appreciation of the needs of the country. . . . To announce allegiance to what has been done, and to abandon the only methods by which it was possible to continue to get it done, was not satisfactory from my standpoint. . . . I very earnestly hope that Taft will retrieve himself yet, and if, from whatever causes, the present condition of the party is hopeless, I most emphatically desire that I shall not be put in the position of having to run for the Presidency, staggering under a load which I cannot carry, and which has been put on my shoulders through no fault of my own. . . . I may add that it looks to me as if the people were bound to have certain policies carried out, and that if they do not get the right type of aggressive leadership—leadership which a Cabinet of lawyers, or an Administration which is primarily a lawyers' Administration, is totally unfit to give—they will turn to the wrong kind of leadership. . . .

In this last sentence, which is found in one of Roosevelt's characteristically long and pregnant postscripts, one glimpses in Roosevelt's mind not merely an anxiety lest the country should turn to the wrong kind of leadership, but the thought that it might become his duty to supply the right kind.

Lodge replies that though it may seem that he, Lodge, has changed his ground, the change is more apparent than real, and he continues:

I have advised you as you know, very strongly, to say nothing which will compromise your future action and to make no promise like that of

1904 (his famous promise after the returns were in on election night that he would not seek the presidency again, which he later interpreted as meaning that he would not run again in 1908), but as the situation has developed, I have become equally anxious that you should so steer your course that no human being could say that you had allowed Taft and the Party to go to defeat in 1910 (in the Congressional elections) in order to clear the way for you in 1912.

Lodge says he does not wish Roosevelt to make a series of speeches; all he wants him to say publicly is that he desires a Republican victory in the congressional election, because Lodge thinks that

on the whole it is the national party and one to which the country can look, despite all its shortcomings, for the carrying out of the policies in which the American people believe. . . .

I saw in the *Outlook* the other day a brief statement of Republican principles: control and regulation of corporations and protection to equalize the difference in labor costs and the great policy of conservation. Those are your principles as they are mine.

From Christiania, Roosevelt writes Lodge on May 5, 1910:

I agree with you that the outlook is black. . . . For a year after Taft took office, for a year and a quarter after he had been elected, I would not let myself think ill of anything he did. I finally had to admit that he had gone wrong on certain points; and I then also had to admit to myself that deep down underneath I had all along known he was wrong, on points as to which I had tried to deceive myself by loudly proclaiming to myself that he was right. . . .

Lodge, shifting tactfully from one opinion to another, in deference to what he thinks Roosevelt wants him to say—and despite his recently expressed desire that Roosevelt should defend the Republican party—soon writes:

You never have said a wiser thing than in this sentence in your letter: "I wish to avoid making any public statements at all for two months after reaching America." This is what I desire above all things and I hope that you will adhere to it rigidly.

This phase of the Lodge-Roosevelt correspondence sees the Colonel back again in the United States, where he is still being pulled vigorously in opposite directions—on the one hand by Lodge and his far more influential counselor Root, and his old-time friends of the old guard faction; and on the other hand by the liberals, who are now trying harder and harder, and, for the time being, successfully, to counteract the standpat influence and start the Colonel on the progressive rampage. Naturally enough, Roosevelt is in an uncertain, if not confused, state of mind. Yet of one thing there is no doubt whatever. He is now thoroughly angry with Taft, who he believes has betrayed his principles (they were never Taft's), and the more so because, having, so to speak, certainteed him to the American people, he finds himself with his hands bound and in no position to attack him. He now remembers, bitterly no doubt, that even before the inauguration Lodge wrote him that he feared Taft would knife him and, in spite of promises, dismiss the Roosevelt cabinet in its entirety, with the possible exception of Postmaster-General George Meyer— a prediction which proved surprisingly accurate, for Meyer and Secretary of Agriculture James Wilson[6] were already the only survivors. The dismissal of Secretary of the Interior Garfield, whose place Taft filled by the appointment of Richard A. Ballinger of Seattle, especially irritated Roosevelt. And the dismissal of Gifford Pinchot, aside from the personal chagrin to Roosevelt, involved an assault on the entire conservation policy, including reclamation of oil lands and conservation of the government's water power holdings. Though the partly foreshadowed indictment of the Steel Corporation, described in a former chapter, had not yet taken place, it was soon to exasperate Roosevelt, perhaps more than any one act of his successor. And yet Roosevelt felt that he could not attack Taft. His position was one of frustration and enforced inaction, and was widened by a new and strange lack of interest in the progressive movement, which he had led during his seven years in the presidency.

The first proof I have of Roosevelt's curiously altered state of mind came in August 1910, when he gave to my brother Gifford and myself a draft of a speech which he proposed to deliver at Ossawatomie, Kansas, on the anniversary of John Brown's birthday [August 31]. Albert Beveridge, who had seen it before we had, had warned us that we would find it a thoroughly negative and un-Roosevelt-like document, not suggesting the Colonel in either literary style or point of view. Most of it, as we afterward learned, had been written by Herbert

Croly,[7] editor of the *New Republic,* and consisted of a fairly scholarly but far from convincing essay on history and social morality. With all his admirable qualities, Croly was never either a clear thinker or writer, his great virtues being his completely fearless integrity of mind and unfailing good will. If Roosevelt should deliver this speech, we believed it would merely shroud his opinions in further mystery at a time when the public, in our opinion, was waiting with eagerness for some pronouncement which would mark his place in the political conflict that was obviously and swiftly developing.

At this period, I made it a point to see Roosevelt frequently at the *Outlook* office at 287 Fourth Avenue, and steadily tried to impress him with the significance of the Insurgent, or progressive, movement in Congress, which had increased immensely in power during his absence, under the leadership of La Follette, Brandeis, and half a dozen Western senators. Though he had never liked the Insurgents particularly, he had often supported their measures and enlisted them in his own projects while he was president. But with Root and Lodge as his two closest friends, it was to be expected that he should have few personal intimacies with the left-wing members of Congress. And with the possible exception of Beveridge, none of them had really been *personae gratae* at the White House. I repeatedly argued that inasmuch as Taft had assumed a reactionary position on almost every question that interested Roosevelt and was siding strongly with the conservatives, the Republican party would, in the natural course of things, bog down in reaction and would be more and more used by private interests as a money-making agency, unless the Colonel drew a sharp dividing line between his thinking and that of the President and proceeded to bring the party back to an understanding of liberal views and ideals of real public service. As his Ossawatomie speech in its original form had little if anything in it that would serve any such purpose, Gifford finally prevailed, first, to let him make changes in it, and finally wholly to rewrite it.

I find in a notebook I kept intermittently at this time an entry made subsequent to this rewriting, dated Saturday, August 13, 1910:

It is my belief that Gifford has saved T.R. from a serious break by getting him to let him re-write the keynote speech to be delivered at Ossawatomie on John Brown's birthday. Roosevelt has written seven thousand words of safe platitudes which would have left people doubtful as to whether he was sympathetic with the progressive movement or not.

The speech, as returned to Roosevelt, was for that time, or indeed for this, an exceedingly radical document, and as I was in New York and Gifford in Washington, I made it my business to haunt the *Outlook* office and try to persuade the Colonel to adopt it as rewritten. To my surprise, he finally promised me that he would deliver the speech as altered, with "a few changes only." I at once wrote to my brother: "I have just been spending an hour with T.R. . . . From the text of the ms. of the Ossawatomie speech he has cut out very little, but added a good deal between the lines." Gifford at this time was also working on his St. Paul and Denver speeches. While Roosevelt, beset on all sides by friends of every political and economic complexion, was still fluctuating between a very radical and very conservative state of mind, the Ossawatomie speech clearly represented the former and, when delivered, drew a howl of criticism from the press of the East and a burst of wild hallelujahs from the more advanced editors west of the Mississippi. For the moment, it accomplished approximately what we hoped. It served as a sort of declaration of war against conservative Republicanism.

It must be remembered that Roosevelt had recently returned from a trip in which his seven-league boots had carried him through Africa and Europe, where he had been immersed in all sorts of fascinating new scenes and adventures, and had enjoyed them with the omnivorous appetite of a child. He had, I think deliberately, tried to forget American politics, which had already become a painful subject, and, in well-deserved lotus eating, had freed his mind of radical trends of thought which, far from being his natural heritage, had been developed by his combats as president with forces which he had opposed, not because they were conservative, but since he had learned by bitter experience that they were hostile to almost every patriotic and forward-looking thing he was trying to do.

On the Dark Continent, he had slain, to the horror of his guides, prodigious quantities of elephants, lions, and other wild beasts, and to their further horror had gone into unhealthy districts, for which he paid the penalty of contracting a severe African fever from which he never wholly recovered. In continental Europe, he himself had been the lion on all occasions, hobnobbing with emperors, kings, snubbing the Pope, and giving new proofs of his established valor by discussing before the world's foremost savants subjects with which he had, comparatively speaking, meager familiarity. His magnetism, his good will, his miraculous self-confidence, and his reputation as the world's first citizen had carried him triumphantly through.

But upon his arrival in New York, where, on June 18, 1910, Mayor Gaynor and the populace greeted him like a victorious Roman consul, he was suddenly thrust back into a harsh world of work and conflict. Naturally enough, it was his earlier friendships and associations, formed before his unexpected presidential excursion into progressivism, that beckoned him most strongly on his homecoming. I think he understood the dangers inherent in the situation, and was eager to be pulled back into the progressive but more arduous role that had once been his.

Meantime, almost everybody who took the slightest interest in politics was asking: On which side will the Colonel now align himself? What changes have taken place in his philosophy? Will his mood be more gentle toward members of the richer classes, with whom in Europe he has hobnobbed on such friendly and delightful terms, the classes which in America he had so often characterized as malefactors of great wealth? Will he take up his cudgels for liberals like La Follette and Beveridge and Gifford Pinchot, or will he support Taft, in spite of the latter's repudiation of the Insurgents and peace treaties with the Bourbons? Has the trip softened him? Has he come back as the champion of the radical West or the Conservative East?

The answer was to come convincingly in the release of his so-called Ossawatomie speech, delivered [on August 31, 1910], in which the Colonel took by far the most radical stand of his life, a stand which, surprising even his more advanced followers, seemed to promise that he would go uncompromisingly forward from the point where he had left off over four years ago.

The Ossawatomie speech dripped with sentences that would even now sound radical, such as:

No man shall receive a dollar unless that dollar has been fairly earned. . . . Every dollar received should represent a dollar's worth of services fairly rendered . . . not gambling in stocks—but service rendered. . . .

115

I believe in a graduated income tax on big fortunes, and in another tax which is far more easily collected and far more effective—a graduated inheritance tax on big fortunes, properly safeguarded against evasion and increasing rapidly in amount with the size of the estate.[8]

In other words, he paraphrased Lincoln's well-known aphorism on the subject: "Labor is the superior of capital and deserves much the higher consideration." And such a remark, he said, was not that of an agitator but of Lincoln himself, and Lincoln was undoubtedly right. He stressed the importance of conservation, referring pointedly to the efforts of great industrialists during Taft's administration to deprive the public of its water power, its forests, mines, and public lands. He said that "the essence of any struggle for healthy liberty has always been and must always be" against those who are trying to enjoy power or wealth or position which has not been earned by honest service to their fellow men.

On the score of progressiveness, the Ossawatomie speech left little to be desired. But alas, its delivery proved the signal for his reactionary friends to close in on him with more determination than ever, and, almost before its echoes had surged back and forth across the country and had died down, he had maneuvered a retreat from Ossawatomie, and was endorsing the Payne-Aldrich tariff bill at Saratoga, and speaking for Warren G. Harding, who was running for the Senate in Ohio.

The morning of the nineteenth of [August?], I had a hectic, indeed almost acrimonious discussion with Roosevelt at the *Outlook* office, ending, as such talks often did, by his good-naturedly sweeping away my arguments with the reminder that we were living in a real and not a theoretical world, and an admonition that I should read Morley's chapter on compromise in his *Life of Gladstone*.[9] After which he drove me uptown in his car and delivered a speech to an audience of Negro businessmen; after which he asked me to lunch with, as I remember, two other men at the Arts Club in Gramercy Park, and we had a long talk on the state of the country in general and of Theodore Roosevelt in particular, which seemed to me a very delightful though politically perilous one. He seemed pretty well to have forgotten that he had recently committed himself in the Ossawatomie speech to what at least half his friends regarded as a career of anarchy. And at that luncheon I got a quite distinct impression that his liberalism was, for the moment at least, as dead as John Brown's body—while his spirit, far from marching on, was taking the back trail for all it was worth to the line of old-fashioned G.O.P. Republicanism.

When I left him, I felt that in spite of his affection for Gifford,[10] and Gifford's influence over him, which was very strong when the two men were together, the Colonel was fast making his escape. That night, in weary discouragement, I entered in my notebook: "Feel that T.R. is in a very unsatisfactory frame of mind. Gifford is his political conscience and when Gifford's influence is absent, T.R. slumps."

Some of the influences which were pulling Roosevelt back from the firing line were easy enough to identify. Root, Lodge, George Perkins, and Frank Munsey were always to be reckoned with, and strangely enough Munsey was one of the most potent forces, as Roosevelt respected his complete fearlessness and described him as "a man of immense personality." What Gary's contacts with Roosevelt may have been at this period is impossible to say. Roosevelt never mentioned him to me, nor did Perkins or Munsey. The colonel's [auto]-biography does not speak of Gary except, briefly, in relation to the Tennessee Coal and Iron Incident, and again briefly in an appendix, in which he attacks Taft for the Steel Corporation indictment.

Miss Tarbell's biography of Gary has nothing to say about politics at this period, although it stresses the friendship between Gary and Roosevelt during the latter's terms in the White House. Nevertheless, it is more than probable that Gary was a factor in the situation, acting through Munsey and especially Perkins, in whose eyes Gary was always a leader to be obeyed.

On the other hand, another set of circumstances was building up Roosevelt's fighting morale, even as the conservative influences were wearing it down. One was the steadily waxing antagonism between him and the President; another, the desertion of many of Roosevelt's middle-of-the-road friends who, under the big-business whip, were rallying to Taft's standard and becoming outspoken in their criticism of the Colonel.

Roosevelt was now once again entering politics in his native state. For in October 1910 he attended the New York State convention, and rashly allowed his friends to propose him for chairman.[11] Through a

117

blunder for which Taft was not really responsible, Vice-President James S. Sherman was put in nomination by the President's friends. And though Taft tried to cancel this seeming affront by putting the blame squarely on Sherman himself in a public letter to Lloyd Griscom, then head of the New York County Committee, the incident created the impression that, by repudiating Roosevelt, Taft was inviting the moment when the two men would publicly lock horns. Roosevelt's return to politics and the Sherman blunder seemed the more convincing when taken as a corollary to his series of speeches at Ossawatomie, Denver, and St. Paul, that minced no words in denouncing the reactionaries with whom Taft had fallen in step. Was this widening breach between him and Taft a personal and private matter, or was it proof that Roosevelt was preparing to declare himself as a full-fledged candidate for the presidency?

On all sides, one heard quoted Roosevelt's statement on election night, four years before: "The wise custom which limits the President to two terms regards the substance and not the form, and under no circumstances will I be a candidate for or accept another nomination. . . ."[12] And almost as frequently it was recalled that again, in December 1907, at the time when he was planning to secure the 1908 nomination for Taft, he made a similar statement. Now, in 1910, the great question among the politically minded was whether Roosevelt would interpret his 1904 and 1907 statements as applying to elections in general, or only to the election of 1908. Charles G. Washburn, one of Roosevelt's friendly but conscientious biographers, writes that the Colonel's secretary, [William] Loeb, told him that at the moment when the 1904 statement was drafted, it was suggested to Roosevelt that he word it so as to refer only to 1908, but that this limitation was rejected since, if he were to say he would not run in 1908, this might be construed as a declaration of intention to run in 1912, which he had not the least intention of doing. Washburn also says that at the time Roosevelt made the 1904 statement, a reporter asked him whether he meant it to cover 1912 as well as 1908. And he replied: "Now, gentlemen, that is something I don't intend to speak about."[13] So far as I can see, Roosevelt was not bound, morally or otherwise, by these statements. Even if he had said in so many words that he would not run in 1908 or 1912, there is not the least reason why he should not have changed his mind later. His statements were mere declarations of intention, offered neither as promises in return for anything nor in the hope of influencing the vote. His 1904 statement was given out on the night of November 4—after the returns were in—after he knew he had won the election. Between 1904 and 1912, when newspapermen, friends, and acquaintances, even political enemies, asked him whether he would ever again run for the presidency, he invariably replied in a way that left the door open. He did not expect to run; he did not intend to run; but he certainly might run if a situation arose where, in his judgment, there was need, and a strong public sentiment, for his doing so.

In 1910 my own belief was, as it is today, that Roosevelt had become once more eager for the presidency; that he was anxious to see Taft defeated, for both personal and public reasons; but, as he himself often told me, he was pretty well, but not wholly, convinced that Taft's nomination could not be blocked. That was certainly the impression he made when I listened to his speech on September 6 at the Water Power Convention at St. Paul. He had the air of a candidate, and spoke like a candidate—and not merely as a man defending conservation and federal control of power development. After the session, I went to Roosevelt's room. He had dressed hastily before the meeting and had not had time to shave. While he lathered and shaved himself, he talked buoyantly and seemed enormously pleased at the warm reception that had been given him. I think he had for the moment determined to throw his hat in the ring and obliterate Mr. Taft, should a turn in events occur to make such an undertaking feasible.

In September of the same year, my brother, William Kent[14] of California, Major Burnham, the South African scout, and myself found ourselves encamped on the crescent black-sand beach of San Clemente Island, about sixty miles out to sea, to the southwest of Los Angeles. On the eighteenth, we were interrupted in our pursuit of marlin fish by the arrival of E. W. Scripps[15] on his steam yacht. As the owner of a large and fast-growing string of papers, Scripps already loomed as a powerful figure in the political as well as the journalistic world. For two days we left the marlin to their own devices and talked politics, Scripps predicting that Roosevelt would not only enter the lists in 1912, but try for a fourth and fifth term. He nurtured a profound dislike for Roosevelt, and to the delight of Kent, who shared his views on the subject, contended that Roosevelt was essentially hostile to the democratic theory of government, and that if he ever got the chance, he would set himself up as a dictator. He cited Roosevelt's contempt for Jefferson and his allegiance to Hamilton's belief in a "monarchical republic," and backed this up by quoting the St. Paul speech in which Roosevelt demanded what he, Scripps, considered an nth degree of executive power. "Some day," he said, "you will see him riding up Pennsylvania Avenue on a white mule and abolishing Congress." One of us offered the suggestion that he would never ride as far as the Capitol, since some old-fashioned Democrat would be tempted to take a pot shot at him. "No," replied Scripps. "All the gun men and assassins, Democratic or Republican, will be riding behind him as major-generals." On the other hand, Scripps despised what he called Taft's "soft-shell" quality, and wanted to see him beaten, but not by Roosevelt.

Neither Gifford nor I thought Roosevelt would actually decide to run, on account of the improbability of overcoming the patronage power of Taft's officeholder machine. Scripps thought Roosevelt would chance it anyhow, and sailed away fulminating good-natured threats to become a regicide should T.R. don the purple.

Though 1910 and 1911 were years of watchful waiting for Colonel Roosevelt, his indecision was mitigated by quasi-political activities which were hard to interpret except as an effort to place himself in a strategic position where, at short notice, he could make a dash for the presidency. If he had not been responsible for Taft's induction to the White House, I think sheer rage at what he felt was Taft's betrayal of the Roosevelt policies would have swept away his hesitation and plunged him into the contest, desperate as it seemed. He believed in the Republican party as the only political force through which worthwhile things could be done, and when I spoke disparagingly of it, he called me to account with the reminder that neither he nor any leader since Lincoln had had anything like a homogeneous or trustworthy political instrument with which to work. He thoroughly despised the Democratic party, which to him was symbolized by Bryan, and feared that if he attacked Taft he would split the Republican party and make it an easy prey for the Democrats.

On September 19, 1910, a secret meeting between Roosevelt and Taft took place in New Haven, at the home of Henry White,[16] which, according to Charles Norton, the President's secretary, was arranged at Roosevelt's request. Per contra, I find my letter to my brother, [dated September 20], in which I note that Roosevelt has asked me to say to him that Taft, and not he, had made the overtures. However this may be, Roosevelt dashed secretly across the Sound from Oyster Bay in a fast motorboat, and spent about two hours with the President, though, due to rough weather, he, according to Archie Butt, "had to turn into Stamford and then come (the rest of the way) by motor."[17] Butt, Taft's faithful chronicler, seems to have been peeking in at the conferees when opportunity offered, for after the conference he writes to his sister, "If they are not farther apart than ever, at least they are no nearer."[18]

So far as can be learned, the first move toward bringing Robert M. La Follette of Wisconsin into the 1912 presidential race was made by Scripps,[19] who, in his feudal domain at San Diego, becoming utterly disgusted with Taft, had sent Gilson Gardner scouting through the country seeking presidential timber.[20]

In this quest, Gardner interviewed Brandeis, Gifford Pinchot, and La Follette, and many other men then in the public eye, and reported to Scripps on their qualifications. Gardner was chosen for this work not merely because he stood in the relation of Colonel House to the Scripps organization, but because he was an astute political observer and a close friend of the three most important men under consideration. And in the event of La Follette's making the race, Gardner would presumably prove useful in adjusting the relations between him and the Colonel, who was also one of Gardner's intimate friends. Gardner found La Follette receptive, and Scripps soon set in motion a political campaign, throwing in his newspapers, but, as was his general policy in most of his enterprises, furnishing as little money as possible.

My brother and I, still believing that Roosevelt would not run and that it was essential to put a liberal in the field, who would at least consolidate the opposition and keep the liberal movement alive, joined the La Follette group, which then or soon after included Louis D. Brandeis, Medill McCormick,[21] later United States senator from Illinois, George L. Record of New Jersey, who had contributed so much to the political education of Woodrow Wilson,[22] James R. Garfield, Secretary of the Interior under Roosevelt, Fred C. Howe,[23] Garfield's ex-law partner and afterward Commissioner of Immigration under

Woodrow Wilson, Charles R. Crane,[24] Rudolph Spreckels, sugar magnate and militant progressive of California, Henry Rickey, one of the leading editors of the Scripps Western newspapers, Alfred Baker of Chicago, Mark Sullivan, who succeeded Norman Hapgood as editor of *Collier's* in 1914, William Kent of California, E. A. Van Valkenburg, editor of the Philadelphia *North American,* John S. Phillips, editor of the *American Magazine,* [Irvine] Lenroot, then congressman and afterward senator from Wisconsin, Walter Houser, La Follette's ex-Secretary of State when La Follette was governor of Wisconsin, and who now became his campaign manager.

The first La Follette meeting of consequence, consisting of several hundred delegates with Insurgent leanings (chiefly gleaned from Western and Middle Western states), took place at the La Salle Hotel in Chicago on the sixteenth of October, [1911]. Record presided and outlined a distinctly radical program, challenging the trusts, demanding government ownership of railroads, and opening up the question of concentration of wealth and both economic and political power, which, already looming as a vital issue, was to grow steadily in importance until relegated to the background seven years later by the World War.

From the moment when Taft had, in our eyes, turned away from liberalism and come under the influence of Crane, Penrose, Tawney, and the older statesmen group, we had been trying to devise some way of keeping the liberal movement alive. Small meetings had been called at various private houses in Washington, where, after seemingly endless discussion, platforms had been drafted and the field searched for some candidate who might head off the now rapidly weakening Taft.

At one of these gatherings, held at my brother's house in Washington, Brandeis and La Follette had proposed amendments to the Sherman law designed to strengthen it generally and in particular to prevent unfair competition and monopoly in the basic industries. These, as will be seen, were the proposals that were actually incorporated in the Progressive platform of 1912 and, after its adoption by the Chicago convention, omitted when the platform was printed, at the instance of Perkins with, I believe, the innocent consent of Colonel Roosevelt, who was persuaded at the time that the plank containing the amendment had never been accepted by the Resolutions Committee, and had been read to the convention as the result of an error on the part of William Draper Lewis, chairman of the Resolutions Committee. Heney[25] of California first called my attention to this deletion, and my efforts to have it restored to the platform later involved me in an acrimonious controversy with the Colonel that eventually lost me his friendship and virtually excommunicated me from the party.

The La Follette campaign, begun in October [1911], at first made little progress either in the East or in the West, largely owing to a lack of the funds necessary to form an organization. Outside of the original group, no contributors of importance came forward. The ill-chosen money-raising committee, consisting of Spreckels, Baker, and myself, did next to nothing. In spite of this, La Follette soon began to show considerable strength in the Middle West and even in the East. And Medill McCormick began writing me frantically from Chicago that with $500,000 we could organize a campaign that might split Ohio, win half the Indiana delegates and a majority in Michigan and Illinois. At the same time he quite truthfully wrote other friends that Baker, Spreckels, and myself had been a complete failure as a finance committee; he devoutly prayed that we would resign—which was exactly what we would have liked to do—and our places be taken by more competent workers.

Meantime, Roosevelt's noncommittal attitude did not worry most of us very much, for we believed that his position was such that he could not afford to oppose Taft's steam roller. He invariably spoke well of La Follette and praised his record, although his praise had a somewhat wintry sound, as if it were drawn from him unwillingly by the Senator's undeniable achievements. He declined to be cornered in a place where he would have to choose between La Follette, a far more radical man than himself, whom he had never liked personally, and his protégé, Taft, whom he disliked still more. He insisted there was no reason to discuss the possibilities of his own candidacy, since he was certain that he could not stop Taft any more than La Follette could. Most of us were satisfied with this, believing what I still think was true, that the Colonel's best opinion was that the chance of his entering the race was practically zero.

La Follette, on the other hand, was consistently hostile and suspicious toward Roosevelt and told me that he fully expected the

Colonel to wait until he had lined up the progressive strength and thrown together an organization, and then step in at the last moment and take it away from him. In justice to both men one should remember that their feelings toward each other were shaped by something outside of presidential ambitions. La Follette's radical ideas, especially on the monopoly question, were almost as repugnant to Roosevelt as Taft's conservative position. Roosevelt believed in huge combinations as part of the modern trend. La Follette, like Brandeis, suspected that the larger mergers were both inefficient and costly to the consumer. Roosevelt distinguished between the good trusts, like the Steel Corporation and the International Harvester Company, and such "depraved and lawless" combinations as the Rockefeller oil trust and the American Tobacco Company. La Follette, per contra, put all the trusts in one basket. He wished to strengthen the Sherman law in order to protect competition and make trusts impossible, while Roosevelt inveighed against competition and characteristically denounced the Sherman law as "immoral." In his last year in the White House, Roosevelt had urged in a message to Congress that the Sherman law be stricken from the books:

It is profoundly immoral to put or keep on the statute books a law, nominally in the interest of public morality, that really puts a premium on public immorality, by undertaking to forbid honest men from doing what must be done under modern business conditions, so that the law itself provides that its own infraction must be the condition precedent upon business success.[26]

In 1910 this obscuring concept still roamed the field of his philosophy like a *mouche volante* in the lens of the human eye. Never could he see that these tremendous aggregations of economic machinery and capital, plus political influence, buttressed by special advantages in raw material, transportation, and finance, must inevitably invest themselves with the further privilege of fixing prices. Nor did he realize that such a power is not merely a monopoly power but, in essence, the sovereign power of taxation exercised by private individuals or corporate persons instead of by the government. He frequently took me to task for my unorthodoxy on the trust question, remarking that men like Brandeis and myself would never be happy until the steel industry had been reduced to the blacksmith shop, and the railroads to the eighteenth-century stagecoach.

Roosevelt (because of the influence of Gary, I have always believed) quite misconstrued the Sherman law, attacking it in and out of office on the erroneous ground that it was designed to prevent all industrial combination instead of merely such combination as induced monopoly. "The effort," he said in an article written just after the Taft administration brought suit to dissolve the Steel Corporation, "to prohibit all combination, good or bad, is bound to fail, and ought to fail; when made, it merely means that some of the worst combinations are not checked and that honest business is checked." In sharp contrast with Wilson, who maintained that private monopoly was "unthinkable" and that competition should be encouraged, he accepted our great monopolies as both necessary and inevitable. Of the Progressives who stood with Wilson on the trust question, he wrote:

These men believe that it is possible by strengthening the anti-trust law to restore business to the competitive conditions of the middle of the last century. Any such effort is foredoomed to end in failure, and, if successful, would be mischievous to the last degree.

While right in believing that competition could not be preserved through the Sherman law alone, he was wrong in thinking that the Sherman law was either useless or mischievous.

Meanwhile, George W. Perkins was more and more in evidence in Roosevelt's entourage, and especially at the *Outlook* office and Oyster Bay. Frank Munsey, sometimes referred to as the unofficial ambassador of the Steel Corporation, had begun to take a lively interest in the Colonel's fortunes. Munsey's excursion into politics was, I believe, absolutely in good faith. He backed Roosevelt not so much on account of the latter's friendship with the steel group as because he, Munsey, outside of his steel affiliations, heartily disliked Wall Street, with which he had suffered costly experiences, and looked on Roosevelt as the only man who could put the Street in its place. Though later events were to clarify the significance of the growing influence of these two men, we did not give it its true place in the political scene until too late to save the only third party movement of consequence which occurred in the United States since 1854.

In the early edition of his autobiography, La Follette refers with great bitterness to his alleged betrayal by his followers in February 1912, and their switch to Roosevelt.[27] In a later edition, he deletes some of his harsher criticisms and writes in a milder vein, realizing no doubt that misunderstandings on both sides should share the blame with the individuals misled by them. Undoubtedly, as the breach widened between Taft and Roosevelt, and the La Follette boom languished under the relaxing rays of Roosevelt's rising sun, many of the Progressives who had flocked to the La Follette camp, in the belief that Roosevelt's relations with Taft as well as his pronouncements against a third term would keep him on the sidelines, began to see that the change in these relations and the growing antagonism between the President and the ex-President were shaking the Colonel's resolve to continue a spectator. It was clear now that Roosevelt would stand a far better chance of capturing the nomination than the Wisconsin Senator, though La Follette had a magnificent record of constructive achievement, indeed a better one in this respect than Roosevelt or perhaps any political leader in any party since Thomas Jefferson. But like most men who are ahead of their age, La Follette was the victim of the grossest misrepresentation by rival politicians and a press that, for years, had pictured him at once as an unreasonable obstructionist and as an advocate of wild and reckless doctrines. The fact is that La Follette was one of the most cautious and studious of men, and, with the single exception of his advocacy of the recall of judicial decisions, which he calamitously proposed in the heat of his presidential campaign of 1920, he never made a political move except after exhaustive investigation, both as to its practicability and remote implications. In the list of laws for whose passage he was chiefly responsible—and he was responsible for more than any other senator in our history—there is hardly one which the ordinary conservative of today would desire to have taken from the statute books.

Despite certain irritating traits, no one who knew La Follette well could withhold a warm admiration and affection for him. Of pioneer stock, and actually born in the traditional log house so coveted by American statesmen as their point of departure, he lived on a farm as a boy, and at an early age studied law and was admitted to the bar, where he soon practiced politics and law with equal success. He had a finely molded head, magnificently carried above broad heavy shoulders. His voice was soft but penetrating, and his way of speaking when I knew him was almost too gentle in that it suggested the restraint that overworked and highly nervous men sometimes impose on themselves in order to avoid seeming overbearing or impatient. And, as his enemies charged, La Follette in public life was in fact at times both overbearing and impatient, and it was hard for him to stand opposition in either private or public life. He was always overworked and always pushed for time. He was a rather short, thickset man, who rarely took exercise yet remained muscularly hard as iron. He habitually worked late into the night, mastering the details of the bills which he fought for or against, with unbelievable industry and persistence. Though his labors told on his marvelous constitution and he was often ill in the later period of his life, he rarely permitted himself rest except when utterly exhausted. In the Senate it was his regular custom to know more about his subject than anybody else, for in addition to his diligence he had a quite miraculous memory, and in speaking his logical mind transformed his store of knowledge into orderly syllogistic forms. He was naturally eloquent, but at the same time a master of every trick of oratory. In action he was by turns fierce, overpowering, gentle, and even pathetic. He had the components of a good actor but used his dramatic art conscientiously, and believed devoutly, almost ecstatically, in the things he was trying to do. At times his emotions seemed to carry him away, and he would tremble, throw back his head, weep, and even groan, descending now and then to bathos. But through all, his mind worked keenly, and the things he said, even in his most impassioned moments, were to the point, always sincere and generally deeply true.

La Follette dramatized his life, and saw himself, as indeed he often was, the central figure in a mighty conflict between right and wrong, truth and hypocrisy, greed and altruism. If he had not, I doubt if he could have endured his titanic labors, especially in later years when his health was poor. He had that ever-present and often exaggerated consciousness of the hostility of the opposing forces which most men acquire who fight their way through seemingly insurmountable difficulties and against the bitter and sometimes vicious opposition of powerful enemies. He often felt himself alone. In the early edition of his [auto]biography, published in 1911, he entitled the chapter describing his fight for railroad rate legislation, "Alone in the Senate."[28]

In 1917, because of his opposition to our entry into the World War, the climax of which came in his speech on the night before the Senate cast the deciding vote, he came very near to being alone. During that tremendous and never to be forgotten effort I sat in the press gallery with Gilson Gardner and heard La Follette speak, hour after hour, to an audience that dwindled when senator after senator rose from his seat and vanished in the direction of the cloakroom. With an enormous eloquence and mastery of facts, he reviewed the course of events that led to the European outbreak. He described what he believed to be the selfish motivations of the combatants, warning us against making the Allies' secret purposes our own, and outlining the probable results of our intervention, both to ourselves and to other nations. He pleaded, urged, exhorted, and threatened, leaving no element of persuasion untried.

"Sir," he said, addressing the presiding officer of the Senate,

if we are to enter upon this war in the manner the President demands, let us throw pretense to the winds, let us be honest, let us admit that this is a ruthless war against not only Germany's army and her navy but against her civilian population as well, and frankly state that the purpose of Germany's hereditary European enemies has become our purpose.

La Follette foresaw that a victorious peace would mean for France only an interlude in her perpetual struggle to reduce Germany to impotence. At the end of his speech, tremendously moved and completely convinced of the immediate and ultimate wisdom of his vision, he stood in silence, tears running down his face. They were not maudlin tears, but angry and despairing ones, drawn from his fear that his colleagues were acting against the good of his country, which he sincerely loved. There was something gentle and appealing, too, in the grief and anger of this despairing man, like that of a person who had failed to keep his child from doing itself an irreparable harm.

Though La Follette hated the war, once we were in it he showed his caliber by refusing to sulk and doing everything in his power to finance it, earning from his old antagonist, Cabot Lodge, the tribute that of all men in the Senate he had been the most useful to the American cause through his untiring work on the Finance Committee.

In the Senate, a Cassandra-like fate pursued La Follette. He seemed doomed to tell the truth in the dangerous early stage before it becomes a truism. For instance, most of the things he said of the war which brought him into disrepute and a still more painful consciousness of isolation are now commonplace. It was La Follette who, a year before the breaking of the oil scandals of the Harding administration, was constantly annoying the Senate with his warnings against the Doheny and Sinclair leases. Though the country's refusal to listen to him until it was too late always pained and angered him, it failed to shake his determination and served only to inspire him to more effort.

Emile Zola, whose political achievements in the Dreyfus case now give him a higher place in the history of France than his novels, had, I think, a reaction to the stimulus of anger resembling La Follette's. While in the throes of writing his Rougon-Macquart series, which he believed were not merely to reveal the world by the light of naturalism, but to make it better, he said to Goncourt: "But when I think of the whole train of novels I am manufacturing, I feel that only the state of struggle and anger can encourage me to go on and finish them."[29] And again he wrote:

Ah! To live indignant, to live enraged at treacherous arts, at false honor, at universal mediocrity! To be unable to read a newspaper without paling in anger! To feel the continual and irresistible need of crying aloud what one thinks, above all when one is alone in thinking it, and to be ready to abandon all of the sweets of life for it![30]

Zola's reflections on the state of mind necessary to effect his functioning could as well have been La Follette's. No other American so often hurled at his antagonists Zola's apostrophe of *J'accuse!* No other, by the sheer power of indignation, so often set forces in motion to shatter unworthy schemes hatched in the shadow of the Capitol.

At the end of La Follette's speech against our participation in the World War, Gardner said: "That is the greatest speech we will either of us ever hear. It will not be answered because it is unanswerable."

La Follette sat down, slumped in his seat, and closed his eyes. One of us scribbled a few lines on the back of an envelope, trying to express in a sentence what we felt, and started to send it down to him but instead tore it up, for the occasion was too solemn for congratulations. Senator John Sharp Williams[31] meantime had sprung to his feet and was pouring forth a torrent of sarcastic but, of its kind, masterly abuse. Blind to the values of the situation, other than in the coin of current spread-eagle patriotism, the Mississippi Senator, who was counted one of the wittiest men in the Upper House, and was in fact the father of senatorial wisecracking, walked menacingly toward La Follette as he spoke, until he seemed about to hurl himself at him.

Mr. President, if immortality could be attained by verbal eternity, the Senator from Wisconsin would have approximated immortality. We have waited and have heard a speech from him which would have better become Herr Bethmann-Hollweg, of the German Parliament, than an American senator. . . . I fully expected before he took his seat to hear him defend the invasion of Belgium—the most barbarous act that ever took place in the history of any nation anywhere. I heard from him a speech which was pro-German, pretty near pro-Goth, and pro-Vandal, which was anti-American president, anti-American Congress, and anti-American people.[32]

Senator Husting[33] of Wisconsin followed Williams, but spoke in a different tone—sorrowingly of his colleague, and proudly of the war, into which his vote was presently to help carry us. "It will be a war," he said, "not for profit or pelf, but for the right, the lives, the honor, the welfare, and the safety of this nation. It will be a war for the democracy of the world."[34]

CHAPTER IV

The Protagonists: Theodore Roosevelt and Robert M. La Follette

By the fall of 1911 Roosevelt's candidacy—still unauthorized but nonetheless fostered by his varied political activities—had grown to proportions that threw many of La Follette's friends into panic. As Gardner put it, while Roosevelt was not an avowed candidate, he was "up on the bit,"[1] and the progressive leaders were turning from La Follette in shoals and calling on the Colonel to lead the attack on Taft.

On December 11, 1911, La Follette invited to his house in Washington a small group of his more intimate advisers, among them William Kent, Charles R. Crane, Louis Brandeis, [Irvine] Lenroot, Senator Moses Clapp[2] of Minnesota, Medill McCormick, Gilson Gardner, my brother, and myself. By this time, things looked so black for the Senator that, in order to avoid a division in the anti-Taft forces, he himself reluctantly prepared to write a letter to Roosevelt, offering to withdraw in his favor, provided the Colonel would at once agree to run. On the other hand, should Roosevelt not so agree, La Follette insisted that he should make it clear he was out of the race and promptly deliver his strength to him. The meeting ended in his asking Kent, my brother, and myself to make a draft of such a letter. Next morning, when the conference reconvened, this time at my brother's house, our draft and one written by La Follette were read. The discussion dragged through the morning and through the afternoon,

Notes begin on p. 285.

with the outcome that La Follette vetoed the letter, a decision in which he was sustained by a majority of the conferees.[3]

At this juncture, in order to reach an understanding between our two protagonists, a luncheon was proposed for December 17 at my house in New York. La Follette at first consented to appear, and then refused on the ground that he could not trust Roosevelt and still believed that he would out-general him and leave him in the lurch. However, he would send his manager, Houser. Roosevelt showed up himself, but as usual was quite noncommittal. He had not made up his mind. The main thing, he said, was to beat Taft. But this he still considered extremely improbable. On the eighteenth, the La Follette group that had met on the eleventh at La Follette's, but with the addition of Dan Hanna, Medill's brother-in-law, and Walter Rogers,[4] foregathered at the Washington headquarters at my brother's request. The session was both stormy and inconclusive. La Follette declined to enter the room until McCormick had left it. Heney said that Roosevelt must be forced at once to declare whether or not he was a candidate. And the proposal was made, but voted down, that even if the Colonel were out of the running, we should try to elect Roosevelt delegates in states where La Follette had little strength and swing them to La Follette at the Chicago convention. In his *Autobiography,* La Follette writes that, after this plan was disapproved, I told him that I was glad it was beaten, since supporting Roosevelt would, in effect, tie us up with the Steel Trust.[5] Here La Follette is in error. For at this stage of the campaign I had no knowledge of Roosevelt's close relation to the steel group, and I learned of it only as events disclosed it after the Republican convention brought it to light.

On January 22, 1912, we again attempted to heal the breach between our temperamental leaders, by the same device of a luncheon meeting at our house, with the discouraging result that now both men flatly declined to attend.

On the night of the [twenty-second] of January, 1912, La Follette was to come to New York to speak at a mass meeting at Carnegie Hall, which I had arranged for. Early that day, I phoned Roosevelt that I would like to see him before the meeting to talk over the necessity, which now seemed very apparent, that one of them should withdraw. I met him about three o'clock in the lounge of the University Club, and said that though I knew he would stand a better chance of beating Taft than La Follette, whose campaign was petering out, I believed it impossible to persuade La Follette to withdraw; that our group considered itself attached to La Follette until he released us; and that the Senator's campaign was at a standstill partly because of the uncertainty as to what Roosevelt would do. He replied that he had not yet decided what to do; he admired La Follette and considered his work, especially during Taft's administration, of immense usefulness. La Follette, in his opinion, had not the remotest chance for the nomination. If he himself should try for it, Taft would almost certainly win anyhow. At the moment he did not think he would run. But he might change his mind at any time, and felt free to do so. But he would not run unless he saw a strong popular demand for him.

It seemed to me, as it still does, that he was quite within his rights. And after the La Follette meeting, where my brother presided—it was a very good meeting indeed, with several thousand people turned away—I went to supper with La Follette at the Plaza Hotel, and told him exactly what Roosevelt had said, as I had promised Roosevelt I would, adding that I thought Roosevelt's position, while unsatisfactory and unfair, in a sense, to La Follette, was fair enough from Roosevelt's point of view. La Follette replied that he was now, more than ever, convinced that Roosevelt was working to draw away the support he had gathered, and that much as he hated the idea of being a stalking horse for him, he would go on with his campaign for the nomination, whatever happened. He said he considered Roosevelt a more or less unconscious instrument of Morgan and the Steel Trust, and that he believed Gifford and I would someday discover he had for years been tied hand and foot by Gary, Perkins, and the other Steel Trust people. Not the slightest progress was made in our efforts to start cooperation between La Follette and the Colonel. They remained in exactly their relative positions—La Follette outspokenly hostile; Roosevelt on the surface friendly and yet noncommittal, and in reality still disliking La Follette personally and opposed on principle to what he regarded as his radicalism.

On the twenty-fourth I had another meeting with Roosevelt, in which I suggested that if La Follette would withdraw in his favor, as now again seemed possible on account of the falling away of his support, it was clear that he, Roosevelt, should treat him with the utmost consideration and courtesy and make his withdrawal as easy for him as was possible under the circumstances. Roosevelt fully agreed to this, and said he would meet La Follette more than halfway should such an occasion arise. At this period, Roosevelt was more irritated with Taft than ever, and when I showed him an article I had written,[6] dealing with the President's part in the Ballinger case, his antedating of the Wickersham brief, etc., he urged me to publish it unchanged and "without any soft pedaling," remarking that it was weak enough as it was, and fell far short of giving Taft his just deserts.

On the twenty-ninth of January, there began another painful and long drawn out series of conferences with La Follette at the Washington headquarters. Most of his supporters were by this time convinced that his strength, always confined to the rural districts of the West and Middle West, had sunk to a point where it was to La Follette's own interest to get out of the campaign as quickly as possible, or, failing this, both men should carry on their campaigns separately, without public hostility, each seeking delegates in the territory where he was the stronger. It was at this point that La Follette delivered his first clear ultimatum, to the effect that he would fight alone if he were "to carry [only] one state and that by a divided delegation." It was after this meeting, as I remember, that [Houser] told me he considered it more than unlikely that La Follette would carry any state delegation but that of Wisconsin.

The final chapter in Senator La Follette's unfortunate but gallant attempt to wrest the Republican nomination from Taft in 1912, an attempt which I am convinced was actuated by no selfish motive, took place at the Periodical Publishers Association's annual dinner in Philadelphia on February 2, 1912. The list of speakers included Governor Woodrow Wilson, Senator La Follette, Dr. Weir Mitchell, and Governor Hiram Johnson of California, and lesser lights such as Mayor Blankenburg of Philadelphia,[7] Gilbert Roe, La Follette's law partner,[8] and that already famous prince of investigators, William J. Burns, who strangely enough was a devoted friend and admirer of Charles R. Crane. Whether or not all these luminaries actually appeared in the firmament that dreary and painful night, I cannot now remember. And what was said by most of them was not of particular importance, except in the case of La Follette himself who, well on in his speech, suddenly began to repeat himself, and talked ramblingly for an hour and a half, despite the efforts of his secretary, John Hannan, sitting immediately behind him, who kept begging him in audible whispers to wind up his address. La Follette had been under a severe strain for months. His health was bad, and his friends had advised him strongly against coming to Philadelphia. The speech, whose climax was an impassioned plea to the magazine writers and publishers to hold out against the lures of commercialized journalism, stands, bereft of its repetitions, as a fine and courageous utterance. Some of it, like much that La Follette said, was not only true but prophetic. But as he went on, and the audience realized that he was not himself, a feeling of anxiety and pity spread through the room. At the end, La Follette sat down, seemingly in a state of collapse, with closed eyes and his chin sunk on his chest. For a few moments there was complete silence. Then Don [Seitz], editor of the *Evening World,* made a brief but scathing attack on La Follette, which, like the Senator's own words, was received in silence, and the guests rose and quickly dispersed. Hannan and I led La Follette from the room. He seemed and was, I think, quite conscious of the reaction to his speech, though not of its cause, which was not so much the ideas La Follette had expressed as the repetition and the speaker's evident condition.

In his *Autobiography,* La Follette writes:

As on one or two previous occasions I had overtaxed my strength. . . . I had just returned from a speaking trip, part of which was made under the most trying circumstances and all of which taxed my reserve. Besides, I was seriously troubled at the evidences I had discovered at headquarters of the studied undermining of my candidacy by some of my supporters. Added to this, the doctors had decided that our little daughter must undergo an operation, the seriousness of which could not be foretold, on the morning following the Publishers banquet.[9]

Next day, February 3, 1912, the press announced La Follette's breakdown, interpreting it as the end of his campaign for the presidency. The following morning I breakfasted in New York with Governor Johnson at the Holland House, lunched with Beveridge, and dined with Mark Sullivan and George L. Record, all of whom took it as a matter of course that La Follette would withdraw from the campaign. That night, Medill McCormick, still in charge of the La Follette headquarters in Washington, called me by phone and said that La Follette was about to give out a statement of withdrawal. The following day, calling again from Washington, McCormick told me that La Follette was too ill to make a statement, but one from his manager, Houser, would appear in the next morning's papers, to the effect that La Follette was definitely out of the race. On the same day, Houser called up George Record,[10] leader of the Progressive forces in New Jersey, and read the statement to him which he said La Follette had dictated himself, adding that Record and all the La Follette leaders might now consider themselves free to turn to Roosevelt.[11] On the following day or the day after, either the sixth or seventh of February,[12] Johnson, McCormick, Record, and myself, after lunching at the Holland House, went to Charles R. Crane's apartment on Twelfth Street, where besides Crane we found Lenroot, Roe, Rogers, and Houser. Houser told us that, while La Follette desired us to feel at liberty to follow any leader we chose, he would not, said Houser, withdraw in favor of Roosevelt, since he did not believe in Roosevelt and could not conscientiously support him. He would, therefore, remain nominally in the running but make no campaign. La Follette's condition, he said, was such as to require a prolonged retirement from hard work, and he discussed with Crane the advisability of a journey up the Nile as the sort of thing that would put La Follette on his feet again. Crane raised the objection that La Follette was too poor a man to afford a trip of this kind, and offered to pay the expense, at the same time remarking that he feared La Follette would never consent to such an arrangement.

In his *Autobiography,* La Follette insists that his breakdown at the Publishers Dinner was merely "a pretext for the desertion which it is now plain to be seen had been under consideration for a long time."[13]

It is quite true that most of us in the La Follette group had been hoping that La Follette would withdraw and release us, since it had long been evident that the primary purpose of the La Follette movement, namely, the defeat of Taft, could not conceivably be accomplished under his leadership.

Upon the publication of the Houser statement, Record, my brother, and myself gave statements to the press, in accordance with what at the time we fully believed to be La Follette's own instructions. Almost at once, however, La Follette repudiated the Houser statement, and,

vigorously attacking everyone who had turned to Roosevelt, continued his campaigning, though in a somewhat desultory manner.

Though La Follette never spoke of the matter to me, even in later
years when our friendship was resumed, I have always believed that
Houser exceeded his authority in telling us that La Follette desired
the statement of February 5 to be interpreted as his withdrawal from
the campaign. For on April 8, after Johnson had at length come out
for Roosevelt (basing this action on the Houser statement and con-
versations), La Follette wired Rudolph Spreckels in San Francisco,
from whom he had received word that Governor Johnson had left
him, La Follette, and was out for Roosevelt, giving as an explanation
for his switch the fact that Houser, La Follette's manager, had released the La Follette men.

. . . The attempt of any of my former supporters to justify their desertion
of my candidacy by making Walter Houser their scapegoat is a cowardly
perversion of fact. They know that no one had authority to withdraw me
as a candidate and that no one ever professed to have such authority or
even attempted to assert it. And they know, one and all, that I persistently
refused to withdraw in favor of Roosevelt or anyone else and stated to
them again and again that once entered upon the contest I would not
back out.

They furthermore know that I refused to permit my own candidacy to
be curtailed with Roosevelt's candidacy or combine with him in any way.[14]

On February 9, I wrote to Brandeis:

February 9th, 1912.

Louis D. Brandeis, Esq.,
Harvard Club,
New York City.

Dear Louis:

I want you to understand my position about La Follette. I gave out a
statement Tuesday afternoon, which you may have seen, in which I said
that La Follette's withdrawal made it necessary for the Progressives to

unite behind Roosevelt. I did this for two reasons. First, McCormick called me up on Monday and told me that Houser intended that his forthcoming statement should be interpreted as a withdrawal on the part of the Senator, and a release to his supporters to do as the local situation suggested. George L. Record says that on Monday night Houser called him up on the long-distance telephone, read the statement to him and said that it meant a withdrawal and a release. Next morning McSween in the *North American* stated that the Senator had virtually withdrawn from the race, and advised his followers to go over to Roosevelt. Second, it seemed to me that as the Senator was out of the race his supporters who believed that the good of the progressive movement demanded that they should turn to Roosevelt should say so, so that the La Follette Progressives would be able to turn somewhere and continue to work for the progressive cause. This was especially true in New York.

In the last two days we have had continual conferences here. Hiram Johnson, Steffens, McCormick, Roe, Rogers, Crane, Lenroot, Houser, Record and myself. With the exception of Roe, I think they all felt that it would be infinitely better to have Roosevelt than Taft. Johnson wrote to La Follette some time ago that he would stick to him until personally released. La Follette wrote back holding him. The probability is that this decision of La Follette's will wreck the whole progressive movement of California, and perhaps bring the Southern Pacific back into power. It will do no good in California for Roosevelt to take his name off the ballot for it can be put back by petition, and Johnson says it would be put back. The only possible way to save the situation in California is for La Follette to release Johnson, and allow him to go in for Roosevelt. Roosevelt is willing to stay till the end, and to make his fight, and to lose or win at Chicago on a straight Progressive platform. He feels that he can afford to be beaten if he takes a high stand. This is very clear in his mind, and he will make it clear to the public before long.

No two men in the ranks of the Progressives have been more radical than Johnson of California or Record of New Jersey. They are as deeply in earnest as it is possible to be. Record has made his break owing to his message from Houser, so that he is free to act as he thinks best. But both Johnson and Record say that if the Senator remains in his present state of mind he will do irreparable harm to the progressive movement and to himself.

I think that you have more influence over the Senator than anyone else at this juncture. He has lost confidence and is unwilling to talk to most of the crowd.

Very sincerely yours,

(A. P.)

Brandeis, as we all knew, had no grain of enthusiasm for Roosevelt, differing with him radically on economic questions. He saw clearly, as Roosevelt did not, the danger in the Hamiltonian theory of concentration of power when applied to corporate organizations. Brandeis had a thoroughgoing distrust of "largeness," and foretold before 1912 the havoc which the merger epoch would cause in finance and industry alike. Refusing to be drawn into the Roosevelt camp, he replied to my letter with an austere brevity that showed quite plainly that he at least would have no truck with the Bull Moose, a position from which he never moved by a hair's breadth.

February 13th, 1912.

Amos Pinchot, Esq.,
60 Broadway,
New York City.

My dear Amos:

I was glad to get your letter of the 9th, having read some part of your statement while I was in the West.

I have not seen Senator La Follette since January 29th, and have not heard from him. The situation is certainly an unfortunate one.

Cordially yours,
Louis D. Brandeis

Though Roosevelt did not officially become a presidential candidate till February 24 (when, in answer to a letter signed by seven governors, he wrote: "I will accept the nomination for President if it is tendered to me, and I will adhere to this decision until the convention has expressed its preference. . . ."[15]), the country was now well aware that an open declaration of war against Taft was but a matter of time, and anticipated with bated breath an intraparty feud that was to prove as bitter as any since the Blaine-Conkling controversy in the seventies. The mobilization of the Roosevelt army was only being held back by the financial difficulty of carrying on a campaign without rich angels. The rampant radicalism of the Ossawatomie speech had estranged all but a few of his well-to-do friends, and caused an uproar in Wall Street which his endorsement of Harding and the Payne-Aldrich Tariff Act had not availed to quiet. As yet we were unaware of the closeness of his relations with Gary, though this might well have been guessed. For, since January, Frank Munsey had been urging Roosevelt to declare his nomination. And, not knowing that Munsey and Perkins would eventually slip forward to shoulder the financial burden, we supposed we were in for a hand-to-mouth campaign for which funds would be raised here and there in small amounts by popular subscription. Whether Roosevelt's decision to run was the result of an understanding that the group which had been affronted by Taft's indictment of the Steel Corporation would see him through, is a matter of conjecture. Yet it is improbable that so experienced a politician would have committed himself to a nation-wide contest for delegates without a definite assurance of an adequate war chest.

However this may be, Roosevelt took a surprisingly soft stand on the trust question in the first draft of the speech he was to deliver on the twenty-third of February at the Ohio Constitutional Convention. On the tenth or the eleventh, he had sent me a preliminary copy of it, and I find clipped to it a note written immediately after reading it:

Read T.R.'s draft of Ohio speech on train. It is very poor. Must be made human and direct.

What is purpose?
  To assure progressives that Mr. Roosevelt stands on a definite progressive platform.

The country has progressed—has he?
  Whether or not they should ask such a question, they *are* asking it.

We all have a right to know. The country should not back anyone *personally*.

Roosevelt must be a candidate of principles.
    Taft need not.
    I cannot gather any definite assurance (from Roosevelt) about what he is going to run on.
    Keeping capital in the community is not an asset.

Page 2:   Real conservative note.

Page 3:   Popular interpretation of Constitution.

Page 5:   Stress on quotation wrong.

Page 6:   Might have been written by Taft.
    There is no new issue now as to protecting trusts. The Attorney-General and the Supreme Court have done that.
    Leave out approval of trusts. We do not know yet whether steel is cheaper on account of steel trust.

Page 7:   The producer is more important than the distributor. Too much stress on useless class. Inconsistent also with praise of combination. Probably we should have independent production and combined distribution.

Page 11: Apologizes for attacking monopoly.

On the fourteenth, Gifford and I went over the speech with the Colonel, after discussing it with Johnson on the thirteenth. At this conference at the *Outlook* office, Roosevelt had a great deal to say in defense of balanced statements to which we took particular exception. Undoubtedly we were crowding him into a position, or rather trying to make him hold to a position, which he had assumed rashly and had now begun to regard as untenable. Though he was patient and receptive as usual, and even amazingly tolerant of our illusions, I went back to my office feeling that the draft was an almost tragic downsliding, and wrote to him hastily as follows:

February 14th, 1912.

Dear Colonel Roosevelt:

I want to make plain to you my position in regard to your Ohio speech. I believe this utterance of yours is of immense importance and will be, perhaps, the chief factor which will decide whether or not the efforts to nominate you for the Presidency will be successful.

However prone Lincoln was to qualifying his statements, it must be remembered he always did this for the purpose of giving an exact literal and clear-cut definition of where he stood in regard to the subject at hand. After reading over both the first and second drafts of your Ohio speech, I found that I had gained no clear-cut and definite impression of your position in regard to the questions which the speech deals with. It seems to me that the qualifying clauses are responsible for this. A certain amount of misunderstanding will result even if you take the most clear and unequivocal position in favor of or against any measure. But if your position in regard to the great issues that are before the people today is modified by conditional and hypothetical premises, no one will know where you stand. Your followers will feel that you have not made plain your platform.

I differ with you, Colonel, radically as to the need of your showing just how progressive you are; just what your attitude toward the tariff, child labor, the trusts, etc., is. No man has a right to be in public life without taking the people absolutely into his confidence. The progressives who have doubted your progressiveness are not few. But their doubts are not as to your progressive spirit or your desire to help the Progressive cause, but as to the methods by which you may see fit to carry on your fight for the people.

In four years we have made enormous strides. When you were in office the tariff question was not an issue as it is today. All of us did not feel that the tariff was, as Senator Dolliver said, the one really grand larceny; Ida Tarbell had not written her articles on the wool schedules, and so it was with many subjects which are definite issues today, dividing class against class and section against section. No one has a right to, and I believe few people do, question your desire to solve in the interest of the people the industrial questions that must be solved now. But everyone has a right and a duty to ask you to make very plain and very simple your views as to these problems and the remedies. I think that the Progressives who are holding off their support of you until they have seen a clear statement of your platform are well within their rights, and in fact acting as their duty directs them to act, as long as their doubts are sincere.

Now as to the general tone of your speech. I would like to see it such that it cannot be interpreted wrong, or at least such that if anyone does interpret it wrong, the document shall contain simple proof that such an interpretation is an unjust one. But it seems to me beyond doubt that your speech should be so easy to understand that no serious misinterpretation could conceivably arise. As you probably remember, Gladstone said that the first duty of a public man was to speak to the people in terms which they could not misunderstand. I feel that through your desire to give everybody justice, you have laid unnecessary stress on giving justice to capital. Capital has had all the justice, or practically all, up to date. You yourself were the first to point out in a large way the injustice and inequality of opportunity with which commercialism and business in politics has saddled the average man. I feel strongly that any key-note utterance at this time by you which did not lay overwhelming stress upon protecting the average man, even at the expense of industrialism, would not only be a mistake, but would be wrong. We have hardly yet commenced in our struggle to regulate the strong and give the average man a show. We have hardly yet fired the opening gun in the campaign to drive the great industrial combinations from the control of legislatures, Congresses and every branch of City, State and Federal government. This is the task which the people now are turning to you to accomplish. Taft has failed because he did not see this great eternal issue—because, being out of sympathy with the needs and problems of the average man, he could never see such an issue and could never feel the undesirability of having the power in the hands of a few.

I think that in your Ohio speech you should make it plain to every man and woman in this country that we are now going through a crisis in that old, unending struggle for human rights. I believe that in this speech you should accept the leadership of a great cause in terms so plain that the people will feel hope.

You have asked me to criticize your speech. I have done so frankly. To recapitulate:

1. I think that you should come out simply and definitely for the things that you are willing to stand for. If there is anything that you cannot stand for in general terms and without qualification, it should be left out.

2. The emphasis all through your speech should be changed so that it will give the overwhelming impression that your first duty as President will be to protect the people and restore justice to them; that this will be done with as little business disturbance as possible; but that the people shall have the preference in escaping suffering.

3. You should bring in the issues that are great and vital issues and in regard to which everybody has a right and duty to ask where you stand.

4. Make the speech so plain that people will understand exactly where you stand and will be able to support you on principle as a candidate verbally bound to the progressive policies of today, rather than as a person whose record implies progress, but who has not yet brought himself up to date. I think that it would be a misfortune if this speech should result merely in a nation-wide debate as to just where you stand.

Very sincerely yours,
(A. P.)

On the following day, he replied:

THE OUTLOOK

287 Fourth Avenue
New York

Office of
Theodore Roosevelt

February 15, 1912.

Dear Amos:

I appreciate your letter, and I thank both you and Gifford for the criticisms. I have adopted about two-thirds of the written memoranda you gave me. I did not adopt the other one-third because it seems to me to embody the kind of statement I am most anxious to avoid, the kind of statement which in my judgment would make the people at large tend to regard the Insurgents as merely an ordinary political party. Take the proposed tariff plank. My dear Amos, I know that you and Gifford are governed by the most intense sincerity of conviction; and yet that plank if I had used it would have made me seem to be uttering a conventional and insincere platitude. Governor Johnson, Mr. Van Valkenburg and

Colonel Nelson all felt this way about that plank; and while Governor Johnson at first advocated my saying something about the tariff in the speech, he seemed in the end to come around to the position the other two so strongly held, that it would be thoroughly unwise and disadvantageous to do so.

Now of course if you are right, and my speech conveys to the bulk of sincere progressives the impression that I am not taking a sufficiently well-defined radical position, then the speech will be a failure. But my own view is that if this is the fact it must mean that from my standpoint the country is not in the right condition to tolerate my leadership at all; that, from my standpoint, the demand is for a man who shall go to one of two extremes, both dangerous to the welfare of our people. After the most careful going over of my speech, I fail to see that I have put in qualifications save precisely as Abraham Lincoln always put in qualifications. I have qualified my statements only so as to try to give an exact and clear view of my meaning. The tendency of all public men—progressives I am sorry to say quite as much as conservatives—is to utter a string of easy, well-sounding, and rather cheap, half truths. These half truths are simple, and it is easy to repeat them and to rail at those who do not accept them as "compromisers"; just as the abolitionists railed at Lincoln as a compromiser for years before he was President, and during his presidency, at the same time that the fire-eaters insisted that he was the worst kind of abolitionist. I have tried to utter as well as I could whole truths, the only kinds of truth that are valuable in the long run, but which are complex and always difficult of statement. It may very well be that you are right, and that I have failed to state them properly, in which case it will prove that I am not the man for this situation. But that I have the right attitude I am absolutely certain, and if I cannot take this attitude to advantage, it merely means that some man of greater power must take it, must state what I have stated, with all the qualifications I have put in, but must be able to do it in a way that will arouse a popular appeal that I cannot arouse.

Sincerely yours,
Theodore Roosevelt

Amos R. E. Pinchot, Esq.,
  34 Nassau Street,
    New York City.

From a political point of view, T.R. was obviously nearer right than we were. He knew that, without office, he would be powerless to accomplish the things we were mutually interested in. He was anxious to avoid taking a stand that would arouse such opposition as to make his candidacy futile. On the other hand, we argued that, since he had already crossed the Rubicon in his Ossawatomie speech, a retreat from its advanced philosophy would gain him little among conservatives, who now knew where he was pointed, and merely weaken the support of the liberals in both parties, who would serve as the shock troops of his army.

We believed that the procession of conservatives and quasi-liberals that foregathered daily at Oyster Bay was profoundly uninterested in the things we wanted the Colonel to do. We considered them stock political reformers of the goody-good breed, with a sprinkling of bankers and industrialists, who talked the lingo of liberalism and hoped to achieve the millennial results without damage to the privileges and profits of their class. With the exception of perhaps a dozen men, his close advisers were men of the stamp of Root, Lodge, Perkins, Stimson, George Meyer, and Frank Munsey. Roosevelt was too keen a politician to be unmindful of the advantages to be gained from the cooperative friendship of rich and powerful interests. In 1904 he had lost the backing of the Standard Oil group by his repudiation of its contribution to his war chest. Now with another presidential campaign in sight he needed something stronger to lean on than the so-called "lunatic fringe" to which Gifford, and especially myself, belonged.

In the internecine war which had broken out within the Republican party since he had left the White House, the Colonel's first impulse was to side with the Insurgent group. But in order to secure the nomination and regain power, this was the great essential: he must have the good will of the financial interests which had been so useful to him in 1904, and these were still conservative. What course should he pursue to consolidate the support of the second element without losing the first? Here he found no clear answer and, like most men in doubt, he oscillated from one opinion to another, and was influenced alternately by his friends in each group. Realizing the importance of his public utterances, and especially of the Columbus speech, Gifford and I did all we could to bring left-wing pressure to bear, resolving at the same time to be with him ourselves as much as possible. Hordes of friends were deluging him with suggestions that ran the whole gamut from orthodoxy to radicalism. I don't know who was responsible for his pronouncement in favor of the recall of judicial decisions which found its way into his Ohio speech. It may have been McCarthy[16] of Wisconsin or Van Hise,[17] for at this period Roosevelt listened with equal cordiality to advanced college professors, bankers, labor leaders, socialists, railroad presidents, trust magnates, and the proprietors of standpat newspapers.

On the twentieth, I dropped in at the *Outlook* office, to find the Colonel wearing a green eye shade, and still poring industriously over the Columbus speech. The morning was memorable only for an incident that showed that whatever may have happened to the Colonel's political sagacity, his sense of humor had not forsaken him. While I waited in the anteroom, an old-fashioned Southern Democrat came in who, for some reason or other, had turned up a few months before as a La Follette man. Though comparatively young, he had all the manners and many of the tricks of the political orator of the *ancien régime*. He had recently gained fame by his speech at a dinner in New Jersey where Governor Woodrow Wilson was supposed to have delivered the principal address. His turn to speak had come just before Wilson's, and losing all sense of the flight of time, he had spoken at great length in a formal, long-winded eulogy of the Democratic party. When at length Wilson was called on, he remarked quite suavely, and without a trace of the irritation he no doubt felt, that his distinguished young friend had spoken so well and that the hour was so late that he would confine himself to telling a story. It seemed, he said, that a noted bad man had been shot by a gambler in a border town of the Southwest, and on his tombstone his friends had inscribed this epitaph:

> Here lies the body of Flint Jones.
> He passed from this life through
>   the intervention
> Of a Colt's Revolver—old style,
>   large bore and brass mounted.
> And of such is the Kingdom of Heaven.

Although it was well known that Roosevelt was now hot on the trail of the nomination, our Southern orator told me as we sat outside the sanctum that he felt quite sure the Colonel, upon due reflection, would decide to abandon his candidacy and fall in behind La Follette; he had, in fact, come to see Roosevelt in order to recommend this course. When he disappeared into the inner office, I could not help wondering what sort of reception he would get. But when he reappeared five minutes later, he was beaming. "I think I moved him," he declared. "In fact, I am morally certain. He spoke of La Follette with unmeasured praise, and when I left him wrung my hand and expressed gratification at my having spoken so frankly."

When I joined Roosevelt, his face bore an amused but slightly wry smile. He looked at me in silence, then he opened his mouth, bared his teeth, and almost shouted: "Amos, who is that man?"

"Whom do you mean, Colonel?" I replied. "That handsome young Southern gentleman who just came out of your office?"

"Yes," he said. "In heaven's name, who was he? He got up and smoothed back his hair and started in making a speech for La Follette. I instantly saw that the only way to stop him was to break in and make one myself. On the whole, I am inclined to think my speech was better than the one he had up his sleeve. Now, what do *you* want with me?"

As Roosevelt's dash for the nomination gathered speed, strange recruits swarmed to the Progressive army, where there was as little accord as among the workers on the Tower of Babel. I remember spending one morning in April with the Colonel, Medill McCormick, Henry L. Stoddard, editor of the *Mail and Express,* Charles McCarthy, then considered a radical of radicals, and the redoubtable William Ward of Westchester County, as reactionary a boss as ever stood beneath the G.O.P. banner. Adjourning for lunch, we returned to the *Outlook* office, where the discussion continued on the subject of the approaching primaries and the difficulty of raising the funds required in contesting them.

Though he was still wobbling on the question of platform, it was a comfort that the Colonel was frankly sailing into Taft. And on the third of March at Oyster Bay, Roosevelt commissioned me to write an answer to the charge of ingratitude which Taft's friends were hotly hurling at him. On the twentieth came his first public meeting in

New York, held at Carnegie Hall. On the twenty-first, I went to the *Outlook* office to show him my revamped article about Taft's part in the Pinchot-Ballinger case, as well as a draft of a letter he had asked me to write in answer to an *Evening Post* editorial charging him with deserting the President.

Meantime, organization work was going on under the skilled touch of George Perkins, who by April had established headquarters at the corner of Forty-second Street and Madison Avenue. Ever tactful and indefatigable, Perkins was taking things more and more into his own hands, despite the growlings of the Western Progressives, one of whom complained to Roosevelt that "our organization is merely George Perkins and a pushbutton."[18]

While not out against Roosevelt, E. W. Scripps refused to support him actively. Having launched the La Follette boom and disliking Roosevelt as he did, he continued nominally to back La Follette and was neutral to Roosevelt. And yet he held his newspapers in a position where they could veer to Wilson should the New Jersey governor land the Democratic nomination, a possibility that seemed pretty remote to most of us but was yet one for which the tacticians in the Scripps group were already preparing.

[Three] letters written in February 1912 sketch with vividness the unhappy tangle into which we had inevitably been drawn. [The first is from myself to William B. Colver], then manager of the Scripps publications and later chairman of the Federal Trade Commission in Wilson's administration. [The second is Colver's reply to me. The third is] William Kent's letter to La Follette, a copy of which he enclosed to me with the notation that it had been written "after a rather painful interview" with him.

February 2nd, 1912.

Dear Colver:

I am very much worried about the situation in Washington. The Senator is indignant to the last degree at Roosevelt's course and I think we are going to have trouble unless we get things straightened out. We went into this game with two definite objects in view—to prevent the nomination of a reactionary and to keep the Progressives in Congress and throughout the country together during and beyond the national Presidential campaign of 1912.

We have all now got to make a decision at once—whether it is better for the country to have Taft or Roosevelt nominated. La Follette says that he has given up all practical hope of the nomination, and that his campaign from now on will be with the purpose of making clear the issues and defining a platform for the Convention. His manager says that if we pursue the policy of fighting others who are Progressives, perhaps not as Progressive as we are, but certainly infinitely more Progressive than Taft, La Follette will have delegates from no state but Wisconsin, and perhaps a divided delegation there.

Nevertheless, without hope of victory for himself and with no purpose which would not be served as well if he would either withdraw from the Presidential race but continue his campaign of education, or remain a candidate and permit cooperation between Roosevelt and La Follette Progressives, the Senator has decided on war between the La Follette supporters and the Roosevelt supporters. I feel sure that he has made this decision on principle, but I also feel sure that he is blinded by his irritation at Roosevelt's course, and hampered in his judgment by his nervous condition. He says, and this is perfectly true, that many of the Roosevelt supporters are not Progressives at all, but reactionaries who are merely trying to get on the band wagon. And he fears that to these men and not to the Progressives Roosevelt will recognize his obligations if he is elected. It seems to me natural, if not inevitable, that the reactionaries to whom La Follette refers should prefer a man of Roosevelt's brand of Progressiveness to La Follette's. It is not that they love Roosevelt more, but because they love La Follette less. I admit that Roosevelt, if elected, may not give as clear and strongly Progressive administration as La Follette would, but nevertheless, I do believe, and I think that everybody believes —certainly the country does—that he will be vastly more Progressive and useful than Taft or Harmon would be, and that his administration will have the human element in it, from the lack of which Taft's has fallen down so utterly.

I cannot but feel that we will make a serious mistake if we support La Follette's nominal candidacy in a manner that will set the Progressives at each other's throats and practically work for the nomination of Taft.

We have got to meet a bad situation. The question as to who is responsible for this situation need not enter into our calculations now.

I do not think that anyone should abandon La Follette. I think we should all help him to do what he can now which will be useful both to himself and to the country, but I do not think we ought to encourage him to demand that his followers in every state should precipitate civil war among the people who have been working together against boss rule, railroad rule and machine politics. If his plan of uncompromising war with all but La Follette supporters is continued, it looks to me like a halt in the Progressive campaign for the things that we believe in, in most of the western states and some of the eastern ones.

Governor Johnson is pledged to La Follette. He will, of course, keep his pledge unless La Follette releases him. This will mean that he will have a very hard fight to hold his people with him. He may win and keep the state for La Follette, but if he does, as he himself must realize, it may mean the destruction of his own influence in the state, and very possibly the return of the Southern Pacific machine to power.

One thing I want you to realize. When La Follette opened his active speaking campaign he agreed that the La Follette Progressives should cooperate with the other Progressives in an effort to send as many Roosevelt and La Follette delegates as possible to Chicago. Houser himself wrote a resolution to this effect, which was similar to the one adopted at the Columbus Conference. I do not think that anything has happened which seems to make that plan less wise than it was when it was adopted. It does not seem to me for a moment that we would be justified in working with crooks or reactionaries. We cannot keep them from following the band wagon, but we need not work with them, bid for their support or accept it if offered. But we can say to the vast number of Progressives throughout the country who want Roosevelt: "Go ahead, get your Roosevelt delegates, we will get our La Follette delegates, and, if we have luck, we will beat Taft at the Convention."

As you doubtless know, La Follette's plan has alienated from him the support of other active insurgents in both Houses of Congress. The people of Illinois and many other states where a Progressive fight is in progress say that they must either revolt against La Follette's decision or abandon the fight in their own state. They think, as I think, that La Follette should not bind them to what they believe is a destructive and short-sighted course.

However any of us may differ as to Roosevelt's course in the matter and whatever his weakness may have been, we believe that he is for the people. I think also that we must not forget that one of his weaknesses is a source of security to the country in our present situation. We are now in a great movement of advance, which is not nation wide only but world wide. Roosevelt has never stood out against the people, he has always led them in the direction in which they desired to go. He will do so again. He will do so, I believe, more strenuously then ever, because, if he is elected to the Presidency, only an advanced radical position can prevent an anticlimax in his career, and the disappointment of the whole people.

Let me recapitulate what seems to me the situation.

La Follette is a real Progressive and a man whom we all honor and desire to support.

Roosevelt is a less real Progressive, a man whom we all honor for his past services to the country, but whose recent course has disappointed many of us. Nevertheless, we believe that he is on the people's side, and that he is perhaps the greatest individual force in the country on that side.

La Follette cannot become the President in 1912.

Roosevelt has a chance to become the President in 1912.

We went into this fight with two objects—to keep the Progressives together and to prevent the nomination of a reactionary.

By working for La Follette in the way he wants us to, we will split the Progressives and help the nomination of a reactionary.

By working for both La Follette and Roosevelt delegates, or by inducing La Follette to withdraw his candidacy, but to continue his campaign for a Progressive platform and Progressive principles, the union of the Progressives may be preserved and the nomination of a reactionary may be prevented.

Without reference to our personal feelings toward Roosevelt and La Follette, it seems to me that we must follow one of the latter courses unless we believe that the nomination of a reactionary is better for the country than the nomination of Roosevelt.

Sincerely yours,
(A. P.)

W. B. Colver, Esq.,
C/o Dr. Kellogg's Sanitarium,
Battle Creek, Michigan.

My dear Mr. Pinchot:

Your special delivery letter sent to Battle Creek followed me here to Chicago.

I was in Washington last week and like yourself was greatly worried by the situation.

I don't believe at this time I will go into much of an attempt to answer your letter. I think I know how you feel and appreciate the agony that all of our fellows are going through at this time.

There are just two things which stand out in my mind. One is that Roosevelt will attempt to heal over the sore spots in the Republican party by bringing together people who are positively incompatible. He will have us, if we join with him, friendly with such men as Walter Brown in Ohio and Elihu Root and Philander Knox and Senator Lodge and that sort of people. This seems to me an impossible thing to do. It means that it will dilute the virtue of the progressive cause and instead of weeding out the traitors from the Senate and from the House and from National and State Committees and from state offices, continue the reactionaries in places of power and obliterate the sharp line that has been drawn by the aggressive fight which has been waged since Roosevelt went to Africa.

The other thing that worries me is that in case Roosevelt is elected we will get instead of a few bitter defeats, to be followed later by sweeping victories, some half way successes, some compromises like the railroad rate bill and other things, where, at the last minute, we will trade some vital point in our legislation for a few votes of scoundrels whose votes we would be much better off without.

Frankly, if I had my way, I would like to see the line-up between Taft and Woodrow Wilson and have Woodrow Wilson win, but in view of the condition of La Follette's health, I am inclined to follow the Roosevelt movement and do what I can in the cause, although my heart will not be in it, I am afraid.

My deepest sympathy goes out to four men in this crisis, yourself, your brother, Gilson Gardner and Senator La Follette. You men have had to go through tribulation and fire and you are tasting the bitterness of a fight that is made for principle and not for selfish ambition.

I shall be glad to go over the whole subject with you some time and already have violated my resolution not to write a long letter, so I will say goodbye. Regards to Gifford Pinchot.

Very truly yours,
W. B. Colver

CC:GG

February 12, 1912.

Hon. Robert M. La Follette,
  United States Senate.

My dear Senator La Follette:

I have done much hard thinking since seeing you on Sunday. I believe it would be absolute suicide for you to fight Roosevelt. The men who have been backing you would feel that you were not fighting the cause of progress, whatever your own judgment might be as to your course.

The situation in California is very acute. I sincerely hope that you will feel like requesting that your name be kept off the California ballot, in the event of the Progressives taking up the Roosevelt candidacy, as they are sure to do.

Governor Johnson asked me to be one of the Delegates, which I naturally refused to do with you in the field. I do not wish to go as a Delegate in any event. I am utterly sick of the whole game and am going to "chuck" it until the situation clears.

There are none of your real friends who do not believe that the bottom has absolutely fallen out of your candidacy as the most active opponent of President Taft. You cannot afford, as you believe, to join forces with Roosevelt; neither can you afford to fight him and thereby accumulate as enemies those who are naturally your friends.

The American people, by a very large majority, thoroughly believe in Roosevelt and it certainly is not your object, as a constructive statesman, to start in smashing him. I believe time will take care of him and his ambitions and that he will not be the nominee of the Convention. In the event of open hostility, you could not possibly be accepted by the Convention, and by fighting him, you make enemies of a large number of people as patriotic as yourself, whose views differ with yours, and in my opinion, cut off the possibility of future recognition and will be considered as an undesirable person willing to jump on anyone.

My advice, at this juncture, is simply to make your fight where it is already laid out without any bitterness and get what Delegates you can from Wisconsin and to go before the Convention with a constructive platform in good temper and without having incurred personal animosities.

The main thing for you is to get away and rest and thereafter to do as little campaigning and as much constructive work in the Senate as possible.

I believe that you must consider me as one of the few people to whom selfish motives cannot be attributed, not because I am any better than anyone else but simply because I have no political ambitions or aspirations of my own and have never cared when I was in the right cause whether I won or lost.

At the present juncture, it seems to me that the best thing is to permit the union of Progressive forces to stick together around Roosevelt, if they so elect. I have resented this action all the way through and feel resentful now. My interest has been with you and your personal well being and in the well being of the country, through your candidacy. Both these considerations now move me to make the suggestions I have made.

Yours truly,
William Kent

As we look back over these stormy yet pregnant days, when two men of exceptionally strong will were opposing each other in a maze of conflicting motives, ambitions, and impersonal objectives, it is hard to do justice to either Roosevelt or La Follette. Both were influenced by a thousand considerations and impressions which no one will ever record. Both were part of a time in which the trends of political and economic thought were inchoate, even more so than today. Each man had a right to his own interpretations and his own views as to the policy that was best for the country and, incidentally, for himself. There was even less agreement then than now on the question whether great industrial combinations were beneficial or the reverse. No one could say to what extent the merger system in industry and finance was retarding or advancing the public welfare.

I think La Follette was unjust in believing that Roosevelt had been captured by the steel interests or was forming alliances with them for selfish purposes. I think he was right, however, in his opinion that these interests were consciously trying to use Roosevelt in order to protect their system of acquisition which, though as polite as men like Gary and Perkins could make it, was nevertheless essentially ruthless and almost completely unconcerned with the public's good. La Fol-

155

lette was obviously much farther progressive in his economic thinking than Roosevelt. He had seen the flaws in the philosophy of industrial giantism, just as Brandeis had seen them. He was economic-minded. His early political work in Wisconsin was set on an economic basis. His campaign speeches for the governorship and the United States senatorship had been fashioned in economic terms. He had waged protracted wars with the railroads, and put over his regulation schemes, which, still later, he was to repudiate as useless. He had the complete confidence of his state, which gave him an unusual freedom of action in the Senate, and this conduced likewise to freedom of thought.

Roosevelt, on the other hand, had played for and won the great stake of the presidency with trump cards that always had been political rather than economic. He had no economic training, and as a member of a comparatively rich New York family, his traditions were intensely conservative and his prejudices, as well as his self-interests, those common to the privileged class in the East. The marvel is not that he fell so far short of intelligent liberalism, but that he so nearly approached it. And this is particularly true when we remember that his nearest political associates had been men like Thomas Platt,[19] Lodge, Root, and Stimson, not one of whom had ever been fired by thoughts more deep or emotions more exuberant than are generally found in the respectable Republicanism of New York or Boston life.

Roosevelt was incapable of understanding La Follette. There was an inflexibility and intellectual sureness about the Wisconsin Senator, who had arrived at opinions which were convictions, which Roosevelt with his unformed ideas and unflagging impressionability could and the great conservatives in politics, whom he saw as men who were never relish. La Follette really hated the great figures of Wall Street undermining American civilization—exposing it, making it susceptible to political and economic disease. Roosevelt, like Lincoln Steffens, looked at big-business men, even the most reactionary and apparently reckless among them, as good men gone wrong, who would return to the fold of righteousness and public service if approached in a friendly spirit. La Follette was sure no one could ever use men of this kind for useful purposes. Roosevelt was under the impression that he, at all events, could so use them. And he did often try so to use them, though, it must be confessed, with little success. Roosevelt was an exceedingly broad man, with all sorts of hobbies and tastes, and an immense if superficial familiarity with books on many subjects. La Follette thought and read on comparatively narrow lines, but thoroughly. He was never willing to take up any subject until he had mastered it, and for this reason set rigorous limits.

Roosevelt was tremendously swayed by personality, by the agreeableness and good fellowship of the men whose paths he crossed, irrespective of their opinions. La Follette had comparatively few friends who disagreed with him on fundamentals—not that he was incapable of hating the sin while he loved the sinner, for he and Boies Penrose were devoted to each other, despite their irreconcilable differences on almost every subject that came before them in a senatorial capacity. La Follette did not care a damn for the pomps and glories of life. He was unaffectedly simple in his tastes. There was no Lorenzo the Magnificent or Louis XIV or William Hohenzollern in his makeup. Roosevelt was a patron of the arts and letters, the friend and protector of scientists, writers, and philosophers. He loved to be cronies with the great, the near-great, and the about-to-be-great. He liked prize fighters, wrestlers, boxers, actors, emperors, anybody and everybody that was pre-eminent. He collected pictures in a small way, and was proud of his Monticellis in Oyster Bay, which were really exceedingly beautiful paintings of their kind. He liked the feeling of having a Gary or a Frick or a railroad president shake him by the hand and put his arm around him. And he also liked the feeling of holding such a man at arm's length, and talking to him like a Dutch uncle. He had plenty of moral courage, though not as much as La Follette. But he did not care to exercise it too frequently. He had a boyish human quality of loving to be fooled, of yielding to the obsession of romantic illusions. La Follette was unromantic to a degree, except in his conception of a Hegelian world, in which the romance was one of the undying struggle between right and wrong, in which he saw himself as a leader in an uphill conflict against sinister forces. Outside of his political activities, his home was his world. His friendships were deep but few, his animosities equally deep, equally unshakable. Both men were egotists. But La Follette was modestly egotistical, while Roosevelt flaunted his egotism with youthful and attractive bravado.

CHAPTER V

The Chicago Convention, 1912

In June 1912 the Republican party held its convention to nominate a presidential candidate. Never shall I forget the gathering of the Taft and Roosevelt armies that jammed the Middle Lake section of Chicago, days before the convention began. It was a gay and noisy carnival crowd that was nevertheless grimly eager for the final drive, that to our small radical group meant more than a nomination, since we believed it would answer the question whether the progressive movement was to go forward or to bog down hopelessly, and perhaps permanently, in reaction.

Quartered for the most part in the Congress and nearby hotels on Michigan Avenue and its intersections were the lesser local politicians and their families, friends, and hangers-on. Less numerous but more imposing than this heterogeneous crowd were the senators, governors, and leading citizens, who appeared from all points of the compass hoping for a deadlock in the Taft-Roosevelt contest that by some happy miracle might put them in the running. Sweltering as was the weather, the streets were gay with the unceasing nondescript processions of humanity—pretty girls dressed in their very best, reporters, foreign observers, college students who had come to the convention for a lark and yet were earnestly curious to see government in the making; labor leaders, farmers, cattle men and miners; businessmen, industrialists, cranks of all sorts and ages who would buttonhole you in a hotel lobby and make you sweat as you listened

Notes begin on p. 286.

158

to their talk of populism or money reform schemes; professional lobbyists representing every kind of interest, some respectable no doubt, who wanted a finger in the platform pie and were willing to pay for it, not in money, of course, but in promises of to-be-delivered votes. There was, too, a goodly assemblage of college professors, economists, and social workers, the cream of the convention crowd, who paid their own way and looked for nothing but a chance to get their ideas and a little order and common sense into the platform deliberations. And then, too, there were to be found, mostly housed in the best suites of the Blackstone Hotel, the really big men of the convention and their handy men and hirelings from the lowest infernos of politics, who wielded mysterious influence, and were followed by an underworld contingent of racketeers, gamblers, thieves, prostitutes, such as flock to convention towns, jubilant in the expectation of rich harvests.

In the Chicago 1912 convention, however, the ordinary excitements of a national convention were vastly amplified by a general anticipation of a dramatic climax in the vitriolic Taft-Roosevelt feud. And the prospect was the more fascinating because Roosevelt was attempting the unparalleled and seemingly impossible feat of blocking the renomination of a man whom he himself had to all intents and purposes appointed to the presidency.

Every lobby along the lake front boiled and bubbled with gossip and the whispering of intrigue, though the real intriguers whose scheming meant anything were far from the madding crowd, behind the locked and mysterious doors of well-guarded suites. In walking twenty yards you could hear as many charges and countercharges of betrayal.

And after sundown, as the surging, whispering, and shouting crowds moved through the streets, bands and torchlight processions made night hideous and sleep difficult. The bill footed by Munsey and Perkins for brass bands for the Progressives alone must have been enormous. For at the time Perkins' secretary told me that it would come to $50,000, which was probably no exaggeration.

Colonel Roosevelt, with George Perkins, occupied a large suite on the second floor of the northeast corner of the Congress Hotel. And to this holy of holies the selected group of Roosevelt's friends and most valued backers were admitted by the doorkeepers as a matter of course at all times of the day and night. Here, in this citadel of progressivism, because of the imponderable elements in the situation, the atmosphere was quiet but exceedingly strained. Though presidential primaries had been held in thirteen states, and in almost every instance resulted in the election of Roosevelt delegations, it was nevertheless probable that, with the National and Credentials committees in the hands of Taft's regular Republican machine, these delegates would be unseated, for the simple reason that the regulars had the sheer power to unseat them, irrespective of the merits of the case. On the other hand, uncertainty as to the action of the Credentials Committee came from the fact that the old guard leaders were aware that the nomination of Taft would spell the defeat of the party at the November election. Yet, as Senator James Watson,[1] a powerful regular from Indiana, said to Gilson Gardner, they preferred even a Democratic victory to losing control of the Republican organization through the election of Roosevelt. "When we get back in four years," said Watson, "instead of the damned insurgents, we will have the machine."

The first important business of the National Committee was to adopt the rules under which the contending Taft and Roosevelt delegates should be seated, and it was at this early point in the proceedings that Roosevelt's cause was virtually lost. In spite of every effort of the Progressives, who were joined by Senator Borah of Idaho, the Taft forces adopted a rule[2] that there should be no roll call on the vote to seat or unseat a delegate except on the request of twenty of the committee's members, of whom it was known only ten or eleven were on Roosevelt's side. This made it easier for the Taft members to unseat the Roosevelt delegates who had been elected in the state primaries. There being no roll call or record of the way they cast their votes, no one could be held individually responsible. For instance, California had elected Roosevelt delegates by a majority of 77,000, but taking advantage of the rule, the Taft majority of the committee unseated these delegates in favor of Taft men and, upon their return to California, no matter how indignant the voters there might be, they could not call the committeeman to account, since there was no way to find out how he had voted. Roosevelt then appealed the decision of the National Committee to the Credentials, where a similar farce was enacted. Excitement redoubled in both camps. Roosevelt gave out statements justly comparing the action of the Taft leaders, of whom he named especially Taft and Senators Root, Penrose, and Crane, to ordinary ward ballot-box stuffing. The political army that had invaded Chicago came near to physical civil war.

While these events were absorbing public interest, a strange comedy was taking place in the Colonel's suite behind doors through which only those bent on urgent business and a few of Roosevelt's more intimate followers were allowed to pass. In the front room near the west wall stood a long mahogany table, and here [councils] of war went on in which were included such men as Munsey, Perkins, Littauer, the glove man, Senator Dixon of Montana,[3] the Roosevelt manager, James R. Garfield, ex-Secretary of the Interior under Roosevelt, William Flinn and Alexander Moore of Pittsburgh, Henry J. Allen of Kansas,[4] then a newspaper editor, later United States senator, Governor Fort of New Jersey,[5] Governor Bass of New Hampshire[6] and his brother [John[7]], the war correspondent, Governor Hadley of Missouri,[8] Governor Stubbs of Kansas,[9] George Record of New Jersey, Bainbridge Colby of New York,[10] Medill McCormick, John Parker of New Orleans,[11] my brother, and [Governor] Hiram Johnson[12] [of California].

In the early phase of the contest, notwithstanding the fact that the Taft machine seemed to have things well in hand, Senator Dixon would sit at the head of the table and quiet the fears of Roosevelt's friends and advisers, his deep calm voice carrying with it a conviction which under the circumstances was hard to account for. As near as I can remember, he would speak about as follows:

Gentlemen, I have only to repeat to you that as surely as we are sitting here, Colonel Roosevelt will have enough delegates to nominate him. He will be named without shadow of doubt. I will not go into particulars, nor will I give you my reasons at this time, but you may rest assured and confident that Theodore Roosevelt will be the nominee of the Republican party at this convention.

To me, and to all of us who were unversed in the ways of conventions, these remarks brought as much of perplexity as of comfort. At this time the general opinion was that though the race might possibly be close, Taft had the nomination already in the bag, and if Roosevelt were to run it would have to be on a third party ticket. The primary elections were obviously to be disregarded by the National Committee and, if this were so, no one could see how Roosevelt could get enough delegates. It was a curious accident that brought me a partial answer to this riddle. One morning I had been summoned to George Perkins' room, which adjoined Roosevelt's, on some matter of no particular importance. As I entered, Perkins, to whom the task of holding in line the delegates from the Southern rotten borough districts, and especially the colored brethren, had been entrusted, was busy with a telephone conversation in which the speaker at the other end of the line was, at first, doing all the talking. As the conversation, which was a long one, went on, Perkins became agitated, and then more agitated, and a look first of incredulity, then of disgust, and finally of consternation, came over his face, and as soon as he began to answer the meaning of the scene became inescapably clear. The body of Negro delegates, whose loyalty to the Colonel had been won in the usual manner, had taken advantage of the critical situation in which the Roosevelt delegates found themselves to raise their figures and demand a payment on account. They loved Massa Roosevelt, but they loved Massa Taft, too. Also, they were not rich men and they had to live, an assertion that, for the moment, seemed more than debatable. Perkins denounced the speaker at the other end of the wire with creditable vigor, but, on second thought, opened the door to further parley by stating that he could not discuss such a matter by telephone, and a decision could be made only after conference with parties whom he did not name. When he had hung up, he characterized the stand of the striking delegates as shameful and humiliating, admitting, nevertheless, that politics being what they were, there was perhaps nothing to do but play the game under the rules laid down by our adversaries. I was soon to learn that these delegates, having taken our encouragement in two installments, held a meeting and decided that they would stick to Taft since he seemed to be the more Republican of the two candidates.

I never told Roosevelt about this strange little backwater in the river of righteousness on which the progressive craft was sailing so gallantly and I doubt if he ever knew of it. It did not shock me then, and it does not now. That the Negro delegates should go to the highest bidder was then as now an established rule of presidential nominations. Buying black delegates for each was certainly no worse than stealing white ones without making any return, which was what Root, heading the respectables of the Taft machine, was doing on a large scale through the National and Credentials committees. Nevertheless, the defection of the Negro delegates, accompanied by a similar breakdown in the morale of certain white delegates, was the final straw that broke the back of the already overburdened progressive camel.[13] For it was on these black and white backsliding converts to progressivism, as well as on the long chance that some vestige of shame would check the unseating of the Roosevelt delegates chosen in the primary elections, that Dixon in the darkest hours was building the otherwise inexplicable hopes he was communicating to us.

CHAPTER VI

Birth of the Progressive Party

Things move quickly at political conventions. In fact, it always seems a miracle that such a raft of bargains can be made, so much business done, such passions roused, and so many pitched battles fought to [decisive and to] indecisive endings in such an incredibly short space of time. As [rulings] flowed in steadily from the Credentials Committee confirming the unseating of the Roosevelt delegates, and as the Negro contingent left us and moved into the Taft column, the rank and file of the Colonel's following, which was milling excitedly in the Gold Room, began to raise the cry of secession. And it was generally believed that Roosevelt was ready to bolt. In the Colonel's suite, the atmosphere had changed from confidence to gloom and anger. Throwing away all pretense of fairness, the Taft leaders were now resorting to unconcealed fraud. Johnson of California strongly advised Roosevelt that, if a third party movement were to be launched at all, it should be done without a moment's delay, so as to take advantage of the public indignation caused by the findings of the Credentials Committee and Root's unfair rulings as chairman of the convention. Standing at the council table, he made his points quietly but with intense earnestness, ending, as I remember, with the words, "We are frittering away our time. We are frittering away our opportunity. And, what is worse, we are frittering away Theodore Roosevelt."

Roosevelt himself did not agree with Johnson but preferred to wait

Notes begin on p. 288.

164

until his opponents had been given time to complete a record that would damn them in the eyes of the country and justify him in leaving the party. He did not like to fire a gun until a time when everyone would say it was in self-defense. Deserting a party that he had led for seven years and starting one of his own was not merely a momentous move, but one requiring a great deal of money. Perkins and Munsey had enlisted their checkbooks in a war to make Roosevelt the next Republican president. Would they fight to make him a Progressive president? They held the key to the situation, and until they reached a decision, Roosevelt could not go ahead, that is, unless he was willing to enter the greatest battle of his career without the support of a major financial power and leaning solely on the slender reed of popular financing.

The moment when the third party was born will, for me, always be an unforgettable one, though at the time I was far from understanding the implications of the scene I was witnessing. Things had gone from bad to worse until the tension in the Roosevelt camp had become unbearable. Before our eyes a nomination was being stolen by gross fraud in brazen defiance of the desire of the mass of the Republican voters throughout the country, as was later finally shown by the result of the election itself. In the Colonel's suite a relatively small group had met, perhaps not more than twenty persons. A dozen were seated around the table, the rest in armchairs or leaning against the wall. Roosevelt was walking rapidly up and down in silence. Munsey and Perkins were standing away from the rest in the northeast corner of the room, leaning over, with their heads together, talking in rapid whispers. Nobody else spoke and most of us were looking at Munsey and Perkins rather than at Roosevelt, as we knew the choice lay with them. Suddenly, the whispered talk ceased, and with a decisive gesture from Munsey, who seemed the more agitated of the two, both men straightened up and moved over to Roosevelt, meeting him in the middle of the room. Each placed a hand on one of his shoulders and one, or both of them, said, "Colonel, we will see you through." At that precise moment the Progressive party was born, but, as we were soon to know, born with a confusion of aims that made it impossible for it to advance steadily in any direction. Though we did not realize it, the Progressive party came into being, a house divided against itself and already heavily mortgaged to men with little sympathy for its professed objective. Looking back, it seems impossible that we should not have foreseen the futility of trying to found a popular party with money given by men of the point of view and associations of Perkins and Munsey. But it must be remembered that at that time we knew nothing of Gary's nearness to Roosevelt or of the steps taken by the Morgan group to safeguard the differential of the Steel Corporation. The Tarbell biography had not been written; the disclosures of the Stanley Committee were as yet undigested. We were riding on a wave of partisan enthusiasm. In the eyes of the more radical members of the progressive group, Roosevelt had so thoroughly burned his bridges by his Ossawatomie and Columbus speeches that it seemed unlikely that anything could dislodge the new party from a radical position, a belief that was reinforced by the fact that the necessity of framing a clear issue with Taft would keep forcing Roosevelt to the left. Some of us, of course, foresaw that the fact that the new party was to be financed by Munsey and Perkins would open it to the charge of feeding on tainted money. This especially worried Beveridge of Indiana who, though a friend of Perkins', said to me at this time, "Perkins, Munsey, and Littauer are too much in evidence. If we're not careful we'll be labeled as a Wall Street promotion." But for the most part, the progressive leaders believed that Roosevelt would either bend the angels of the party to its liberal purposes or, failing that, at length separate them from the organization.

Sincere as I think Munsey and Perkins were in a desire to do something worth while, it would have been hard to find two men in the entire country whose philosophy diverged more sharply from that of the insurgent movement out of which the third party grew. Their careers formed a perfect antithesis to the ideas Roosevelt had voiced in the Ossawatomie and Columbus speeches. Roosevelt had denounced swollen fortunes, wealth gained by stock gambling, oppression of labor, exploitation of the public. He had declared that no man ought to have a dollar unless he earned it. In tones that carried to the remotest corners of the land, he had inveighed against invisible government. He had promised the "square deal." He had declared against privilege. He had pointed to the power of money in politics as the paramount issue. He had quoted Lincoln to the effect that the rights of labor are above those of capital. He had made the foundations of plutocracy rock with threats spoken, I believe, in a spirit of sincerity. He had denounced Taft, Root, Crane, and Penrose as servants of plutocracy. He had drawn a line in the sand which his radical friends had devoutly hoped would separate him forever from the influence of Wall Street and all its hangers-on. But now, in spite of this, the decision to form a new party had virtually been made by two men who, though undoubtedly of good intentions, were, with the exception of Morgan the elder, John D. Rockefeller, Sr., and Judge Gary, the most conspicuous figures of America's moneyed oligarchy. Besides being chairman of the Steel Corporation's finance committee and Gary's alter ego, Perkins, acting for Morgan, had organized the giant Harvester Trust which, of all combinations, was the most hated by the farmers on account of its monopoly and price-fixing policies. Four out of six of the finance committee of the Harvester Trust were also members of the finance committee of the Steel Trust. Soon the International Harvester Company was to be convicted for illegal monopoly on . . . counts.[1] In [1912] Robert Wagner, now United States senator, as chairman of an investigating committee of the New York State Legislature, was to sign a scathing report on the conditions of labor and, in particular, the bad treatment of women employees in the Harvester Company's New York plants.[2]

Munsey's relation to high finance was mainly through the Steel Corporation. He was a close friend and sincere admirer of Gary's. He occupied a peculiar and rather mysterious position and was often spoken of as the Steel Corporation's unofficial ambassador. In March 1912, the Stanley Committee examined him for two sessions on his relation to the Steel Trust and especially on a remarkable article lauding its resources and position in the trade, which he had written in April 1908 and published in June of that year.[3] The article, which confessedly was composed with "the aid of officials of the Steel Corporation,"[4] set the value of its inventory at $1,782,000,000. Nevertheless, it listed the Tennessee Coal and Iron Company at but $50,000,000, a figure $850,000,000 below John Moody's estimate of its value made at about the same time. From these two items, the committee inferred that Munsey was serving the Steel Corporation in a double sense, first, by overvaluing the property it held before the panic, and second, by undervaluing the Tennessee Coal and Iron Company, so that the enormous profit won through Gary's deception of Roosevelt would not strike the reader. Munsey denied that Gary had helped him in writing the article but admitted that he had shown it to him after it was finished, and the latter had approved it. George F. Baker, another member of the finance committee of the Steel Corporation, had given him an opinion as to the value of the corporation's ore holdings. Apparently the article had the double purpose of increasing the market for the stock and yet of confirming the impression, which the Steel Corporation was most anxious to give, that their purchase of the Tennessee Coal and Iron Company for $45,000,000 was far from a bargain and was actuated only by a desire to check the panic.

In January of that year, Brandeis had told the Stanley Committee of the amazing policy of the Steel Corporation. Fifty thousand employees were working twelve hours a day, "every day in the week, including Sunday," although the English steel industry had already adopted a 55.2-hour week for workers of the same grade. The Steel Corporation was advertising for the grade of laborers from eastern Europe, because they would stand for this severe regime, and they could more easily be kept from organizing than could Americans. Both Brandeis and John Fitch, investigator for the Sage Foundation, told the committee that the strain of the twelve-hour day and seven-day week made men derelicts at forty. "Under such conditions," said Brandeis,

the astonishing thing is that they should live until forty. . . .[5] It is not merely the fact that he becomes a useless individual and a burden to his family at forty; it is the fact that he is the father of a family and transmitting . . . through many [generations] the evil weaknesses and the degeneration which have come to him through the life to which he has been subjected. . . . I ask you, gentlemen, to remember that these persons, however they may differ from us in race or in their habits of living, are individuals. Imagine what would be our condition if we, seven days a week, undertook to work twelve hours a day.[6]

He insisted that "their condition was worse than that of the Negro under slavery." Under slavery, only owners of little foresight and of exceptionally brutal nature treated their property so as to destroy its value. He quoted statistics of the Department of Labor and showed, as did Fitch, that 65 per cent of the employees were paid a wage too low to keep themselves and their families in health. He told of the system of espionage and black-listing in vogue to prevent employees from organizing to better their miserable conditions. He asked why the Steel Corporation preferred the lowest class of foreign labor to American labor and put in evidence an advertisement issued by the Steel Corporation, reading in part as follows: "Tinner, catchers and helpers, to work in open shops, Syrians, Poles and Roumanians preferred."[7] He asked why the Steel Corporation did this in a country "where there are so many hundreds of thousands unemployed persons" and continued,

I say these are the conditions which have driven out American labor; and the most important thing I want to impress upon you in regard to that is not merely the long hours or the low wages, but it is that it has been and is attended with conditions of repression the like of which you can not find, I believe, this side of Russia.[8]

He told of the corporation's political activities and of how, a short time before the primary elections of 1908, orders came from the New York office to the general superintendent of the Edward Thompson plant at Braddock, directing him to order the department superintendents to line up their employees for Penrose candidates for the legislature. He quoted Fitch to the effect that it was well known that the Steel Corporation was the dominant force in politics in the mill towns; that workmen were repeatedly discharged for refusing to vote as the company wished.[9]

Whatever motives actuated Munsey and Perkins in espousing the Progressive cause, their connection with it was a source of weakness in the farming and industrial sections of the country, if nowhere else. Munsey was known to be one of the largest holders of Steel common. The story ran that during seven days in which he was on a steamship between Cherbourg and New York he had, on one occasion, lost seven million in steel. Like all great gamblers, he had the admirable traits of willingness to take chances, and ability to lose without self-pity. On the other hand, he did not easily forgive anyone by whom he thought he had been wronged, and he held a grudge against the Wall Street crowd in general because he considered they had deliberately "done him" in the market. He believed in Gary, however, and in the Steel group, and, I think, joined the Progressive party largely because he recognized in Roosevelt a powerful fighter who would make war on Wall Street but exempt the Steel Corporation from his attack. Though he made most of his money in stock trading and in business enterprises, he was best known as a newspaper editor, and in this capacity might have been very useful to the new party, had it not been for his perhaps unmerited reputation as a Wall Street supporter. He wrote clearly and in a style that conveyed the force of a personality that was quite remarkable. I remember Roosevelt saying to me one day in connection with our inability to get someone to take a certain stand on some matter, "Why not set Munsey on him? When he wants to, he can exert tremendous pressure through the strength of his personality." Largely because of his shyness, Munsey has been erroneously pictured as a cold, calculating person. In reality, he was rather warmhearted and capable of sustained enthusiasm for the things he cared about. He had decided ambitions to shine both in the social and business world, and Gary may have proved useful to him in the latter sphere. But he never put on side and was always glad to talk about his obscure beginnings in Maine and the days when as a messenger boy he used to deliver telegrams on a bicycle.

Passing over the Roosevelt bolt, the nomination of Taft by the Republicans, the hectic weeks in which the new party went through the throes of formal reorganization, and the unexpected choice of Woodrow Wilson by the Democratic convention in Baltimore (brought about through Bryan's final dropping of Champ Clark, who had been slated for the nomination, and his dramatic attack on Tammany Hall), we come to the Progressive convention called to order on August 5, 1912, with twelve hundred delegates and alternates and a great throng of sympathizers who met in Chicago to nominate Roosevelt. Looking down from the gallery of the Coliseum, it must be confessed that the sea of upturned faces was not, on the whole, reassuring. It was true that there was a large number of superior, intelligent, and deeply earnest people, who had seen the inside of the political cup and were disgusted with the uselessness of the Republican party as an instrument for attacking social problems. They were public-spirited businessmen, farmers, lawyers, college professors, instructors, students, schoolteachers, social workers, inconspicuous Insurgent politicians, editors who had been carrying on losing battles against corrupt local machines, radical thinkers who believed in old-fashioned American ideas and objected to the inroads of plutocracy, socialists impatient with the futile tactics of their party, and a sprinkling of rash, liberal-minded clergymen on the verge of losing their pulpits through their disagreement with rich parishioners. This admirable group furnished the moral fibers of the new party, but outnumbering them was a distinct majority made up of people bent chiefly on riding to power or prestige on Roosevelt's broad back: sharp-faced Southern Republican politicians looking for a turn of the wheel that would let them fill their bellies long starved of patronage; Eastern disgruntled hangers-on of the old party, some too good and some too bad for it; Far Westerners and round-headed Middle Westerners shouting for industrial justice, but mainly attracted by the idea of getting in on the ground floor of a growing concern. Then there was that raft of restless sentimentalists who always clutter a new movement that may possibly satisfy their craving for good in the abstract, only to disappear the moment they are asked to work for a concrete proposal.

This nondescript army, with aims as far apart as the poles from the equator, was miraculously kept united by the magnetism of one electric personality, and the pervasive thought that somehow something worth while and exciting was about to eventuate through their chief's magic. And through them all a sort of rage for righteousness presently began to surge. Soon the convention was keyed to the pitch of a crusade. A religious fervor took possession of it. "Onward Christian Soldiers" and the "Doxology" swelled in the Coliseum as solemnly as in a cathedral. The Progressive party, under Roosevelt, was going to free the United States not only from political and economic but from spiritual night. It was to rout Taft's Republican hosts, but this was merely a prelude to routing all the hosts of darkness. It was to stand at Armageddon and battle for the Lord, and manifestly in such a struggle, God, working his mysterious ends—ends no less mysterious than our own—could be counted on the Progressive side. And yet, a curious thing about it was that for this goal of glory there was no program of any definition, nor, apparently, was one necessary, for in the innocence of our hearts we believed that all that was required to reach the holy city of our dreams was to huddle ourselves and our aspirations under one great umbrella and to advance, saint and sinner, patriot and politician, with arms entwined and voices raised in song.

For all its legal status, the Progressive party cannot really be said to have been a political party at all. Rather, it was a faction, a split-off fragment of its mother star, the Republican party, which, like a meteor, flamed momentarily across the sky, only to fall and cool on the earth of solid fact. It was composed almost exclusively of Republicans with here and there a stray Democrat, over whom there was more rejoicing than over ninety and nine deserters from the Republican fold. New parties that have lived to tell the tale have always been built on some one central idea that distinguished them from the old parties. This was true of the Democratic party which Jefferson, Madison, and Monroe founded on the idea that the fundamental principles of individualism, free speech, and free press must be preserved from the assaults launched against them by the Whig party through the Alien and Sedition laws. At the moment of its birth, unlike the Progressive party, it drew its strength not from one but from all political groups. Its appeal was, in fact, so universal that soon after the election of 1801, the Whig party, though it had been the party of Washington and Hamilton, and had fought the Revolutionary War, disappeared, never more to be heard of. It was followed by the Republican party, which also owed its existence to a single dominant idea, as shown by its first platform which emphatically stated that all issues must be subordinated to the slavery issue. The Socialist party, the Prohibition party, the Labor party, and all other parties that have survived their first defeats, have each possessed one single paramount concept that has upheld them through their vicissitudes.

The Progressive party, on the other hand, had no such central point of attraction. Aside from the personality of Roosevelt, the ambitions of the men who hoped to profit by his return from his self-imposed sojourn at Elba, and a hazy vision of a better world, its members were hopelessly split on almost every question of importance. Its platform hedged on every important issue but conservation. It was filled with irrelevant details and needless changes in political machinery. Between the June defeat at the Republican convention and the Bull Moose convention, everyone who had a cherished *ism* had gone running to Roosevelt, or Perkins, or some influential member of the *Outlook* entourage, and his pet scheme had been shoveled into the platform, on the theory that the more hooks baited, the more fish would be caught. However, when the Resolutions Committee of the new party began the task of drawing the platform, there was one subject which it refused to hedge on, even though pressed to do so by Roosevelt, Perkins, and Munsey. Here was the first test of the Gary-Perkins-Munsey influence, and be it said to the credit of the Resolutions Committee, this influence was defeated, although the setback proved to be a temporary one. All the night before the day when the platform was to be read to the convention and, in fact, well on into the morning of that day itself, the Resolutions Committee labored at the impossible task of writing a contract with the people which should have taken weeks, if not months, to produce. Whenever planks were completed they were sent up to the Colonel's apartment where Roosevelt, Perkins, Munsey, and a few other trusted advisers sat with blue pencils and, after approving the planks, or revising, or wholly rejecting them, sent them back to the committee, which in most cases bowed to their judgment. Early in the morning, however, when the nerves of the committee, among whom I was sitting as an unofficial member, were frayed by what was considered too much interference from above, as well as by the fatigue of an all-night vigil, the framing of the so-called industrial plank was reached. In this plank it soon became evident that the most important question was the manner in which the party should treat the Sherman Anti-Trust law. Professor Charles McCarthy of the University of Wisconsin, who was not a committeeman but an expert in economics of such standing that he was welcomed as a valued counselor, especially as he was implicitly trusted by Roosevelt, believed that the Sherman law would be read out of the new party unless the platform was approved in so many words. McCarthy, myself, and some members of the committee had taken part the previous year in Washington conferences that had been called especially for a discussion of the trust question. The result was that McCarthy presented to the Resolutions Committee a plank embodying what had been agreed on in these conferences and reading as follows:

We favor strengthening the Sherman law by prohibiting agreements to divide territory or limit output; refusing to sell to customers who buy from business rivals; to sell below cost in certain areas while maintaining high prices in other places; using the power of transportation to aid or injure special business concerns; and other unfair trade practices.

Now, this clause was considered important not so much because it was thought that the means it suggested for strengthening the Sherman law would prove effective as for the reason that in standing for *"strengthening the Sherman law,"* it thereby endorsed the Sherman law and pledged the new party to use it against monopoly. It was clearly a challenge to the Morgan interests as well as all interests operating with an illegal monopolistic technique or one that stood on the borderline of illegality. Roosevelt had agreed to a plank of this sort. For the time being, he was under the influence of McCarthy's economic thinking, and he had said he would approve strengthening the Sherman law in the speech he was to deliver to the convention next day. The committee was, therefore, very much surprised when the industrial section came down from Roosevelt's rooms with the Sherman law clause cut out. But, knowing that Perkins was closeted upstairs with Roosevelt, and realizing that besides endorsing the Sherman law, the clause struck directly at the Harvester Trust which was then under fire for using the very practices the clause forbade, it attributed the blue-penciling to Perkins rather than to Roosevelt, though it seemed hard to believe that Roosevelt was not party to the change.

Here was a new party being financed by men who had been fighting the Sherman law for eleven years. This law was the one ever-present threat to both the Steel and Harvester trusts. From the day in 1901 when Morgan, after consulting his lawyers, had told his directors that the crowning venture of his career would be outlawed if attacked by the government, the Steel Corporation had been up to its neck in politics, with the most skillful lobbyist in the country in command. Shortly after that memorable directors' meeting, Perkins had taken Gary to the White House; a close friendship had commenced between the latter and Roosevelt; the Garfield investigation had been steered into safe paths, so that in Gary's words, quoted by Roosevelt in his letter to Paul Morton, "It had done good instead of harm." Roosevelt had been taught that the Sherman law was immoral and had repeatedly advised Congress to wipe it off the books. Gary's government price-regulation theory had been endorsed by Roosevelt, as had his good and bad trust distinction. The Harvester Trust had received a coat of shining white from the presidential brush. The Steel Trust exchequer had come to Roosevelt's rescue in the Parker campaign, following which Roosevelt had succored the trust in the 1907 panic, to its profit of several hundred million, while the absorption of the Tennessee Coal and Iron Company, by presidential permission, had freed the trust from its last visible danger of competition. Roosevelt's cabinet and key undersecretarial positions had been heavily loaded with Morgan henchmen,[10] including two Steel Corporation directors who were also Morgan's partners, one president of a subdivision of that corporation, and two members of the Steel Corporation's legal staff. On retiring, Roosevelt's first choice of a successor had been Morgan's ablest lawyer, Elihu Root, and his second choice was Philander Knox, the Steel Corporation lawyer who, when Attorney-General of the United States, had befriended Morgan by consenting to a decree in the Northern Securities case continuing the combination of interests which the government's victory was supposed to forbid. Upon the accession of Taft, Roosevelt's third choice for the presidency, the Steel Corporation had remained politically potent enough to install another Steel Corporation lawyer, George W. Wickersham, in the all-important post of Attorney-General. Wickersham, following the Roosevelt tradition, had given Gary to understand that he would take no action against the Steel Corporation. But, yielding to public clamor aroused by Brandeis and Stanley, he had indicted the Steel Corporation, and thereby broke down an immunity which should, with ordinary luck, have lasted four or eight years more.

And now, at the end of Taft's four years, the Steel Corporation, as never before in its brief history, needed the offices of a friendly federal administration. The stake it was playing for was no less than the perpetuation of its differential and price-fixing power, through which, in a period of a little more than ten years, it had according to Brandeis' calculations, besides paying interest on its bonds and preferred stock, put back almost a billion dollars of earnings into the company, transforming its water into real value. Taft was on the rampage, having in his four years wrought more havoc with the Steel Corporation than Roosevelt had in seven. He was committed to a militant prosecution of the Steel Trust. The public was watching his Department of Justice with a jealous eye, since prior to the indictment hostile newspapers had gone so far as to call for the impeachment of the Attorney-General for allowing the trust to go unpunished. If safety lay anywhere, it lay in Taft's defeat and in a new president who, acting honestly and under the sway of his own convictions, would stay the hand of his Attorney-General and give the trust every chance to justify its existence. Such being the case, endorsement of the Sherman law in the new party platform would complicate matters by committing the Progressive administration to push the prosecution. If Roosevelt himself insisted on approving the Sherman law in his speech, that was bad, but it could not be helped, and after election he could truthfully argue that, though he believed in the law, he had no sympathy with invoking it against an innocent corporation which he had always classified as the most worthy of the good trusts. The main thing, from the point of view of the Morgan interests, was to start the new party with a sound attitude on big business. The industrial plank was a test of this attitude, and therefore it was of immense importance that it should not be tainted by the economic fallacy of Brandeis, La Follette, McCarthy, and the rest of the lunatic fringe.

In view of the futility of the conviction of the Standard Oil Company in May 1911, it may be asked what Gary had to fear from a similar conviction of the Steel Corporation. The answer to this is that in 1912 it was not known that the Standard Oil Company would be able to defy the dissolution decree and continue business on the old lines. Whatever the ultimate effect of the dissolution, the government's victory had been a great blow to the Rockefeller interests. The government's charge, as paraphrased by Chief Justice White in his opinion, was that the Standard Oil Company

took its birth in a purpose to unlawfully acquire wealth by oppressing the public and destroying the just right of others, and that its entire career exemplified an inexorable carrying out of such wrongful intents, since . . . the pathway of the combination from the beginning to the time of the filing of the bill is marked with constant proofs of wrong inflicted upon the public and is strewn with the wrecks resulting from crushing out, without regard to law, the individual rights of others.[11]

And the testimony, to which immense publicity had been given, in the main backed up the charge. If the Steel Corporation were convicted, no one could say what the consequence would be. It might be forced to return the Tennessee Coal and Iron Company to its original owners, who were always hostile to the trust, and especially so since 1907 when they believed they had been bilked out of their property. Professor Berglund had shown,[12] as had the minutes of the directors' meeting of the corporation, that possession of the Tennessee Company was a matter of life and death to the trust.

The next day came the grand finale of the Progressive convention. A packed, ecstatic Coliseum listened to the reading and adoption of the platform which, though generally a tame affair at conventions, drew bursts of applause from the audience. At the moment when Dean Lewis, chairman of the Resolutions Committee, read the industrial plank, Roosevelt, as I remember, was not in the hall. Perkins sat next to me in the front row of seats, facing the speakers' table, but far to the right. "We favor," read Lewis,

strengthening the Sherman law by prohibiting agreements to divide territory or limit output; refusing to sell to customers who buy from business rivals; to sell below cost in certain areas while maintaining high prices in other places; using the power of transportation to aid or injure special business concerns; and other unfair trade practices.

But before he reached the end of the paragraph, Perkins turned to me and whispered excitedly, "Lewis has made a mistake. That doesn't belong in the platform. We cut it out last night"; and springing to his feet, he disappeared through a nearby exit. What happened then, I do not know of my own knowledge, but I learned later from various sources, and at length from Roosevelt and O. K. Davis, secretary of the National Committee, that a conference was quickly called and Davis dispatched to the press associations and newspaper offices with instructions to see to it that the offending plank should not be printed. So far as I know, the omission of the Sherman law clause from the press accounts passed unnoticed until McCarthy began to ask what had become of his favorite paragraph. To the party as a whole its inclusion or exclusion meant little or nothing. The Progressives were not thinking in economic terms then. For all but a small minority, whose influence steadily shrank after the convention, Roosevelt himself was the issue. It would have made no difference to the bulk of the party if it had had no platform at all.

Under raking fire from Wilson, who centered his attack not on Roosevelt but on his economic doctrines,[13] from Brandeis, from

McAdoo, Borah, Taft, and the infuriated old guard leaders, who saw in the Progressive bolt their own certain if temporary downfall, Roosevelt was conducting himself gallantly and devoting every energy to a brilliant campaign. Everything else he left to Perkins who, as chairman of the Executive Committee, not only authorized the expenditures, but chose and routed the speakers and, with Munsey, controlled the principal organs of publicity in the East. The National Committee he ignored. It held no meeting between the Chicago convention and Election Day. National headquarters was soon transformed into a propaganda bureau; the platform was distributed in immense quantities with the Sherman law clause omitted. Rafts of pamphlets were sent out containing reprints of the editorials Perkins was writing for the party Bulletin, denouncing the Sherman law, praising Morgan, Harriman, and Perkins, and stating that what politics needed was the guidance of great industrialists and railroad builders. Edward P. Costigan, Progressive leader of Colorado,[14] now United States senator, complained to me that upon writing to headquarters for campaign literature he had received large crates of pamphlets which set forth the Perkins view of monopoly, defended the Steel and Harvester trusts, and explained a contribution of $48,500 which Perkins had made to the Republican party in 1904 out of the funds of the New York Life Insurance Company. The Democrats, meantime, were playing up Cortelyou's[15] alleged shaking down of the corporations in Roosevelt's behalf in 1904, the secret visit of Frick and Harriman to the White House, and their contributions to the Roosevelt war chest in New York State at the time Roosevelt was running against Parker. They dug up the story of the Tennessee Coal and Iron Company and printed it in their *Campaign Book*[16] as proof that Roosevelt had been the patron saint of the Steel Corporation, and cited the report of Assistant Attorney-General Townsend, which recommended prosecution of the Harvester Trust on the ground that it has "maintained a persistent campaign to destroy competition" and "monopolize trade in 'everything that the farmer buys.'" They also printed Commissioner Smith's warning to Roosevelt that prosecuting the Harvester Trust would throw the Morgan interests "into active opposition,"[17] and Roosevelt's instructions to Attorney-General Bonaparte not to institute a suit until he had conferred with Perkins and Commissioner Smith.[18]

Again and again I went to Roosevelt and begged him to consider the almost certain consequence of the vulnerable position the party was being placed in through Perkins'[19] activities. It seemed a cruel injustice to the minority of intelligent, decent people who were giving their best to the new party without self-interest, and solely in the hope of forging a weapon with which they could fight for the things they believed in, that Roosevelt should allow the party to be so undermined in public esteem that it already seemed impossible for it to survive the defeat in November, which all but the most sanguine of us expected. If the Progressive party had had no purpose beyond landing in power in 1912, it might have been practical politics to try to soothe the fears of the business interests by featuring the big-business element that had thrown in its lot with us, although it seemed to me that Roosevelt was making a tactical error even if this were the only goal, since his political radicalism, and especially his attack on the courts, had alienated Wall Street beyond recall. But, on the other hand, if the plan looked beyond the first reverse, if it had to do with a permanent liberal organization, through which men and women of good will could strike at plutocracy and realize at least some part of the vision they had seen at Chicago, then nothing could have been more impractical than the path Roosevelt was taking.

In October 1912 Roosevelt's patience, which was truly extraordinary, was taxed to the utmost by my constantly urging him to bring liberals to New York and let them speak from headquarters in order to counteract the conservative atmosphere. Failing to win Roosevelt's approval of this move, I went to Hiram Johnson, who was campaigning as vice-presidential candidate in Ohio, and asked him to help me persuade Roosevelt that the situation was extremely serious and that such men as Van Hise of Wisconsin, William Allen White of Kansas, my brother, Heney of California, Beveridge of Indiana, Raymond Robins of Illinois,[20] should make flying visits to New York, successively taking the center of the stage at headquarters, visit Roosevelt at Oyster Bay, give out interviews, and answer attacks. Johnson approved the plan, and to make it easier for Roosevelt to act, I saw Perkins and told him frankly that a good many Progressive leaders felt that he was unnecessarily drawing fire on the party by his constant public activity, and on October 17[21] I wrote him a letter to which, as I remember, he replied by word of mouth to the effect that the men I mentioned could not possibly come to New York, as their speaking dates in distant cities were unalterably fixed.

The month of October 1912 was on the whole one of the most miserable in my life. In a humble capacity, I had been working in the progressive movement since 1909, giving practically all my time to it. Though I was one of the least influential of Roosevelt's host of advisers, and never felt that he liked me, I had performed numberless small errands for him, helped with some of his speeches, hindered him with others, answered attacks, written magazine articles and pamphlets defending him, turned out boiler plate for rural consumption, worked on platforms, sat in on scores of conferences, and had run for Congress in a hopelessly Democratic district, purely [for the sake of conducting] an educational campaign. I think I wanted nothing for myself. Certainly I did not expect anything beyond the satisfaction of taking a part in building something which appealed to my imagination. In 1909 I had seen for the first time, in the Ballinger case, the inside of the secret game of grand politics and found it a very shoddy game, a too long tolerated fraud at the expense of a helpless and credulous public. In the Progressive party, quite aside from defeating Taft came the possibility of substituting something for this fraud that might in time play a shining part in the country's history. But in October 1912 came the realization that, barring miracles, the party would disintegrate after November 4, and things would go on exactly as they had been before its appearance.

For this I blamed Roosevelt and was angry with him. As I look back, unjustly so. He was acting neither badly nor well, but in accord with his nature and lifelong training. Roosevelt, for all his good points, was not a statesman. Statesmen are dominated by ideas. Ideas merely harassed Roosevelt; he always could shake them off when necessary. The radicals in 1912 were trying to thrust Roosevelt into the role of a statesman, notwithstanding the fact that he was essentially a politician, and a mighty good one up to the moment of his return from Africa. On the whole, he was a conspicuously honest politician and remarkably decent and public-spirited. Unlike the general run of politicians who have risen to the presidency since the Civil War, he could never be used by private interests unless they had first succeeded in deceiving him. As a politician he was convinced that he could get nowhere without the support of some strong economic group. An alliance with what he allowed himself to believe was the most decent as well as the strongest of these groups was thrust upon him in 1901 by the fact that the Morgan interests needed him even more than he needed them. But he never yielded to economic pressure meekly, as did Harding in the case of the oil interests, or slyly, as Coolidge did to any interest that required his passive cooperation, or timidly, as Hoover has to the hydroelectric and utility people. Roosevelt, on the contrary, took the bull by the horns, set his seal of approval on his good trusts, and let his critics make the most of it, meantime working for what he conceived to be the public good with an enthusiasm that was quite unfeigned. He was not radical. He believed reasonably that results could be effected only by a compromise. The part of John Morley's *Life of Gladstone* that deals with the necessity of compromise in politics[22] had made a deep impression on him, and he referred me to it more than once. The mistake our group, the lunatic fringe, made was in treating Roosevelt as if he belonged to the left wing and trying to get him to work through a technique that was foreign to his nature, which was to start on a long-pull program that might, at length, with luck, bring a radical party into power.

CHAPTER VII

Decline of the Progressive Party

Notwithstanding the magnificent tribute of 4,119,582 votes, Roosevelt was discouraged by his 1912 defeat, and quickly lost interest in the Progressive party. A month after Election Day, he wrote to an English friend, "What the future of the Progressive party will be, nobody can say. . . . At present, however, I do not see how the party can triumph under me; but I will have to take a certain interest in it until a new man of sufficient power comes along."[1] He was unhappy with the ragtag and bobtail element of which the party was largely composed. He liked the great and had been used to moving in the halls of fame and power. But now, with the exception of my brother, Heney, Johnson, Beveridge, Perkins, and Jane Addams, there was hardly a nationally known name on the new party roster. It was a dreary fate for the first citizen of the world to have to sit and twirl his thumbs indefinitely among mediocrities. Dean Swift, through his ironical contempt for men in high places, brought himself into a similar uncongenial position. "I am hated [mortally] by every creature in power," he wrote sadly to [the Earl of Oxford], "and by all their followers. . . . I do not visit one Lord either temporal or spiritual, nor am acquainted with above three squires and half-a-dozen parsons."[2] Not merely the 1912 episode, but his long-continued abuse of

Notes begin on p. 291.

the elite of the political and economic world had at last banished him from the haunts he loved best. Like Napoleon at Longwood, he now lived in exile surrounded by [a] few former generals and a handful of faithful servitors. In justice to him it must be said that, the campaign over, there was very little in the Progressive party to hold his interest. Unfortunately, he had thrown no durable issue into politics, and his trust regulation theories had been thoroughly squelched by both Republicans and Democrats.

Perkins, on the other hand, was still full of fight, and, as Henry Stoddard said, "could act faster than you could pull a trigger." With 1916 in mind, he went bravely ahead with the reorganization of the party, and as his first step called a meeting of the shattered hosts of Armageddon in Chicago on the tenth of December. It seemed to many of us that, if the Progressive party were ever to escape from the leadership under which it was quickly dwindling away, this Chicago reorganization meeting was the time for Roosevelt to act uncompromisingly. If he could only be persuaded to get Perkins to resign as chairman of the Executive Committee and replace him with a man of different type, there seemed a chance, so to speak, of changing the chemistry of the party and bringing it back into line with the insurgent movement, out of which it grew. Escaping from Perkins' leadership and revamping the party's program would, no doubt, mean the loss of Perkins' financial assistance. But in broaching the subject to Roosevelt, I asked him to consider whether a party with a clear objective, such as the destruction of the power of wealth in politics, would not in all probability create its own financial resources. Not thousands, but millions of people, I argued, might contribute to the party if they could feel certain of the integrity of its intentions. On the other hand, if we went on as we were going, with Roosevelt sinking more and more into the background, and the big-business emphasis becoming daily more pronounced, but one outcome could be expected—in fact, so far as I was concerned, desired—the party's early and deserved demise. All this, and much more, I tried to say to Roosevelt in a letter which was the last of my futile attempts to steer him in a way that he had no intention of going.

December 3, 1912.

Colonel Theodore Roosevelt,
289 Fourth Avenue,
New York City.

My dear Colonel Roosevelt:

I want to write you apropos of our conversation about Perkins last Friday, because I feel that I can express myself more clearly in writing. If you care to show this letter to Perkins, I shall be glad to have you do so, as I know he will understand the spirit in which it is written, and as I do not want to say anything about him which I would not say to him.

In my opinion, it would be a serious, if not fatal, error to have him remain in the position of titular head of our party. And I firmly believe that if the facts are presented to Perkins, he will see this as plainly as many of us do and be the first in urging that he should withdraw from the Chairmanship of the Executive Committee.

I do not like to burden you, Colonel, with my anxieties. I know the burden you already carry in leading a great movement, in keeping us all together, and in planning for the future, is more than any man, however strong, should be asked to bear. But in this Progressive Party, with its thousands of earnest men and women giving their strength to the cause of humanity, and with the millions of struggling people who see some hope in a cause dedicated to economic justice instead of to politics, we have something so fine and so full of possibilities of real usefulness to our country, that I feel justified in laying before you what seems to me so fearfully plain.

From the beginning of the organization of the Progressive Party, we have set a high standard and made the claim that we are going to be something a little different and better than the old parties. We have frankly stated that we are not out for political victory only, but to establish social and economic justice. As Lincoln freed the chattel slave, so are we going to free the industrial slave. We have gone into battle singing hymns and announcing that we will stand at Armageddon and battle for the Lord. From the very beginning, we have framed our campaign rather as a crusade than as a political fight. In short, we have assumed a heavy responsibility toward the people and placed ourselves on a plane where any suspicion of insincerity would be utterly ruinous to the cause.

To speak more specifically, we are today solemnly pledged to carry on an active campaign against the system of exploitation which the trusts have fastened upon the American people. It is the same old struggle for economic justice which has gone on from the beginning of time—the few who are strong and rich and organized against the many who are poor, weak and unorganized. In the old days it was the Crown and the privileged group surrounding the Crown against the people. Today it is the industrial oligarchy, the trusts, against the people.

We have outlined a magnificent program. In the first place, we plan to have real popular government, and in the second place, we have announced a campaign of social and industrial justice. Under the latter head we advocate decent hours of labor, minimum wage, industrial insurance, old-age pension, safety devices, employers' liability, etc. All of these things will, we hope, make the lives of wage earners during their hours of labor safe and healthy. They will make our factories a better place to work in, labor safer, and old age more endurable. But all these reforms when established will be costly, and will make the production of the necessaries of life more expensive. If we put every one of these measures into practice, and do not at the same time prevent the trusts from simply shifting the burden of the additional cost of production onto the shoulders of the people, as they have frequently done in the past, we will accomplish little or nothing. It will be as hard as ever for the average man and woman to pay for food, clothing or fuel. The wage-earner, though perhaps working under better conditions in the factories, will be as near starvation as ever in the home. We will help the consumer not at all. The trusts will continue to make a killing out of selling the sheer necessities of life at prices the people can ill afford to pay, and our whole program of social and industrial justice will be open to the criticism of woeful incompleteness, if not of insincerity.

We have got to meet this trust question frankly and immediately. It is the cost of living question—the bread question. If we weaken or falter in regard to it, our party will fail.

We cannot keep the people's confidence or support by preaching mere palliatives. We have got to stand for something different and more fundamental than the old parties have stood for, or quit claiming that our cause is the cause of humanity and justice.

All of this is what you have seen and taught the people to see. And each day they are seeing and feeling it more intensely. There is but one great issue in America, and that is the economic issue whether our industrial system shall serve or exploit the people.

The Republican Party has just crashed to the [ground] because it stood with the corporations instead of against them in this struggle.

The Democratic Party has just won a sweeping [victory] because the people hoped that it would fight the corporations instead of protect them. Nothing that Wilson [said] in his campaign gave him the confidence of the people to such an extent as his telegram in reply to Bryan's question whether he would stand for the election of Judge Parker, a corporation man, as temporary Chairman of the Democratic Convention.

We may have a party as highly organized as Perkins' and Munsey's money and Perkins' great business ability can make it—perhaps as highly organized and perfectly co-ordinated as the G.O.P. itself. But unless we keep the great issue clear—unless we make plain beyond a suspicion our stand on the great economic question whether the trusts shall or shall not be allowed to exploit the people by dictating the terms upon which the people shall obtain food, fuel and clothing, we will lack a cause and our party will be a flash in the pan. I believe that under the circumstances the selection of a trust magnate as leader (titular or otherwise) of our party would be bad politics and bad ethics. Mr. Perkins has been a director of the Steel and Harvester trusts. These two particular corporations are the ones whose unsocial and monopolistic practices have been most thoroughly exposed in the magazines, in the daily press, in the publications of the Survey and the Sage Foundation, and in the investigations of two congressional committees. The Executive Committee of the Steel Trust, of which Mr. Perkins I believe has been Chairman, has openly, and I think, indefensibly been instrumental in stamping out labor unionism from the steel corporation. I understand that more or less of the same thing has gone on in the Harvester Trust. The record of both trusts in regard to their treatment of employees is public property today.

Since Mr. Perkins has been Chairman of the Executive Committee of the Progressive Party, he has been more active than any one man in any party in the defense of big business. His signed columns in the daily papers have been largely pleas in behalf of big business and attempts to show that big business is after all the people's best friend. He was quoted (I do not know whether accurately or not) in a public statement as advocating that the Industrial Commission called for in our platform

should be made up of men like James J. Hill. He has shown bad judgment by attacking Bryan in the state of Colorado, by making himself
and the justification of big business an issue everywhere, by circulating
two pamphlets entitled *Is Perkins Honest?* and *Is Perkins Sincere?,* and
by offering to become our party's expositor of the trust question in a
series of signed aricles in *Collier's,* answering Brandeis. His unceasing
activity and his large contributions, together with Munsey's contribution,
have given the impression that our party has fallen under trusts' and Wall
Street influences; in short, that Munsey and Perkins hold a kind of
mortgage on the Progressive cause.

I realize that we should be and are most grateful for Perkins' tremendous generosity and hard effective organizing work. Any one that knows
him cannot help liking him and admiring his energy, perseverance, and
ceaseless industry. Personally, I believe that Perkins will not demand a
controlling position in the party as a condition of remaining in it and
working with it. I cannot believe that he, or any man who really cares for
the Progressive cause, would require a fifty-one percent interest in the
party, or refuse to take any interest at all.

Nothing that Perkins has done or said has suggested that he was not
strictly on the level and acting conscientiously and in accordance with
his deepest convictions. Nothing that we could give Perkins or do for
him would be too great a reward for his hard work and financial support.
But Perkins, like the rest of us, must be governed in this crisis by only
one thing—the good of the party and the Progressive movement. It will
be hard for him to relinquish a controlling position in the party, but
hard things happen to all of the Progressive leaders. It was hard for you
to go into this terrible gruelling fight with the almost certain knowledge
that you would be defeated, and hard for you to have been shot in the
body at the end of it by a would-be assassin. It has been hard for Ben
Lindsey to make his fight against the Evans-Guggenheim crowd; hard
for Heney and Johnson in their struggle; hard for Gifford wearing himself out in fifteen years of incessant effort for the cause of the people. But
no man, whatever his services, can deserve anything from the party which
will endanger the party's welfare or even its existence.

What I have mentioned above seems to me to contain serious objections
to Perkins' leadership in the Progressive Party. I think he will see that
himself if he is talked to plainly about it. But there is one matter in
comparison with which I feel that all others are minor considerations.

Unless I am much mistaken, the episode of the elimination of the anti-trust plank from the Progressive platform is bound to come out, either at Chicago, or subsequently. McCarthy's interview has started people talking, and anyhow, practically all of the Resolutions Committee are probably familiar with the facts.

If Perkins remains in a position of control it will be said that our party has chosen as its leader the man who went to Chicago and succeeded in having cut from our contract with the people the one clause which bound us to fight the trusts and protect the people. It will be said that he not only fought the anti-trust clause and succeeded in having it eliminated after the Committee on Resolutions had adopted it on the night before the platform was read, but that when the Committee put it back again and repassed it, and after he himself next day heard it read to the Convention and formally adopted, and after it had thus become actually and legally part and parcel of our platform he was instrumental in once more having it cut out in defiance of the Convention's action.

In addition to this, it will be pointed out that, although our Convention adopted this anti-trust clause and made it a part of our platform, and although you yourself were in favor of the plank and in essence embodied it in your speech to the Convention (and Perkins knew this to be the case, for he heard the plank read to the Convention by Dean Lewis, and he was familiar with your Convention speech), he caused to be printed and spread broadcast throughout the country a false version of the platform intentionally omitting the anti-trust clause.

We know what the result of this was. We were placed in a false and fatal position in regard to the whole trust question, and especially in regard to monopoly. Our sincerity was questioned. The Democrats scored upon us heavily. And in spite of the fact that your own position was right, and that our real platform was right, we could not justify our shortcomings and were obliged to spend every ounce of our energy in defending ourselves and explaining to the people that we stood for something which our contract with the people omitted, and that we were really not opposed to the prosecution of monopolistic and anti-social combinations.

On the whole, we came out of the trust controversy with only fair credit. What the result would have been if the facts of Perkins' fight against the anti-trust plank had come out during the campaign it is hard to say. But it is probable that there would have been an immediate crisis if it had become known that the omission of any reference to the anti-trust law in our platform was not through inadvertence; that an anti-trust plank had been adopted by the delegates to the Convention, but cut out at the instance of a director of the Steel and Harvester trusts.

I believe that Perkins will see all of this as clearly as we do. I believe that he will see that the great essential in the Progressive Party is to keep our people together and develop an undivided, effective fighting force, united in personnel, but above all united in principles and policy. I believe that he will see that the probability of being able to do this is practically nil as long as the cause is led by a man who differs so radically with the majority of the party upon a fundamental question of policy, and who doesn't command the confidence (I do not mean personal confidence, but confidence in regard to the trust questions) of the rank and file and of the majority of the leaders of our party.

If the fight against Perkins on the ground that he unjustifiably emasculated our platform in the interest of big business is not made at Chicago next week, it will certainly be made at some time, for his leadership, unwelcome as it will be to a large element of the party, will surely result in discord, and this discord will just as surely develop into an attack upon him on the grounds I have stated. We cannot stand such an attack and Perkins himself is the only man who can save us from it by doing the fine thing which I think he is willing to do, and putting us in a position where our cause will not have the sword of Damocles hanging forever over it.

In order to succeed as a party we must have a program representing an actual economic need of the people. This actual economic need of the people is today what it has always been since history's beginning—freedom from industrial exploitation at the hands of special privilege. The only difference is that today, owing to the educational work which has been going on in this country since your first administration, the people know exactly what is the matter and are fully determined that something shall be done about it.

For us to go into this fight unnecessarily handicapped, weakened, and threatened by the leadership of a man whose record even up to and since the Chicago Convention shows him to be unsympathetic to the cause as understood by the majority of the people, seems to me to be in the first place unjust to the cause upon purely ethical grounds, and in the second place, to be political folly. No amount of financial support or organizing ability can for an instant counterbalance the loss of respect and the blow to the sincerity of our aims which such an arrangement would result in.

You said to me the other day that it was folly to propose that Perkins should resign as Chairman of the Executive Committee until we had found someone else to take his place. It seems to me that it would be better to even leave the office vacant for a while than to have him continue in it. But there must be men who could fill this position effectively, altho not with quite the same degree of brilliancy or ability. Bristow, Chester Rowell,[3] Merriam, Herbert K. Smith, William Allen White occur to one's mind and there must be several other men who could be called on and made to feel the obligation to serve.

It is the fundamental question whether we will start right or wrong, whether we will have such support as is accorded to parties of men who are known to be sincere and right-thinking.

If we believe that the mission of our party and the business of our generation in America is to destroy privilege and fight an oppressive industrial system which makes the lives of men, women and children harder than they should be, we must draw the issue clearly and simply, and leave no place for doubts of our singleness of purpose.

If our party should fail now it would be a public calamity. It would seem to mean a humiliating defeat of those forces in America which are represented not only by patriotic politicians, but by the splendid list of social workers, educators, etc., who have found a home for their efforts and aspirations within the party.

If Perkins wants to take a position of leadership in the party, let him first identify himself with progressive social and industrial work, so that in the mind of the public he will be something besides a trust magnate— so that his name will bring to mind other organizations than the New York Insurance Company, J. P. Morgan & Co., the United States Steel Corporation, and the International Harvester Company. He could easily take a position of leadership in industrial work in this state and in the nation if he feels as we feel about these questions. He has in the highest degree the ability, the attractive personality and the energy necessary for such leadership. There is plenty for him or any man in his position to do. Let him clean up the unfortunate conditions of labor in the Harvester Trust. Let him make a fight in the Steel Corporation in favor of labor unionism and against the terrible system of industrial oppression that the Sage Foundation publications so vividly portray. Then he can assume leadership in the Progressive Party, with the confidence of the people and with a record which affirms rather than denies the propositions for which our party stands.

Sincerely yours,

(A. P.)

The following is Roosevelt's reply, which made plain that his decision had already been made:

December 5th, 1912.

Dear Amos:

All right, I shall send Perkins your letter and this answer.

I certainly do not regard Mr. Perkins as the "titular head" of the party, and I know he does not so regard himself. Therefore I do not feel that we need bother ourselves about his remaining in such a position inasmuch as he is not in it now. He is not the titular head; the trouble is that he is so efficient that wherever he is he attracts attention. Flinn is our other man of the same powerful business type; he has more political knowledge; if he had been in Perkins' place, he would have done admirable work, and would have been, if anything, even more viciously attacked than Perkins was. On the other hand I emphatically feel that he should remain as chairman of the executive committee. Now, my dear Amos, you speak (what I know you feel) with great sympathy of the task that I am trying to carry through, the task of taking a part in leading a great movement and in keeping its supporters together and planning for the future. Moreover, I absolutely agree with you that this Progressive Party, with its thousands of earnest men and women giving their strength to the cause of humanity, and with the millions of struggling people who see some hope in a cause dedicated to economic justice instead of to politics, offers something very fine and very full of possibilities of real usefulness to our country. I moreover agree absolutely with what you say as to the Progressive Party's claiming to be something different from and better than the old parties, and standing not only for political victory but to establish social and economic justice. As you say, our purpose is to free the industrial slave as Lincoln freed the chattel slave. But I utterly differ with you as to your belief about the source of the dangers with which we are threatened. (I believe that our vote would have been cut in half at

191

once if we had not been able to persuade two or three millions of good men and women that we were not engaged in an assault on property, or in wild and foolish radicalism. I believe that the suspicion that we were over-radical, were jeopardizing property and business, cost us a million or two of votes. I further believe that if we put out Perkins, and then did the only logical thing by putting out all the men like him, we should gain one or two hundred thousand votes and lose two or three millions. I mean in all sincerity that I think that if the policy you advocate had been adopted at the outset of this campaign—for of course Perkins is simply a symbol, and it is idle to put out Perkins if you don't put out all the men of the same stamp—that we would have been a rival to Debs in the running, and would have lost every particle of power to fight for a good cause.)

In your letter you say that Perkins has acted conscientiously, disinterestedly, and with no thought of personal advancement. I can add that he is in absolute and entire sympathy with our attitude toward the trust problem as it is set forth in our platform, as I have set it forth in my speeches, and as men like Jim Garfield, Joe Alsop and Ben Lindsey understand it. I know of no point as regards the trusts on which Ben Lindsey and Perkins disagree, for instance. If Perkins is all right, if he is fighting valiantly for the common cause, then we should be worse than foolish to throw him over. Perkins and Flinn have both been peculiarly valuable men to our cause. I have the utmost confidence in the zeal, the disinterestedness, the high purpose of both, and I know the efficiency of both. I am proud to have them as my friends. I do not believe we could have made any fight to speak of if we had not had them, and men like them with us. One is attacked only as the other is attacked. I stand by both with my whole heart.

Now I agree entirely with you that we are solemnly pledged to carry on an active campaign against the system of exploitation by the trusts. But I disagree absolutely with you when you say that the trust question means the cost of living question, the bread question. I am not certain that the carrying through of such a programme against the trusts would have any effect upon the cost of living whatever, and I am certain that it would affect it only in a small degree. The one argument which it is difficult to answer when advanced on the trust side is that the trusts cheapen production. I think it can be answered. I think that we can show that on the whole the consumer is not better off because of the action of the trusts. But there is real doubt in the matter; there is a genuine argument to be made on both sides. There is a genuine doubt whether if we broke up all the trusts on the Brandeis plan the result would not be that the cost of living would go up instead of down. (Please look at Hobhouse's[4] article in the recent *Contemporary Review;* I know of no competent authority who treats the trust matter as more than one (and not the most important one) among a score of factors in raising prices.) At any rate I am as certain as I can be of anything that the trust problem is a wholly minor problem in the cost of living problem, and that any promise to the people of benefiting them as regards the bread question, the cost of living question, by action on the trust business is a fallacious promise, with but little more merit in it than the Democratic promise to reduce the cost of living by the alteration of the tariff. The rise in the cost of living has been world-wide. It has been almost as great in countries where there are no trusts as in countries where there are trusts. In Italy, for instance, there is not a trust of any kind; but in proportion the cost of living has advanced there as much as elsewhere. The articles making four-fifths of the average small man's expense are not produced by trusts at all, and the control exercised over them by trusts, in some cases real, has never been proved to be materially instrumental in raising the price. (Altho I think it has raised the price in some cases.) Eggs have gone up greatly in price, but no trust has any effect upon them. Chickens have gone up greatly in price, quite as much as meat; yet there is practically no trust in chickens. So about milk; and servants' wages—which I am glad have risen. It is debatable whether the Millers' Trust has had any marked effect in raising the price of bread. Now my point is, not that the trusts have not been responsible for a small part of the rise in these products, but that even if this is true, it is for so small a part that the solution of the trust question would really have almost no effect on the cost of living question. You say we cannot keep the people's confidence and support by preaching mere palliatives. You are right. But we can forfeit their support much quicker by preaching something which is not so, and by promising what cannot be performed.

I agree that we must keep the issue perfectly clear, or rather, one of the issues, which is that the trusts shall not be allowed to exploit the people by dictating the terms upon which the people shall obtain food, fuel and clothing. I do not wish to see a trust magnate, or, to drop the terms of the stump, a big corporation man chosen as the real or titular head of the party *unless he ought on other grounds to be the titular or real head of the party*. If any trust magnate develops who on other grounds ought to be the head of the party, I shall vote for him to be such. But as neither Mr. Perkins nor any other corporation man is now the titular head or the real head of the party, and as no human being whom I know is thinking of making such a man the head, I do not regard this point as having the slightest applicability at present. You say that the Steel Trust and the Harvester Trust are the worst of existing trusts, or at least those which have been more exposed in magazines and the press. I know nothing of the Harvester Trust excepting the decision of the Supreme Court of Missouri that its whole behavior was excellent, and that it had offended in no way at all excepting by being big, that is, successful. As for the Steel Corporation, I think it has done some evil. It has done very much less evil, however, than the Pueblo Iron and Fuel Company, a comparatively small rival. Yet what you apparently support as the real remedy, the Brandeis remedy, would not in the smallest degree affect the Colorado Iron and Fuel Company (Mr. Guggenheim's company), and in my judgment would not work the very smallest improvement from the standpoint of cost of living.

Now as to the episode of the elimination of part of the trust plank from the Progressive platform. You say this episode is bound to come out, either at Chicago or subsequently. I hope it will come out at once, and the sooner the better. Mr. Perkins had nothing more to do with that episode than, for instance, Beveridge and Dixon and myself.

First as to your saying that the elimination of the lines of which you complain placed us in "a false and fatal position" in regard to the whole trust question, and especially with regard to monopoly. I do not agree with you. Unquestionably the successful mendacity of our opponents was exercised against us on the trust question as well as on various other questions. My own judgment is that if the sentences omitted had been kept in, the result would not have been different in the smallest degree. The attacks against us were not made in good faith. They were made with the deliberate purpose of perverting the truth and of clouding the issue. They were made without any reference to what we had actually done. As a matter of fact the classes among whom we failed to do well were the classes of small business men, prosperous farmers and the like, who thought that our platform and the candidates upon it were too radical, and not that they were too conservative. I may add that the ex-

perience of my colleagues on *The Outlook* absolutely bears out this statement. This was a Democratic year, and the Democrats were contented
with Wilson. The mere fact that the exposure of Wilson's trust record
in New Jersey did not damage him a particle is enough to show that we
could have gained mighty little from any further development of anti-
trust sentiment. My own feeling very strongly is that the difficulty we
had to encounter when we developed our programme about the trusts
was much less the difficulty of making people believe that we were not
cheap, and that all anti-trust talk was not cheap.

Now as to what actually happened about that anti-trust plank. I was
consulted freely by various men as to various planks in the platform. Mr.
Earl[5] of California and Senator Flinn consulted me about the Christian
Science business. You and Gifford consulted me about many things.
McCarthy consulted me about many things; he was violently opposed to
Miss Jane Addams on the colored question. Innumerable other people consulted me. Everyone asked me to interfere with the committee and to get
them to do or leave undone something. Among the people who consulted me on certain points were Perkins and Beveridge. By the time
that this trust plank came up our chief concern was to eliminate all matters of surplusage from the platform. At that time there was danger of
the platform being twice as long as it ought to be. I was trying hard to
cut out everything redundant. The action in connection with the trust
plank was merely one of innumerable similar actions, and when the question was first brought up at the end of the campaign I remembered little
about it. After much cudgelling of my brains and talking over with
various people, I think the following is substantially accurate. The committee sent up to me most of the planks as they passed them, with the
idea of getting any suggestions from me, inasmuch as I was to be the
candidate and as my speech to be delivered before the convention had
already been prepared. The planks I took most interest in were the social
and industrial planks and the country life plank. But I also took much
interest in a number of the others, including the trust plank. I suggested
in the case of each plank any amendments or changes which I thought
advisable. Perhaps once in twenty times these changes or suggestions
would be original with me. On the nineteen other occasions they represented efforts on my part to meet the protest of some Progressive who
felt very deeply on that particular subject. My own constant and harass-
ing care was to try not to let our party split open—and usually the split

was threatened on something about as important as the difference between Tweedle-dum and Tweedle-dee. (Keeping in or leaving out the sentences of which you speak in the trust plank was a mere case of Tweedle-dum and Tweedle-dee). I was also steadily trying to keep each plank cut down to be as short as possible. I do not know what course was taken as regards some of the suggestions I made, but I was notified in most cases that the suggestions had been adopted by the committee. It was thoroughly understood that I was not trying to embody my own ideas so much as that I was trying to get something which we could all in common stand on. I believe it was Dixon who brought up the trust plank, although I am not certain. Some man, I think it was Beveridge but it may have been Perkins, objected to the lines that are at issue. Perkins certainly recorded the objection. I did not and do not think that they strengthen the platform. I thought and think that they went needlessly into detail, and that to include such details, and leave out other equally important details, might make it look as if we would not oppose practicing much we had not specifically said that we would oppose. I said at once that as far as I was concerned I was entirely willing to have them struck out because they represented needless amplification, needless going into detail, and because to enumerate these particular inhibitions without enumerating others quite as important, might cause people to think that we did not intend to make the latter illegal. I also added with entire explicitness, and with the entire assent of my hearers, including Perkins, that in my speeches I intended to advocate just such action as that contained in the lines to be excluded, but that I agreed that the platform ought to be as short as possible and that we should state general purposes and not try to go specifically into details as these particular lines did. On the other hand, I felt that the first part of the plank dealing with the commission did not speak with sufficient explicitness as to the power that the commission should have over the trust. I suggested that one or two sentences should be inserted to strengthen the anti-trust plank at the beginning, and that these particular sentences to which you refer should be omitted from the second part of it. The suggestions were taken down in writing, either by [me] or by someone else present. Senator Dixon then took the amended section downstairs and returned shortly afterwards and said the committee had adopted the amended plank. I was told the same thing by two or three members of the committee later on. Afterwards I was informed that by mistake the unamended plank which had not been adopted was read in the convention. I was further informed that Senator Dixon immediately pointed out (to Dean Lewis, as he informs me) that the plank as read to the convention was not the one adopted by the committee; and that accordingly the sentences in question were dropped out of the platform as it was finally printed. I called up O. K. Davis and asked him to see that the press associations got the platform as thus printed. How utterly unimportant the matter was, and how utterly unimportant it then seemed, may be gathered from the fact that no human being as far as I know was impressed one way or the other about the matter, or raised any question about the matter. As far as I know, no member of the resolutions committee raised any question about it. Dean Lewis corrected the proof of the platform as finally issued. Frankly, I think it was utterly unimportant. I think it is a mere case of Tweedledum and Tweedle-dee whether those lines were left in, or whether, as I believe would have been wiser, they were cut out, although used in our different speeches. It is very undesirable to try to make a platform contain everything that can be put in speeches.

However, toward the very end of the campaign somebody spoke to me about these lines having been improperly left out. The first inquiries I made satisfied me that they had been properly left out, and that they had not been adopted by the committee. Dean Lewis now tells me that he believes that through some mistake the amended plank was not read to the committee after being brought down by Senator Dixon from my room, and that the committee did adopt the plank as unamended. As long as there is the slightest doubt on the question (and while I regard it as supremely unimportant) I feel that the lines to which you refer should be restored to the plank. I used the exact language of these lines again and again in various speeches, including the statement I made on November 2nd. I may add that my so using them was cordially approved by Mr. Perkins on the explicit ground that as a matter of course all the practices named would be effectively stopped under the Progressive proposal.

I feel a keen sympathy with Charley Thompson[6] of Vermont when he said that this was a typical mare's nest. I strongly feel that the course I recommended should be adopted and the lines re-inserted in the platform; but frankly I do not think they improve the platform at all, and I am not certain they were originally in it. I advocate the course only because it is well to put ourselves in such shape that suspicious souls shall not be able to make mountains of molehills.

Let me repeat, my dear Amos, that I do not for one moment believe that Perkins is attacked any more strongly than Flinn, than you and Gifford, than Medill, than Professor Merriam, than any number of other men, excepting in so far as he is more prominent. He has been the most useful man, not even excepting Flinn, in this whole fight. You couple Munsey with him. There would not have been any Progressive Party east of Philadelphia about which to make any complaints at all if Perkins and Munsey had dropped out of the fight. There would not have been any Progressive Party in Pennsylvania if Flinn had dropped out of the fight. Wilkinson made the fight for us in Syracuse. He is a steel man too, the head of the Crucible Steel Company. Of course if you rule out Perkins, Munsey and Flinn, you have got to rule out Wilkinson too. Wilkinson is in this fight for precisely the reason that Perkins and Flinn are. He told me substantially what they told me, namely, that he had become convinced that something must be done to help the condition of the wage workers, and have justice done so as to better the condition of the small man; and that he was in the Progressive Party because the triumph of the Progressive Party and the adoption of all its principles meant the elimination of the possibility of his children having to face revolution.

If Perkins or anyone else in this movement acts badly, I will turn against him. As long as he does not act badly, I will positively refuse to turn against him. I feel that this whole assault on him has been not only thoroughly unjustifiable, but contains the greatest element of menace which we now face as to the future of the Progressive Party. I must speak frankly, my dear Amos. I believe that the spirit, however honest, which prompts the assaults upon Perkins is the spirit which if it becomes dominant in the party means that from that moment it is an utter waste of time to expect any good from the party whatsoever, and that the party will at once sink, and deservedly sink, into an unimportant adjunct to the Debs movement or some similar movement. The great test of reformers always comes when they are required to work together. You have quoted Lincoln as being against chattel slavery. Have you forgotten that Lincoln was not for the abolition of chattel slavery until he had been President for two years? Do you not know that Lincoln's fight was half the time a fight to prevent foolish extremists from ruining the anti-slavery cause and ruining the union by insisting upon ostracising the moderate men? Do you forget that in 1864 Senator Wade of Ohio, Congressman Davis of Maryland and Wendell Phillips and Fremont did their best to break down Lincoln and the Republican Party on the ground that they had not gone far enough against chattel slavery, at the very time that Greeley and Raymond (the chairman of the executive committee of the then Progressive, that is, the Republican Party) were complaining bitterly that the party was being ruined because Lincoln had gone too far against chattel slavery. The reason that you quote Lincoln with such admiration now is because he succeeded. He succeeded. His success was in large part because he declined to submit for one moment to the constant proposals to rule out the Perkinses, the Munseys, the Flinns, the Wilkinsons of his day and generation who were in the Republican Party. My dear Amos, you and those like you who are engaged in this assault upon Perkins are following precisely the course which Wade and Davis and Fremont and Phillips followed forty-eight years ago. In the name of radical progress, in the name of lofty aspirations for the toiling masses, they did their best to alienate the moderate men without whom the Union could not have been preserved nor slavery abolished. Any man who agitates this business is doing everything he can to wreck the Progressive cause, and to make it a movement utterly impotent for accomplishing anything of good whatsoever. I shall oppose any such effort with every particle of strength I possess; and as regards the action on the trust plank at the Progressive convention I shall be delighted to have the whole matter made public at any time, and the sooner the better. It will be hard enough to make the Progressive Party win out on any terms; it will be infinitely harder if there is fighting among ourselves. We are the one party trying to serve the cause of the plain people; and it will be a dreadful thing if we render ourselves impotent to serve this cause.

My dear Amos, as I have said above, remember that the ability to think and act independently is no more essential than the ability to get on with others in work for a common cause. In my judgment every man who now gives any encouragement to our foes by inciting war among ourselves is simply rendering aid to the reactionary elements in this nation. He is acting precisely as the well-meaning extremists acted who in 1864 tried to break up the then Progressive Party, the Lincoln Republican Party. You know how fond I am of Gifford and of you. I believe I am advising you for your own good when I say that you impair your power of future usefulness if you give the impression that you never can work with any people for an achievable end. You tried to work with Taft, and broke with him. I think you were absolutely justifiable. You tried to work with La Follette and broke with him. I think you were absolutely justifiable. But if you now prove unable to work with the only body of people in this country who offer a chance of really achieving anything in this country, I think you will gravely impair all power to serve any good cause. Let me reiterate that the trouble has not been in the least, as far as this movement is concerned, due to not being radical enough, or not taking a sufficiently extreme position or not giving enough power and prominence to the radicals; our trouble has come because we were forced into the necessity, the lamentable necessity, of breaking up an old organized party, and taking what seemed to most people to be altogether too radical action. We did not get enough of the moderates among the Republicans with us; and we only got the strong, but sane, radicals among the Democrats. If we in any way at this time acted in more radical fashion than we have acted, we should make ourselves a laughing stock; and we should above all make ourselves a laughing stock if we took any action looking toward the ruling out of the moderate men who are with us.

Faithfully yours,
Theodore Roosevelt

Amos Pinchot Esq.,
  60 Broadway, New York.

This letter, though dated December 5, did not reach me until after the Chicago conference. It was begun in New York, but Roosevelt rewrote it several times on the train en route to Chicago, the first drafts being of such a nature that Charles Thompson of Vermont and other friends of Roosevelt insisted on destroying them, and persuaded the Colonel to keep rewriting until his anger cooled and he produced something less violent in tone. The letter as finally sent was very far from reassuring. Its explanation that the clause endorsing the Sherman law was struck out of the platform as redundant was an unfortunate one. The platform treated the regulation remedy at great and disproportionate length. It bulged with redundancy on the most immaterial subjects. Following the appeal to the largest-number policy, it was a catch basin for everyone's *ism;* since you could find in it wordy paragraphs on almost anything, from the shorter catechism to how to build a birchbark canoe, it certainly should have been able to give six lines to the Sherman law, which was pre-eminently the most vital and hotly discussed issue of the time.

As to the argument that to forbid certain unfair trade practices was by implication to approve those not mentioned, this did not in the least meet the case, for the clause was drawn inclusively, ending with the words "and other unfair trade practices."

Again, the letter says that during the campaign he (Roosevelt) made inquiries that satisfied him that the Resolutions Committee never adopted the plank approving the Sherman law. If this was true, it did not belong in the platform, and yet he felt that it should be put back. He himself repeatedly used the excluded lines in his speeches, and yet the exclusion or inclusion of an endorsement of the Sherman law is a mere matter of Tweedledum and Tweedledee.

In the meantime, not having heard from Roosevelt and believing that he did not intend to answer my letter of December 3, I sent word to him that in my opinion the first business of the Chicago conference should be for Senator Dixon, who was to preside, officially to restore the Sherman law clause, and that, if he failed to do this, I would con- sider it my business to rise and make a motion for its restoration. I was thoroughly distressed and deeply angry at the turn of events. I did not know the inside history of the relations between the Steel group and Roosevelt's administration from 1901 to 1908. Clear as it may seem now, I was, like the great majority of the Progressives, un- aware of the reasons for the dominance of big business in the party and of the strategy which was to keep the party alive till 1916. What I did know was that it was being used as a means of legalizing and respectabilizing industrial monopoly, and this seemed to me a cruel injustice not only to the liberal movement of which the party was the expression, but to the individuals who had joined in good faith.

On my arrival in Chicago, a delegation of outraged Progressives, including Oscar Straus[7] and Dixon, bore down on me at the La Salle Hotel, and warned me that an open attack on Perkins—which I had no intention of making—would disrupt the party. I replied that I did not propose to mention Perkins at all, but that if Dixon did not restore the Sherman law clause when the meeting began, I would make my motion, which, if unopposed, I thought would carry with little or no comment. I offered to go with them to Roosevelt's room and talk the matter over; and I sent a message to Roosevelt, but the latter refused to see me. The discussion raged furiously, while the gathering in the ballroom waited impatiently for the proceedings to begin. Surrounded by a group of Progressives, mostly protesting vehemently, but a few taking my side, I at length reached the meeting and took my place with misgivings no doubt comparable to those entertained by Judas when he sat among the disciples. The tension, however, subsided when, after a flying visit to the Colonel's room, Dixon mounted the platform, and, explaining in a few words that by inadvertence copies of the platform had been printed omitting a part of the industrial plank, he read the troublesome Sherman law clause in a monotone, and announced that if there were no objection he would consider it the will of the conference that it should be incorporated in future printings.

On my return from Chicago, I wrote a letter to Roosevelt, dated December 23, running in part as follows:

December 23rd, 1912.

Dear Colonel Roosevelt:

Your letter of December 5th was handed to me at Chicago the day before I left. There are several things in it which I want to take up with you, especially as I feel there has been some misunderstanding between us in regard to them.

In the first place your letter argues strongly and repeatedly against the proposition to "put Perkins out" (of the Progressive Party), against "ruling out the Perkinses, the Munseys, the Flinns," etc. You say:

> "I further believe that if we put out Perkins, and then did the only logical thing by putting out all men like him, we should gain one or two hundred thousand votes and lose two or three millions. I mean in all sincerity that I think that if the policy you advocate had been adopted at the outset of this campaign—for of course Perkins is simply a symbol, and it is idle to put out Perkins if you don't put out all the men of the same stamp—that we should have been a rival to Debs in the running, and would have lost every particle of power to fight for a good cause."

As far as I know neither Gifford nor myself, on any occasion, have directly or indirectly favored the proposition which you combat. When I talked with you about Perkins at your office on Friday, the 29th of November, which was a few days before the Chicago conference, I said to you, and I tried to make it as clear as words can make anything, that I thought that having a trust magnate act as the mouthpiece of our party and allowing him to have a controlling voice in the party councils was a grave mistake, and that I believed that if Perkins could be persuaded to resign from the Chairmanship of the Executive Committee and play a less conspicuous part in the Progressive campaign from now on, we would stand much better in the eyes of the public.

I said that I could see no objection to Perkins remaining on the National Committee, or on the Executive Committee of the National Committee, and I repeated twice with emphasis in answer to an objection made by you against driving Perkins out of the party, that there was no question of driving him, or anyone, out of the party, and, moreover, that an open attack upon Perkins at this time was of all things the most important to avoid as our party was not strong enough to stand such a split.

In addition to this I said, and I think you will remember, Colonel, the emphasis with which I made this remark, that for us to accept Perkins' money and support during the campaign and then when the election was lost to show him the door was entirely out of the question, and that we were stopped from doing so by every consideration of common decency.

On December 3rd I wrote you a long letter on the subject of Perkins, and the missing anti-trust plank. In this letter, as well as in the conversation to which I refer, I took the stand that the only possible way to solve the difficulty was for you to show Perkins that his leadership was hurting the party, and persuade him to resign from the Chairmanship of the Committee voluntarily.

In my letter I also said that owing to the cutting out of the anti-trust plank of our platform at the instance of Perkins, it was probable that an attack would be made upon him at the Chicago conference if he remained in the position of Chairman of the Executive Committee. This prediction, by the way, was amply justified, for when Gifford and I reached Chicago a number of people came to us advocating such a move.

This we successfully discouraged. Whether or not we were wise in doing this the future will show, but at all events this is what happened.

Almost as soon as the New York special arrived at Chicago several people, including Mr. Straus, came to me and said that they understood from your letter and from you that I was about to make an open attack upon Perkins at the conference. I told them that I had never had any such thing in mind. On the way home from Chicago still other people, who had seen your answer to my letter without seeing my letter itself, wanted to know if I had really been on the point of openly attacking Perkins at the conference, and if so, why. From all of this I feel that there has been a misunderstanding which should be corrected.

Let me repeat, in order to make myself entirely clear, while I hold and have held right along that it is a serious mistake to have a trust magnate speak for the party or influence its policy, and while I contend that the great majority of the party feel as I do, and that it is a contradiction of the fundamental principles of democracy to have a leader whom the majority do not desire and whose motives they are inclined to question, still I have made no objection at any time to Perkins being in the party, or on the National Committee or the Executive Committee. There is a difference between a man being in the party and being Chairman of the Executive Committee, spokesman, holder of the purse strings, controller of publicity and organizer of its political machinery.

We must remember that Perkins and Munsey have not only been the financial supports of the Progressive Party, but that they control to a large extent the newspapers and magazines which are favorable to our cause. To my mind it is exceedingly unfortunate that two men, both allied with trust and Wall Street interests, should have such tremendous power through money and publicity over a party founded largely as a protest against the oligarchical control of our political and industrial institutions.

As you probably know, Charles R. Crane has long made it a rule not to exercise control over the policies of any local or national political organizations to which he is a large contributor of money. After all, experience teaches us that the power of money is a peculiar and subtle thing, and that in actual life, just as in melodrama and cheap novels, it is difficult either for men, women or political parties to maintain their independence if they are under a heavy weight of financial obligation.

I think that to add to the power Perkins already has through finance and publicity by giving into his hands the organization of the party is a mistake of a very serious and dangerous character. But as this has been done we have got to make the best of it, working all the harder to make the party succeed in spite of everything.

In defense of the Harvester Trust you quote the opinion of the Supreme Court of Missouri, to the effect that its whole behavior was excellent, and that it offended in no way at all except by being big. The Supreme Court of Missouri has been, perhaps, our most perfect example of a court owned and operated by the special interests. It has been one of our best arguments for the recall of judges and judicial decisions. In the Ogglesby case, for instance, mentioned in C. P. Connolly's articles in *Everybody's*,[8] it established a record which has hardly been equalled for inhumanity and partiality to corporations.

In Kansas, the Harvester Trust has been prosecuted criminally and convicted on seventy-five counts.

The Factory Investigating Commission of New York State has just been informing itself upon the Harvester Trust's factories at Auburn in this state. In the statement of the Chairman of this Investigating Committee appears the following:

> "The appearance of the women workers was very disheartening; they were worn looking and pale, and their clothes, faces and hands were covered with oil and hemp dust. No attempt whatever was made to remove the dust by any system of exhaust, but it is breathed in all day long by the workers, some of whom testified that they frequently suffered from colds and sore throats. The women receive salaries as low as five dollars a week, out of which their board and living expenses have to be paid. . . . They work a total of 64½ hours a week, according to their testimony, which is in violation of the labor law. . . . There are more women than men on the night shift, and most of the night workers are married."

Mr. Perkins' reply was in part as follows:

> "This night work has been rendered necessary largely because of the government's perfectly unreasonable attitude toward large corporations, which has made it impossible for managers of large concerns to know whether they are on foot or on horseback, whether they could expand their plans to keep up with the increasing demand or not."

In the Philippines the record of the Harvester Trust is well known. Its lobby has succeeded in securing a law fixing a prohibitive tariff upon hemp exported to foreign countries, with a rebate on hemp shipped to the United States. It controls the United States market, and therefore the price. The result of this has been, as manila hemp is from sixty to sixty-five per cent of the total exports of the Philippines, that people in whole sections have been greatly impoverished, and that the Harvester Trust has a monopoly and in addition practically receives a subsidy of about half a million dollars a year.

Both the Harvester and the Steel trusts have a system of pensions conditional, in the case of the Steel Trust, upon twenty years' continuous employment, and in both companies conditional upon "loyalty" and a proper interest in the company's affairs. By such a system of bonuses and pensions, delayed until old age, and depending upon passive acceptance of the company's hours of labor, wages, etc., the Steel Trust has stamped out unionism, and both the Steel and Harvester trusts have fastened a system of practical peonage upon their employees.

In the second place, my dear Colonel, I want to enlarge a little upon my reasons for emphasizing the importance of restoring the anti-trust plank to the platform, although in doing so I must take direct issue with you. You say that the question whether the anti-trust plank is in the platform or out of the platform is as trivial as the difference between Tweedledum and Tweedledee, and that the trusts have practically no relation to the cost of living.

There isn't a single law on the statute books that gives the people protection against the trusts except the Sherman law. If that law is not retained upon the statute books and strengthened the people are left absolutely impotent to fight for industrial freedom, or for economic betterment.

You yourself, while President, in practically every message to Congress, endorsed the Sherman law and asked that it should be retained and enforced. Practically all of the Progressives today admit that regulation of trusts and price fixing by a commission alone is impracticable. You have taken this position on the stump and in published statements in *Collier's* and elsewhere.

It seems to me that if we are going to have any trust plank at all in the platform, the one thing that cannot possibly be left out is endorsement of the Sherman law, To cut this out in order, as you say, to save space, or for any reason, seems to me like cutting out the part of Siegfried from Götterdämmerung, or Ulysses out of the Odyssey.

Two things are certain in regard to our trust policy. The people will not for a moment stand for a commission, even of arch-angels, with power to fix the prices of necessaries of life and to say which trusts are good trusts and which bad trusts. In the second place they will not stand for any party that fails to stand by the Sherman act. The charge that we were not going to enforce the Sherman act, that is to say, that we were in favor of legalizing monopoly, was the strongest weapon that the Democrats used against us in the recent campaign. The next strongest was, I believe, that the trust influences within our party would be powerful enough to prevent any hostile action on our part against predatory wealth.

The chief importance of the part of the trust plank that was omitted was not that it forbade certain unfair practices upon the part of the trusts, but because it was an enforcement of the Sherman law and a recommendation for strengthening and making it effective. Surely the difference between a plank which enforces the Sherman act and one which leaves out the Sherman act, and by implication may be construed to endorse monopoly and limit our trust policy to regulation of monopoly by commission, seems anything but trivial.

I cannot get it through my head either, that the trust question has not a very important bearing upon the cost of living. Take the Standard Oil Company as an example. For the sake of argument, let us concede that oil is cheaper under the Standard Oil monopoly than it would be under competition (although I do not believe this is true). Be this as it may, we know that the Standard Oil Company will earn about one hundred million dollars this year. We also know that an earning of fifty million dollars a year would be more than a generous return to its stockholders upon the value of the property, and that the fifty million dollars which it takes from the public above this generous return is a sheer economic loss to the community. In other words, assuming that these figures are approximately correct, the Standard Oil Company takes fifty million dollars a year out of the pocket of the average man which it could afford to leave in the pocket of the average man by reducing the price of oil. Practically the same condition exists in the case of scores upon scores of trusts, big and small, that manufacture and distribute the things men and women must buy in order to live and work.

The sugar trust, the steel trust, the harvester trust, the meat trust, the coal trust, the butter trust, the wool trust, the light and water-power monopolies, and the cold storage combinations that get together to keep up the price of almost every kind of perishable food, are milking the public, just as industriously as the Standard Oil. The result is that the trusts are exploiting the common people, and concentrating wealth in the hands of our industrial oligarchy. Whether the public are better off or worse off than they would be if trusts had never been formed is not the main question. Whether or not the trusts have raised or lowered the cost of living in the past is not the main question. But the main question is whether the trusts through monopoly and their power to fix prices are today keeping prices away up above where they ought to be and thus making it hard for the average man and woman to buy the necessaries of life with the wage that he or she earns. And the fact is that we know, and that everybody knows, that this is just what they are doing.

In Hobson's article in the *Contemporary Review* of October, to which you refer me, he says, speaking of the trusts:

"For though the business men who form these combinations are motived partly by economics in business methods which may assist and not retard production, the main object at which they aim is the maintenance of high prices by means of a control of output. The normal result of the formation of combines is to restrict the rate of production, making it lower than it would be under an era of free competition."

As I said to you in my letter of December 3rd, it seems to me that our whole program of social and industrial justice will be discredited, and ought to be discredited, unless we can prevent the trusts from charging the increase in the cost of production (which shorter hours, higher wages, pensions, insurance, etc. will bring about) to the public—unless we can prevent them from using the industrial improvements required by our platform as an excuse for putting up the cost of commodities of daily use.

When Lloyd George, in 1909, introduced the budget providing for practically the same planks which are in our platform now, he was careful to explain to the English people exactly how he would defray the cost of industrial reform by taxation upon unearned increments, incomes, inheritances, and some kind of special privilege or abuse.

It seems to me that it is necessary for us, both as politicians and as economists, to assure the people that the cost of our industrial reforms will be defrayed in some way other than by diminishing the purchasing power of their wages. The endorsement of the Sherman law is perhaps the most important measure contained in our platform along this line. For this reason, also, it seemed to me important that the plank endorsing the Sherman act should be restored.

As far as I know only two methods of trust regulation are proposed. One is to fix prices by a commission, and the other to enforce the Sherman act. We have come out flatly against price fixing by a commission. There remains the Sherman act with a commission merely as an executive arm. Therefore, if we are not for the Sherman act we are not for any trust regulation at all, but for unrestrained power of the trusts to exploit people by monopoly, or any other means that they can devise.

For this reason I have felt that it was important to put back the Sherman act in the platform.

You say that you fear that our party has lost votes because it has been too radical. I believe that the trouble with us has been that we have not been anything like radical or fundamental enough. It seems to me that we have been making a great fuss and preparing to cure cancers with porous plasters. As far as Gifford and I are concerned, I know of no policy which we have advocated that you have not also advocated. If you can mention any view in regard to a public measure that I have held that you do not approve of, I will either try to justify myself or revise my opinion.

The great danger has seemed to me all along, not that the people would fear the Progressive Party would go too far, but that it would repeat the performances of the old parties by not going far enough.

We have a splendid program of popular government. Our program of industrial justice is accepted on every hand. There is no issue in regard to it. With the exception of our conservation policy, which is splendid, we have not got down to fundamentals along economic lines. And we must get down to fundamentals before we can make a deep and lasting impression upon the community.

It is poverty that is the curse of this country; it is poverty that we have got to fight. It is a fairer distribution of wealth that we must achieve before we can do anybody any real good. Everybody knows this in his heart, and the sooner we make it as clear as sunlight that the Progressive Party knows and feels this too, the greater will be, and ought to be, our support from the people. If we do not make this plain our party can have no real permanent strength, it will be merely a temporary resting place —a sort of "safe and sane" happy-medium island of refuge for those who are unable to decide whether they are going to join the people or the special interests in this fight.

We cannot at the same time appear safe and sane to the people and to the interests that are preying on the people. We cannot successfully ride two horses, especially when they are going in opposite directions. Our party has got to make an open choice whether it is to be a radical party or a conservative party. Its very existence depends almost wholly upon its being dominated by radical rather than conservative men and ideas.

Of course our party, like all parties, will necessarily be divided into factions, we must expect that. There will always be in every party the conservative wing and the radical wing. We will never be wholly united in our ideas of what is the best for the country and for the party. We already have our factions now and will continue to have them, and there is no harm in this. But one question must be answered, for the people are asking it today. Is the radical wing or the conservative wing of our party to shape its policies?

I have written to you very frankly and fully because I feel that there has been a good deal of misunderstanding not only between you and me, but between you and Progressives that feel a good deal the way I do. I believe this misunderstanding will, in the end, be simply a means of coming to a better and more satisfactory relation between all of us.

Very sincerely yours,

(A. P.)

Colonel Theodore Roosevelt,
   287 Fourth Avenue,
      New York City.

On January 1 I received the following letter, answering mine of December 23:

December 31st, 1912.

Dear Amos:

I was glad to get your letter. Now Amos, I am not going to answer it in detail. The important thing is that, as far as I can make out, you and

I and Gifford are really at one on most of the matters of policy to be pursued, and so I am not going to take up the matters of difference unless they become more important than they are. For instance, my concern over what you said about the trusts was due to my understanding that you regarded the trusts as practically the sole cause of the increased cost of living. I think, although I am not sure, that they are one of many causes (I have just been talking with Fisher of Yale, who is inclined to combat me even on this point), and as I will go with you heartily to remedy this cause, as far as it exists, it is not of much consequence exactly what we individually think is its relative importance.

Thank Heaven! we have re-instated everything about the anti-trust plank that was, or may have been, cut out, and so that leg's off! Therefore on this point we are now a unit.

Now from Frank Heney I understand that at the last meeting here in New York to arrange as to who should be the "spokesman, the controller, the publicity man" and so forth, was entirely satisfactory. Probably you know that it was I who got Heney on to that meeting by wiring to Lissner either to come on himself or to make Heney his alternative.

You make out a strong case against the Harvester Trust. In Kansas I was informed by Stubbs that the Harvester was now behaving well, and that it was only behaving well because they had established over it in Kansas by indirect methods just the kind of power I want to see a National Commission establish over it.

I wish to Heaven we *could* get other people besides Mr. Munsey interested in establishing Progressive papers. Outsiders do establish papers here and there and I am backing them as heartily as I know how. As for the further matter you say about Messrs. Perkins and Munsey, I think I will wait until I see you. I am in great haste.

A happy New Year to you and yours,

Sincerely yours,

Theodore Roosevelt

Amos R. E. Pinchot, Esq.,
   60 Broadway,
    New York City.

P. S. I need not say that I feel that the Progressive Party must be the radical party. We have no excuse for existing excepting as the radical party;

but I want to keep it as the party of sane and tempered radicalism such as that of Abraham Lincoln.

Roosevelt's letter, friendly, moderate and, from his point of view, eminently sensible, left the situation precisely as it had been. It is true that the Sherman law was back in the platform. But with Perkins still at the helm and Roosevelt a mere passenger bent on leaving the ship at the first port, the party had practically lost headway. In the 1913 and 1914 state elections the Progressives made a lamentable showing. Soon Roosevelt was speaking of the party in a reminiscent and reconciled mood, as when one remembers bygone mistakes: "There is," he wrote his son, "just one element of relief to me in the smash that came to the Progressive Party. We did not have many practical men with us. Under such circumstances, the reformers tended to go into sheer lunacy."[9]

In 1913 Roosevelt went to South America, returning in May of the following year. He then made a trip to Spain, arriving in the United States in June 1914. In the meantime, Perkins was losing no time in pushing the evangel of monopoly. In June 1913 he gave out an extraordinary interview during the government suit against the International Harvester Company, to the effect that people were being knighted in Canada for doing exactly what he had accomplished in building up the Harvester Company in the United States. This was the interview which contained the famous sentence that was greeted with derision by the farmers of the Northwest, "Wherever we (the Harvester Company) have gone, the land has bloomed." In February 1914 he carried on a written debate with Senator Borah on the monopoly question, in which he contended that a successful attack on the Steel Corporation would prove a national calamity.

In May 1914 I made one more abortive effort to dislodge Perkins from the chairmanship of the Executive Committee, this time in the form of a public letter to Senator Dixon,[10] summing up the position of the party very much as I had in my correspondence with Roosevelt. However, the latter only served to sever my already strained relations with Roosevelt and to end my contacts with the Progressive party as a national organization. Though he had lost his initial interest in the Progressive party, Roosevelt—and Perkins—now seemed bent on keeping it in existence till 1916 for reasons which, strange as it may seem, the vast majority of the party did not fathom. Though by this time it had little of its original significance, it could still be used as a weapon with which to force the Republicans to nominate him, or someone agreeable to him, under the threat that if they refused, Roosevelt would repeat the 1912 performance. Notwithstanding the signs and omens, which should have been clear enough, most of the Progressives were blind to the real situation and wholly certain that if Roosevelt did not win both nominations, he would, nevertheless, run as a third party candidate. To this course he seemed to be irrevocably committed by the fact that he was allowing Perkins to make preparations for a Progressive convention to be held at Chicago, at the same time as the Republican convention.

It must be said in justice to Roosevelt that as the 1916 convention approached, he never by a single categorical statement encouraged the Progressives to believe that he would run for the presidency if nominated by them alone. Over Oyster Bay hung a cloud of mystery which was only thickened by the unsatisfied inquiries of Progressive leaders, Republican leaders, and newspaper correspondents. Roosevelt, now only fitfully active in politics, was losing the aura of power that had hitherto surrounded him in his days of glory. Like Ulysses, he had wandered far since the events of 1912, to return comparatively unregarded except by his most devoted followers. At this period, though he could be classed neither as a Progressive nor as a Republican, his dearest associations, his ways of thought, and his most intimate friends, except for a handful, were of the Republican genus. Though he still remained outside the old party's fold, it was with one foot on the threshold. Would he cross over to Republicanism meekly, as a returned prodigal? Or, protected by the threat of a third party bolt, would he boldly force the old guard to accept him rather than face more lean years with Wilson in the White House?

His general mildness, his continued association with Perkins and Gary, his intimacy with Lodge and other stalwart Republicans, his avoidance of radical utterances in his magazine work, his absorption in the World War, were giving rise to the belief that his days of political radicalism were past. That advances were being made to him by important industro-financial interests had long been rumored. But in the winter of 1915 an event took place that brought him once more into the forefront and headlines of speculation. On December 17

Gary gave a dinner at his home, 856 Fifth Avenue, in Roosevelt's honor, which was attended by a selected group of the country's most distinguished bankers, industrialists, and politicians. Though Gary tried to keep the dinner secret, rumors of it leaked out and into the press within a day or so. Gary, Belmont, McCormick, and Roosevelt himself refused to answer questions on the purpose of the dinner except to deny that it was political. Later on, Roosevelt explained to John Leary of the *World* that the only topic discussed was military preparedness.[11] But on what theory it had been unanimously decided that a friendly symposium on preparedness should be so carefully hidden from the public, neither he nor anybody else explained. At all events, no one believed that it was a preparedness dinner and the interpretation of both the press and the public was that Gary had fired the opening gun in Roosevelt's campaign for the Republican nomination of 1916. The *New York Times'*[12] account of the dinner is as follows:

ROOSEVELT GUEST OF BIG FINANCIERS

Hint of 1916 politics in the dinner given by E. H. Gary
But nothing is revealed

———

PERKINS, MCCORMICK, G. F. BAKER, VANDERLIP, GUGGENHEIM
AND HEPBURN THERE.

ALSO LIVINGSTON BEECKMAN

———

Despite attempts to keep the matter secret, it was learned yesterday that Colonel Theodore Roosevelt was chief guest at a dinner on Friday night at the home of Elbert H. Gary, head of the Steel Corporation, at his home 856 Fifth Avenue. Many persons prominent in financial affairs were present. Although most of the guests were Republicans, several were prominent Democrats, and there were a few Progressives.

When the news of the dinner became known those present who could be reached were extremely reticent about it. There was a rumor that the dinner was held for purely political purposes, and that the possibility of Colonel Roosevelt becoming the candidate of the Republican party for the presidential nomination next year was discussed. Colonel Roosevelt, through his secretary, John McGrath, said last night that he was at the dinner but did not care to discuss what had taken place. Secretary McGrath added, however, that the dinner was purely a private affair and that it had no political significance.

Among those present at the dinner besides Mr. Gary and Colonel Roosevelt were August Belmont, Jacob H. Schiff, George F. Baker, R. Livingston Beeckman, Republican Governor of Rhode Island, Medill McCormick of Chicago, former Bull Moose leader of Illinois, who has gone over to the Republican party, George W. Perkins, chairman of the executive committee of the National Progressive Party, A. Barton Hepburn, Frank A. Vanderlip, Cornelius Vanderbilt, Frederick W. Whitridge, Frank T. Kellogg of St. Paul, Daniel Guggenheim, C. A. Coffin, Henry Walters, Richard Lindabury of Philadelphia, E. C. Converse, Clarence Mackay, and George B. Cortelyou.

When Mr. Gary was asked if he cared to say anything about the dinner, he replied: "I don't care to say anything about it. It was purely a private affair."

"Was Colonel Roosevelt there?"

"I will not talk about it."

"But if Colonel Roosevelt was there, it is a matter of public importance, isn't it?"

"I have said that I cannot say anything about it," replied Mr. Gary. When a list of names of those present was read to Mr. Gary, he still insisted that he would not discuss the subject.

Mr. Belmont was next asked if he cared to discuss what had taken place. "I will not discuss the dinner in any way," he said.

It was learned that Governor Beeckman of Rhode Island had a conference with Colonel Roosevelt recently. It was said he told the Colonel he favored his nomination by the Republican party. It is also known that Medill McCormick and Theodore Douglas Robinson, the Colonel's nephew, who has also returned to the Republican fold, had a conference with the Colonel at his office on Friday afternoon. Mr. McCormick was seen last night, but would not discuss the conference.

Politicians, when they learned of the dinner, said yesterday they considered it of extreme significance because of the standing of the men who attended. They saw in it an indication of the beginning of a real attempt to amalgamate the Republican and Progressive parties, and perhaps place Colonel Roosevelt in command as the Republican nominee for the presidency. At all events, it seemed to be agreed by men of all political beliefs that the importance of the meeting would become more and more evident as political affairs progressed toward the next presidential election, and that its influence would be far-reaching. One man, who declined to have his name used, said: "That dinner will prove to have been one of the biggest events of the campaign when we look back on it after the next election. The absence of politicians from the dinner means nothing. Or rather it means everything, depending on your viewpoint."

A survey of the names of those who were present with Colonel Roosevelt shows that the financial side of the Republican party was well represented, and if the financial side has decided to cast its lot with Colonel Roosevelt again, the politicians will be brought into line.

Whatever else it does, the dinner will exert a tremendous influence in the future course of the Republican and the Progressive parties, and it undoubtedly shows that men of the first importance politically are considering a fight under Colonel Roosevelt's leadership.

Irrespective of the subject discussed at the dinner, there is no doubt that Gary's object was to launch a Roosevelt boom. Not only the Steel Corporation but the Harvester Company, also a Morgan promotion whose finance committee was headed by Gary,[13] were being hounded by the Wilson administration. Investigated, prosecuted, and muckraked, their antisocial practices bared, and the illegal differentials on which their monopoly power rested dangled before the public gaze, these two huge and fantastically profitable consolidations needed a change in federal politics as never before in their history. The feverish zeal with which Perkins had been defending them from his desk in Progressive headquarters had not stemmed the tide of public opinion. Wilson, Borah, Brandeis, and the Democratic administration were hot on their trail. It did not require men of the shrewdness of Gary and Perkins to see that the solution of their difficulties would be the election of a president who could be trusted to use his power to mend this distressing situation, to use it vigorously, and, what was more important still, to act with the authority of a man convinced that he was doing right. Hughes, the other leading aspirant for the Republican nomination, though a well-tried defender of big business, had certain objections in Gary's eyes. He was essentially a Rockefeller man and the European war had enlarged the already wide divergence between the Rockefeller and the Morgan points of view. On account of their rivalry with the British oil interests, the Rockefellers were anti-English, while the Morgans were proverbially pro-English. Shell was then as now in effect the British government, and the Rockefellers had been fighting pitched battles with Shell, often getting the worst of it in various quarters of the globe. The Rockefellers were looked on as pacifist and pro-German, the Morgans as warlike and pro-Ally. Though it was true that the Morgan and the Rockefeller groups were economically allied by many common intranational interests, they diverged politically, especially since the 1904 presidential campaign, in which Roosevelt repudiated the Standard Oil contribution. Hughes might therefore be expected to favor the Rockefeller philosophy.[14] Indeed, he was already favoring it and was rated as distinctly of hyphenated philosophy.

Roosevelt, on the other hand, could be relied on in every way. He was fiercely pro-British and pro-Ally, so that if he were elected the Morgan group would have reason to feel that its loans to the Allied governments would have whatever security came from the support of the White House. He had accepted Gary as mentor of his economic thinking soon after he succeeded to the presidency in 1901, and had wholeheartedly adopted Gary's business doctrines, his good and bad trust distinction, his regulation scheme, and his government price-fixing plan. He was against the Sherman Act, which the Morgan interests had always feared, and now more than ever. While president, he had repeatedly demanded the repeal of the Sherman law in his messages. He had steered the 1906 investigation of the Steel Trust into safe channels,[15] and had given the Steel Trust a clean bill of health. He had held up an adverse report on the Harvester Trust and prevented its indictment in 1907,[16] in spite of the recommendations of the Department of Justice. He had secretly accepted the financial help of Gary and Henry C. Frick, the most powerful figure in the Steel Trust except Morgan, in the dark days of his campaign against Alton B. Parker, while E. T. Stotesbury, Morgan's Philadelphia partner, had acted as his ———— in the same campaign. On the advice of Morgan's lawyer, Elihu Root, he had saved the Steel Corporation's monopoly power by permitting it to buy its only formidable rival, the Tennessee Coal and Iron Company, and had promised it immunity from prosecution. He made Henry L. Stimson, Root's partner, Federal District Attorney in New York and secured his nomination for the governorship. He had put in his cabinet Robert Bacon, a partner of Morgan's and a director of the Steel Corporation, Truman H. Newberry, president of a subsidiary of the Steel Corporation, Elihu Root, Morgan's ablest lawyer, and Philander Knox, also a distinguished Steel Corporation attorney, and he had made Morgan's son-in-law Assistant Secretary of the Navy. When he left office, his first two choices for his successor were Elihu Root and Philander Knox. When the Steel Corporation was indicted in 1911, he had written a violent protest denouncing Taft for permitting such a crime against common sense. In 1912, yielding to the advice of McCarthy of Wisconsin, myself, and other liberals, he had publicly favored keeping the Sherman law on the statute books, but, yielding to Perkins and Munsey, he had permitted the Sherman law clause to be stricken out of the Bull Moose platform. He had allowed Munsey and Perkins, both spokesmen of Gary, to finance his 1912 campaign, and the latter to turn Progressive headquarters into a propaganda bureau for the Steel and Harvester trusts. Finally, in 1915, as shown by his correspondence with Lodge, he had promised a Pittsburgh millionaire to do what he could to throw the Progressives behind the candidacy of Philander Knox, despite the latter's alleged pro-Germanism, at the time expressing the belief that Knox would give the country a first-rate administration provided he would put another Morgan attorney [Root] in his cabinet as Secretary of State.[17] Now in 1915 he was allowing Perkins,[18] still in full charge of the party's machinery, to prepare for another Progressive convention, and soon he was to authorize George Meyer, the man who in 1904 James Speyer had told Lodge would be useful in keeping Morgan in line, to establish the Roosevelt Republican headquarters in Chicago on the eve of the Republican convention.

Whether or not this summary casts light on the much-mooted purpose of Judge Gary's dinner in the winter of 1915 is a matter for the reader to decide. At all events, the spring of 1916 saw a redoubled political activity on Roosevelt's part, similar to that of the spring of 1912. In April and May, though not declaring himself a candidate, he launched into a series of speeches in Chicago, St. Louis, Kansas City, Detroit, and other large centers, on such subjects as "Righteousness in Peace and National Preparedness," "National Duty," and "International Ideals," which can be interpreted either solely as an effort to bring the country into line with his preparedness ideas, in which he was deeply engrossed, or as also motivated by a desire to put himself in line for the Republican nomination now but a few months off.[19]

On the eleventh of May, in reply to an inquiry from Guy Emerson, secretary of the Roosevelt Non-Partisan League, Roosevelt gave out a statement which was generally interpreted as a declaration that he would seek both the Progressive and Republican nominations:

As you know, I have refused to endorse the use of my name in the primaries or in any way to enter into any factional contest which has for its object my nomination in Chicago in June. You also know that I have emphatically stated that it would be unwise to nominate me unless with the full understanding that such nomination means the hearty endorsement of the principles for which I stand—the principles set forth in the Chicago speech to which you refer.

I do not have to improvise my convictions on either Americanism or preparedness. I have fought for them all my life long, and when I was President I translated my convictions concerning them into governmental policy.[20]

On June 7, 1916, the two conventions were held in Chicago, the Republican in the Coliseum, as of yore, and a sadly shrunken Progressive convention housed in the Auditorium adjoining the old Congress Hotel. The hostile armies had begun to swarm into the city by the third, and at once began maneuvering for favorable positions. Roosevelt himself was in command of the Progressives through Perkins, though he remained in Oyster Bay, his intentions still veiled as to whether he would run on the Bull Moose ticket should he fail to capture the Republican nomination.[21] Once more a devoted army of crusaders composed of the same strange admixture of idealists and disgruntled political adventurers marched through the streets with flags flying, still hoping for the triumph of the Progressive cause. Few bands, however, enlivened the proceedings. The faithful were more hard up than in 1912. Munsey and his money had gone home to the Republicans, and Perkins remained as a lonely angel, still bearing the burden on the chance that Roosevelt would head both tickets, in which case plenty of funds would be available for pressing the war against Wilson. The 1916 convention proved to be strictly a steamroller affair. Raymond Robins, as chairman, would brook no opposition to Perkins' program. Only delegates who were known conformers gained recognition, and all iconoclastic talk was cut short with crashing regularity by the Robins gavel.

The first business of the Republicans and Progressives was the appointment of a joint committee to sound the possibility of agreement. To the dismay of the Progressive appointees, who were for Roosevelt and Roosevelt only, Reed Smoot is said to have opened the meeting with the remark, "We will take anyone you want but Roosevelt,"[22] and from this position the Republicans could not be dislodged. At the beginning of the second night, the deadlock was still unbroken. Both conventions were becoming restless and it was feared they would kick over the traces and cast decisive ballots next day. No one but a few insiders knew what was going on. Contradictory reports spread electrically through the crowds, though the belief prevailed among the Progressives that the Colonel would head the party in any event, especially if the Republicans should nominate Hughes, since Roosevelt's dislike for him because of his stand on the war was notorious.[23] Late on the second night, when all hope of agreement was abandoned, the Conference Committee called up Oyster Bay and put the question squarely up to Roosevelt, with the astounding result that he urged them to unite on Senator Henry Cabot Lodge of Massachusetts, a staunch old-school reactionary who, as representative of New England's industrial interests, had been fighting progressivism for thirty years.

I attended the Progressive convention as an onlooker, and next day was witness to the extraordinary scene when, keyed by suspense to a condition of almost frantic excitement, the Progressives, after listening in unbelieving silence to Perkins' account of the Conference Committee's talk with Roosevelt, suddenly realized that the jig was up, and that the founder of their party was leaving it, at the same time administering its final and ungentle *coup de grâce*. From the moment the convention had been called to order on June 10, rumors had been rife that Roosevelt would not run, that he had been talking over the long-distance telephone with Perkins about compromise candidates, that he was inclined to support Hughes. But these had been hotly rejected. The crowd was fanatically loyal to Roosevelt, and it believed that Roosevelt would be equally loyal in turn. When the blow fell it was almost too bizarre to be credited. But when Oscar King Davis read a written communication asking for the endorsement of

Lodge, signed Roosevelt, the gasp of incredulity was followed by passionate cries of dissent. Suddenly the crowd surged from astonishment to anger. It felt that in naming Lodge, Roosevelt had done something not merely fantastic but grossly insulting. They were taken by surprise. They had been kept in the dark, treated like children—pawns in a game into the nature of which they had had no inkling. I saw men and women sitting as if stunned, like unjustly punished children, with tears streaming down their cheeks.

Clinging to the possibility that something unforeseen might yet alter the Republicans' decision to have nothing to do with Roosevelt or anyone he might choose, Perkins had for hours been fighting despairingly to keep the crowd from nominating Roosevelt, but now it broke away from him in a rush. Bainbridge Colby advanced to the front of the platform and in deliberate tones, in which there was a touch of irony, put Roosevelt in nomination. Johnson seconded the nomination in a ringing speech calling on Roosevelt to meet his responsibilities. Perkins, still vainly trying to put off the nomination that was now inevitable, announced to an unheeding audience that the Republican convention had taken kindly to the Lodge suggestion. But the delegates shouted him down and Roosevelt was nominated in a deafening commotion; the convention adjourned in disorder.

Heartened by Johnson's speech, in which he expressed the hope that Roosevelt was still open to persuasion, the Progressives met again in the afternoon and raised a campaign fund of $100,000, partially, I think, as a means of rebuking Roosevelt and showing they were ready to fight. It was shortly after the collection that Roosevelt's answer to his nomination arrived:

Oyster Bay, New York, June 10th.

To the Progressive Convention:

I am grateful for the honor you confer upon me by nominating me as President. I cannot accept it at this time. I do not know the attitude of the candidate of the Republican Party toward the vital questions of the day. Therefore, if you desire an immediate decision, I must decline the nomination.

But if you prefer it, I suggest that my conditional refusal to run be placed in the hands of the Progressive National Committee. If Mr. Hughes' statements, when he makes them, shall satisfy the committee that it is for the interest of the country that he be elected, they can act accordingly, and treat my refusal as definitely accepted.

If they are satisfied, they can so notify the Progressive Party, and at the same time they can confer with me, and then determine on whatever action we may severally deem appropriate to meet the needs of the country.

THEODORE ROOSEVELT

This was the end. Everyone knew that his conditional refusal meant that Roosevelt had decamped and was on his way back to the Republican party. Hughes had been nominated by the Republicans at 12:49, two minutes after the Progressives nominated Roosevelt. The convention broke up in a sullen mood; a crowd without a leader, it filed slowly out of the Auditorium. Among those who had joined the movement for selfish interest, there was probably a deep feeling of disappointment. But for the many men and women who had followed Roosevelt for four years with great hopes and unselfish motives, there was the added grief of disillusionment. From now on politics might grow better or worse; political parties might rot in materialism, or soar from earth to sing hymns at heaven's gate. It was immaterial to them. They did not know what would happen, nor did they care to speculate for the moment. One thing, however, they were sure of. It would be many a long day before they would serve in the rank and file of another Progressive movement only to be disbanded in a *cul-de-sac* while the old parties marched triumphantly on their way.

That was Saturday evening. The following Tuesday Roosevelt dined with Hughes in New York and renewed his pledge of support.

I left the Auditorium after the adjournment of the convention on June 10 accompanied by Hiram Johnson, who was soon to play a singular part in the defeat of the candidates endorsed by Roosevelt. The situation was not a pleasant one for Johnson. He was vastly chagrined by Roosevelt's defection. He liked neither Hughes nor Wilson. He had a fight on in his own state, and could expect little support from the Hughes Republicans. Johnson made no pretense of accepting Hughes, and while he won in his own state, Hughes was defeated, throwing the fifteen electoral votes of California into the Democratic column. Meanwhile, E. W. Scripps, the original sponsor of La Follette, and now in Wilson's camp, again effected a telling political intervention by sending Gardner into Progressive-Republican states where governors, senators, and congressmen were up for election, with the message that the Scripps papers would support them in the exact proportion that they withheld support from Hughes' campaign. It was in these states, especially Oregon, Washington, and the Dakotas, where Gardner had sowed the seed of Republican revolt in ground already harrowed by rage at Roosevelt's attempt to turn the liberals over to Lodge and then to Hughes, that Wilson won the doubtful electoral votes that swung the victory from Hughes.

There are generally extenuating circumstances for every political act in which the element of betrayal seems present. It is true that Roosevelt used the Progressive party in 1916 as a weapon to frighten the Republicans into nominating him. When he failed in this he discarded the weapon with an alacrity that was nothing less than cruel. It is true, I believe, that at no time in 1916 did he intend to run on the Bull Moose ticket unless nominated also by the Republicans. It is true that notwithstanding this, he allowed the Progressives to believe that he would carry their flag through thick and thin. It is true that, though he never directly promised the Progressives he would run, he promised by the implication of his actions and used the Progressives as pawns in a maneuver they did not understand till too late. All this was bad; at the time it seemed unforgivable. And yet, in the light cast on these events by Roosevelt's own peculiar philosophy, there was a certain justification. As described in his own letters, Roosevelt's position was as follows: he believed that the most important thing in the world was for America to enter the war on the side of the Allies. Comparatively speaking, domestic issues did not exist for him. He was wrapped up in the war. Even the good and bad trust issue was subordinated to the international situation. In 1916 Wilson was a pacifist. He had skillfully encouraged antiwar feeling and was running on the slogan, "He kept us out of war." Roosevelt felt—and how much his personal animosity toward Wilson warped his judgment cannot be told—that the essential thing was to get rid of Wilson.[24] For him to run as a Progressive would have meant to re-elect Wilson. Therefore he refused the nomination.

So far Roosevelt was consistent. From the very outbreak of European hostilities he had been promoting the World War as a war of democracy and justice. He was of the opinion that a German victory would mean the debacle of civilization. On the other hand, his staunchest friends were unable to assert that he was quite single-minded in his desire to defeat Wilson. If that had been his only object, he would have worked for the nomination of some candidate, other than himself, more "American" than Hughes or Knox, who would unite the Republicans and the Progressives. If he had not been in one of his worst periods of self-deception, he would have realized that the hatred he had aroused by his assault on the Republicans in 1912 made it impossible, even if he had secured the nomination, to poll the full strength of the Republican party.

Roosevelt was historically interesting as a politician of good character, fair intelligence, and high executive ability, whom a major economic interest, with a questionable system of acquisition to defend, felt obliged to corral by shrewd diplomatic approaches. Because of his remarkable talents, his native sense of justice, his desire to play a righteous part in the eyes of the world, his unique genius in advertising his ideas, as well as himself, he should have been one of our greatest presidents. He failed first on account of the limitation of an unreflecting mind. He never got off by himself and thought things out to the end. The sessions of sweet silent thought were not for him. He was too much on the go. He believed in action for action's sake— the strenuous life was his undoing. He failed in the second place because of the untoward accident that he came into power at the same moment when Morgan's mammoth steel consolidation came into being under the Damoclean sword of the Sherman law. Overcapitalized, oversized, a mushroom growth rather than a natural development, the Steel Corporation could live and prosper only through the maintenance of an illegal monopoly system built on differentials in transportation, fuel, and raw material. Bereft of these differentials, it would have been as helpless as a stranded whale. Morgan knew this; so did Gary and Perkins. That was the beginning of Roosevelt's undoing, if undoing there was. History may hold otherwise. It has already put him in the Hall of Fame. It may place him in the company of the great. But whatever may be the ultimate fate of his name, it will forever be associated in the minds of those interested in the inner workings of our politico-economic system with the simple formula set down at the beginning of this book: society in the industro-financial age is governed by wealth. Not wealth in every form, but surplus wealth over and above what is required to conduct business. Differentials of a sort that are either illegal, or apt to be adjudged illegal, destroy competition and build up monopoly. Monopoly, the most effective wealth-producing agency known to the world, creates exorbitant profits and surplus wealth, and the latter reaches out to control the political and other phases of society in order to protect the technique that has created it. By this formula may be traced the story of Roosevelt's rise and fall, and the rise and fall of the party he headed. How innocent a pawn he was in the mighty and intricate system in which he was caught is a question on which we may differ, my own opinion being that he was surprisingly innocent about it. He had a talent for innocency. All things with which he associated himself fell in his mind easily into the category of goodness.

The failure to secure the Republican nomination in 1916 was a severe blow to Roosevelt. Two days after the 1916 election he said rather sadly to Leary of the *World*, "This was my year—1916 was my high twelve. In four years I will be out of it. This was my year to run. I did not want to run in 1912. Circumstances compelled me to run then. This year it was different."[25] Roosevelt in defeat was as courageous as in victory. In spite of increasing ill health, he went on working for what he most believed in, preparedness and the war. He battled for Hughes heroically, though he thoroughly disliked him. Notwithstanding advancing years, he tried to raise a division and take it to France. He bore no grudge against anyone, not even against myself for all the unkindness with which I had treated his pet theories and his favorite friends. He thought I had gone utterly to bad on the war, on radicalism, but I am told he was sorry rather than angry, and I think he had, perhaps, a few kindly recollections. His thinking progressed steadily to the right, and he won back the regard of the conservatives, who a few years before had hated the mention of his name. Though out of power, he kept his friends, both humble and exalted, through the charm of his personality and the fact of his good will. He had the most kindly and considerate manners in the world. If he was not a great man he was at least a great gentleman. He was extraordinarily courteous to the people who worked for him in a humble capacity. Of the night he died his man servant wrote, "He did not talk much. A little later he said, 'James, don't you think I might go to bed now?' That was his way of asking for a thing."

CHAPTER VIII

Reflections on the Rise and Fall
of the Progressive Party

In the preceding chapters I have outlined the history of the rise and fall of the Progressive party, beginning with the repudiation by Taft of the Roosevelt policies and ending with Roosevelt's final farewell to presidential ambitions. Whatever human interest such a narrative may have, there is implicit in it another interest that is perhaps sufficiently plain without pointing it out. Also, to those interested in the more profound currents of American life, the purely political thread running through the story will be subordinate to the economic thread. Both, however, are worth touching on briefly.

The lesson taught by the Progressive incident seems simply to be the familiar one: that a party cannot be founded without a definite cause, or solely upon the personality of an individual. To survive the hardships of the initial years, a new party must be a party of ideas, not of men. If the Progressive party had framed an issue that was at the same time clear and of large actual consequence, it would not have died upon the defection of its leader. On the contrary, it would have gone on and bred its own leaders. There is never a dearth of leadership if the cause is vital. The party, however, had an aspiration instead of an issue, a most creditable aspiration, but one for whose accomplishment its platform provided no understandable means. Social and industrial justice! The square deal! Destruction of invisible government! The dawn of a new day! But how realize these ends?

Notes are on p. 295.

The answer of the Progressives was, "Make Roosevelt president." And when it became clear that they could not do that, the Progressives disbanded and the country knew them no more.

It is true that the platform contained the Gary scheme of government regulation of monopoly and government price fixing. But, failing to stand up against the onslaughts of Wilson and Borah, this scheme in due time took its place as a fallacy borrowed from the shelf of Karl Marx, though neither Roosevelt nor the rest of us then recognized this as socialism. Roosevelt, though in his heart a socialist, did not have the least idea of what socialism meant.[1] The Steel Corporation people, on the other hand, irrespective of *isms,* put their price-fixing plank forward pragmatically, and simply as a means of getting themselves into a position where they would practically have a government guarantee that, because of their peculiar advantages in transportation, raw materials, and fuel, they would forever sell metal at four or five dollars a ton more profit than the manufacturers who possessed no such advantages.

In its platform, the Progressive party attempted to make an issue of "invisible government." "Behind the ostensible government sits enthroned an invisible government," it declared, "owing no allegiance and acknowledging no responsibility to the people." It asserted that, since the old parties had failed to destroy this invisible government, a new party was required to carry out this great purpose. As a matter of probability, if the new party had come into power, it would have been no less or more conducive to invisible government than the old parties, except that, on account of the influence of men like Gary, Perkins, and Munsey, and of the Colonel's debt to the Steel Corporation and some of the railroad leaders, the Progressive party might have proved as subject to invisible government as the other two.

How, then, is it possible ever to establish a party independent of the moneyed interests and devoted, to a reasonable extent, at least, to the public good will? How avoid an infiltration of strong, nonpopular interests such as has taken place in the Democratic and Republican parties, such as also took place in the Progressive group even before the party came into existence? There is only one possible way of accomplishing this seemingly impossible feat. It is to found the new party (at its very beginning) on a clear, understandable, and brief program which will be so obviously unacceptable to the interests that

227

carry on the invisible government that they will have nothing to do with it. The issue must be drawn so clearly between the public and the economic interests that prey upon the public that there will be no confusion. The issue will automatically assign to liberals and conservatives, to believers in democracy and to believers in autocracy, their respective positions. Moreover, a new party should be founded on a single issue, for if there is more than one, its strength will be divided. You may find in a gathering of a hundred intelligent people, we will say, fifty who believe in issue A and fifty who believe in issue B, but you will probably not find more than twenty-five, or perhaps ten, who believe in both A and B. The first mistake of the Progressive party was that it had no definite paramount issue. Its second was that it had a raft of little issues: federalism, equal suffrage, recall of judicial decisions in state courts, minimum wage, eight-hour day, six-day week, old-age and unemployment insurance, commission regulation of corporations doing interstate business, currency reform, physical valuation of railroads, government-owned and operated railroads in Alaska, protection of the farm or business by the tariff, repeal of the Canadian reciprocity act, graduated federal income and inheritance taxes, and so forth, and so forth. Nothing in the platform stood out as the central objective of the party. It was a conglomeration of unrelated parts, worthy enough in themselves but representing many divergent philosophies, and capable, as a whole, of driving away as many people as it attracted. In reality, with the exception of the small controlling group that wanted a party that would sponge out the Sherman law, nobody paid much attention to the platform. It was thrown together at the last minute, with Perkins and Munsey and the Colonel blue-penciling it from above, not because it mattered much what it contained but because, since the Colonel was going to run as the candidate of the new party, a platform was required, or at least was a conventional part of the proceedings. The theory on which the platform was framed was the old and silly one of putting a hook out for every variety of fish. There was no realization of the proven fact that a multiplicity of hooks drives away more fish than it attracts.

If the Colonel had said, "We will found a new party in order to repeal the Sherman law and facilitate and regulate industrial combination," that would have proved an issue. He could never have won in an election, at least not till he had conducted several campaigns of education and proved to the people that he was right, but he would have had a durable organization, for there were enough people, both capitalists and socialists, who believed in such a program to ensure that the party would last, at least for a while. An old party does not have to have a dominant issue after it survives the early stages, in which a dominant issue is necessary in order to get men to stick by it through early defeat, to sacrifice time and money, in short, to keep it alive. It can go along by its own momentum, through the force of tradition, habit, and party loyalty. It can be dull and noncommittal. It requires no flaming attributes to gain and hold its following. But a new party is a different matter. It can exist only through a sharp differentiation from the old party. Why should a man leave his old party and join a new one if the latter neither offers anything radically different nor proposes a new solution to some pressing problem? Why should a man pull up stakes and repudiate and break his old associations, unless something important is to eventuate? Roosevelt said, "Elect me, and something important will eventuate. You will have social and industrial justice, and so on." But the voter said, "How are you going to provide social and industrial justice? What is your technique for abolishing invisible government? You ask us to trust you and follow you. Why should we until we know not merely what you are going to do but how you are going to do it? Your intentions may be of the best, but how do we know that you will succeed in carrying them out? If you have a practical scheme, why do you hold it in the background?"

The Progressive party, then, failed because it had an aspiration and no issue, that is to say, no described, understandable program for transforming its reveries into facts. In the second place, it failed because, under the leadership of Theodore Roosevelt, it attempted the impossible feat of reaching a goal through means that were politically antagonistic to the goal. It was always one of the Colonel's pet theories that he could perform this miracle—make men serve ends despite the fact that they disbelieved in them. To found a popular party with the money of Perkins and Munsey and promote it through their efforts did not seem to Roosevelt an impossibility, but it proved one nevertheless. It must not be concluded that Roosevelt cared anything about the Steel Corporation or the steel men with whom, since 19[01], he had had such close intimacy;

229

nor should it be supposed that the theories which Gary and Perkins imposed on him meant a great deal to him. On the other hand, he realized with crystal clearness, having lost the support of the Standard Oil interests in the 1904 campaign, that he must retain that of the other dominant economic group, or as much of it as possible, if he were ever to make another successful dash for the White House. Therefore, when Roosevelt was asked to free himself from the burden which the presence of Steel Trust men and women in the Progressive organization had saddled on him, a request was being made that he was unable to comply with, even if he wanted to. Roosevelt was shrewd enough to know that with the hostility of both the oil and the steel interests, nothing but a miracle could land him in the White House, and if he did not reach the White House, manifestly his whole program of social and industrial justice, and the like, would never be realized. He would use Steel Trust money and profit by Steel Trust ability, but it would all be for a righteous end; and then again it was to be remembered that the Steel Trust was a good trust, not a bad one, and that therefore there was after all no antagonism, for him, between his ends and his means.

If Roosevelt had read the monograph published some years ago by Professor Holt of Harvard[2] on this particular question, he would, perhaps, never have fallen into this error. Holt, with a variety of examples, shows an unlikelihood amounting to almost impossibility of ever reaching an end by means which are inconsistent with it. The difficulty is that the means you employ gradually color and transform your end until the end has, to all intents and purposes, vanished.

There is something strange about the power that money has over us. If you take money from a man, it is not the baseness but the very decency in you that rises up against your following any course that will injure your benefactor. The average human soul revolts against taking something and making no return.

The third and most interesting subject for reflection in the story of the rise and fall of the Progressive party is the following. It is the illustration it provides of the way in which the process of accumulation of wealth by the politico-industrial means which I have already discussed in Chapter [I][3] seeks to protect itself. Here was an industro-financial organization making a great deal of money through a process that was forbidden both by law and by public opinion. Through its transportation differentials and ore supply advantages, it had reached a pinnacle where it could prevent competition and fix prices. This, by the way, is the much sought-after position that in the case of a producer of a major necessity of life opens the door to an almost limitless acquisition of wealth. This important achievement, conceived and built up by Mr. Morgan, was menaced first by the appearance of Theodore Roosevelt, and second by the probability in 1911 that a new party would come into the field. Its high degree of vulnerability came from the fact that both the suppression of competition and the fixing of prices were illegal and that, galled by extortion, the public was apt at any moment to raise a hue and cry which might, conceivably, result in the dissolution of the trust, an undesirable proceeding since it would naturally be accompanied by investigations that would lay bare its methods, or in the possible separation from the Steel Corporation of the railroads and their transportation facilities, which were the main sources of its monopoly power. How the danger was averted in Roosevelt's first and second terms has been described in Chapter —.[4] The story of the rise and fall of the Progressive party is, from one point of view, a narrative of how the Steel Corporation went about averting a second danger and turning the situation to its own account. Even before the party's birth, men whose philosophy, interests, and works were inconsistent with a desire to create a bona fide liberal force in politics appeared unaccountably. At the birth of the party they were on the scene and practically purchased it before it had given its first cry of life. They paid for its keep, cared for its education, and went to the length of robbing its platform in order to keep it from error. They carried it through years of vicissitude and when, as the 1916 election approached, it was evident that the new party could not itself win, they used it as an instrument and finally sacrificed and destroyed it in an effort to force upon the Republican party Theodore Roosevelt, a man whom they educated to their own way of thinking, persuading him openly to champion the Gary price-fixing proposal. . . .

Section III

APPENDIXES

APPENDIX I

Amos Pinchot on Henry Stimson
Confidential Memo, 1-19-32*

For my sins, I inherited Harry from Gifford, who was in college with him. We three belonged to the same secret society. Harry was in Yale '88, Gifford in '89, and myself in '97. Later we developed a common interest in the strenuous life generally, which was increased by our admiration for Roosevelt who, at the time I left college, had begun to boom his way into public life with a riding crop and a sporting rifle under his arm.

I graduated in 1897 and that summer, about the happiest of my life, Gifford and I spent in traveling through the West—Montana, Idaho, and Washington mostly—looking over forests, reporting on and photographing the great timber areas of the Northwest. We started out late in June, and after packing up through the Rockies into the Cascades and over to the coast, we wound up our first long hike at Seattle. There I took the train east for Kalispel, Jim Hill's home town (Gifford went off on some other business), and with a trapper friend, Jack Monroe, bought four horses for $56, packed over the main range of the Rockies in a blizzard, and rode down into Browning, Montana, just east of the divide, on, I think, the first or possibly the fifteenth day of September. It was there at Browning that Harry, his wife, and his sister met us. Gifford met us in a few days, and we took a magnificent trip across the foothills to the edge of the Rockies, and thence up through what is now Glacier Park, camping finally above the head of the upper Saint Mary's Lake, on the moraine of the great Jackson Glacier, and, I think, arriving back East early in November.

* According to his own account, Pinchot dictated this "memorandum, personal in character," on January 19, 1932. He sent it to Senator Hiram Johnson and subsequently to a few other friends. See AP to Hiram Johnson, January 19, 1932.

That was the first of three or four grand hunting excursions I took with Harry and Gifford. Harry and I became fast friends—at least I did. I liked Harry enormously, though he had his peculiarities, unrealized by me at this time, but clearer in retrospect, the chief of which was that he had continually to be killing some poor damned animal or other, and when he was out after grizzly bear, the whole camp was subordinated to his paramount object—a dead bear. Nobody could rest till he got it. Horses were killed for bait; the cook had to get up before daylight to get Harry's breakfast; and sit up late to rustle supper for him after he had come home, having watched at the sacrificial horse till dark—a tryst which the bear generally refused to keep, to the infinite sorrow of everyone in camp. Sometimes, if there was a moon, Harry would stay out till morning. It never entered our heads that any of us needed a bear but Harry. The whole trip centered on one thing—Harry's bear. In fact, we all became, so to speak, procurers for the securing of a nice fat grizzly for Henry L.

However, Harry had many real virtues. He was a tireless hunter, equable when he had his way—and we always gave him that. He was fond of Gifford and, I think, of me, quite unaffectedly.

After the Spanish war, in which I acquired some germs and a busted hip joint but little permanent glory, I went on a hunting trip in New Brunswick with Harry and Gifford by way of recuperating. This time the issue was moose, not bear. After Harry got his moose, we all relaxed and got ours, which was not difficult for hardy Nimrods like ourselves, as the slaughter of moose, like that of bear, is, with good guides and good rifles, about as difficult and dangerous as the killing of spring lambs in a well-equipped abattoir.

After that, my intimacy with Harry grew. He and Mabel, his wife, visited us in the country. Mabel—a childless, agreeable matron who worshipped Harry rather heavily—had been discovered by him among the dizziest peaks of New Haven, Connecticut, society. Her maiden name had been White, and she was related to some other White (I'm ashamed to say I can't remember to whom) who had been in the diplomatic service or a judge or something of the sort—it was quite important, however. Harry's talk was generally of guns, wild beasts, and tales of destroying the latter by means of the former. He liked to talk about government too, and was extremely public and civic-spirited—naturally, being a junior partner in Elihu Root's office. He was a good conservationist at that time, on account of Gifford, and because it was standard Rooseveltian doctrine. He truly admired Gifford, yet looked at him a little askance because of his radical ideas, and never ceased to hope that Gifford would cool down and be a good sterling Republican.

At that time, aside from his slightly unorthodox devotion to Roosevelt's rising star, Harry represented the essence of old New York musty conservatism, blended with a conviction that, as a gentlemanly college-bred man, whatever he did was, per se, the right thing to do. His father was an able, respectable, well-to-do family doctor. The Stimsons were well connected, unfashionable, self-respecting.

Soon Harry began to prosper through his law firm, which grew fast under the warming rays of Root's genius and the real ability of the younger men in the office, especially Harry and Bronson Winthrop. Harry bought a rather nice place down on Long Island, and some horses—he, of course, joined the militia as part of his civic duty, but had not had time to attend the Spanish-American War— and I used to go down and ride with him now and then. Some of the Long Island set took him up as a hopeful young man of affairs, of sound Republican persuasion, and made a good deal of him. Before long he became a typical country squire, modeled on the solid, unostentatious pattern, and learned to stand before the fireplace and flick his riding boots with his crop.

In 1906 Roosevelt, by now, next to Root, Harry's chief inspiration, appointed him United States Attorney at Root's request. He prosecuted the sugar trust in good shape and, with the assistance of the bankers, sent Charlie Morse to jail because he had defied the canons of sound piracy by robbing not only the public but his associates.

In 1909, Taft now being president, Harry had the first real test of his loyalty to the Republican party, whose ticket he had always voted piously, going to the polls vestryman-wise in black coat and silk hat. This test came as the result of Taft's conflict with Gifford in the so-called Pinchot-Ballinger controversy over the Alaska coal fields. Gifford and his assistants, Price and Shaw, were fired for objecting, over the heads of their immediate superiors, to the President's conclusion that Ballinger was without blame in the matter of granting certain suspected and very valuable coal claims to the

Morgan-Guggenheim syndicate. Glavis' head also fell. He had discovered and reported the coal fraud; and Taft and Wickersham, in order to sustain the decision against Glavis, antedated Wickersham's report on the case, so that it would appear to the Senate as though Taft had made it before deciding to dismiss Glavis. *Collier's Weekly,* that is to say, Norman Hapgood, at the instance of Louis Brandeis, took up the case in behalf of Glavis, whose counsel Brandeis became. The House insisted on voting its own members for the joint investigating committee, instead of having them appointed by Speaker Cannon. (This, as I remember, being the first overthrow of Cannon's iron rule.)

As the investigation approached, it became obvious that Gifford had to be represented by counsel. The fight was going to be particularly important, as well as bitter, and an able, courageous lawyer was sorely needed. So, after a great deal of discussion, it was decided to ask Harry Stimson to take the job, Harry apparently being well qualified, by his long friendship for Gifford, by his standing as a lawyer at the bar, as well as by his court experience during his term as United States Attorney for the Southern District of New York. So, at all events, we reasoned.

Gifford being busy in Washington preparing for his appearance before the committee, I was delegated to see Harry and persuade him to lead our forces. By this time I thought I knew Harry as well as almost anyone in the world. I had not only had years of close association with him and hunting experiences in the West and in Canada, such as bring people pretty close, but after my admission to the bar and while Mr. Root was in the Senate, I had occupied Mr. Root's room in the Root, Howard & Stimson offices, though not associated in any way with the firm.

After a long discussion of the case with Harry, he finally agreed to serve, and at once wrote and posted a letter to Gifford to that effect. I left his office in good spirits, and wired Gifford of the favorable result.

Our satisfaction was short-lived, for Harry at once changed his mind, and dispatched Felix Frankfurter, then a clerk in his office, to the Post Office Building, and had the letter fished out of the mail. Upon learning of his refusal, I went back and had another try at Harry, without result, except that, though he repeated his determination not to act himself, as a sop to Gifford he agreed to allow Frankfurter to serve as an assistant counsel with whomever Gifford should choose to represent him. This seemed a good deal better than nothing; but a few days later, Harry likewise revoked this decision on the ground that he could not afford to have a clerk in his office associated with a radical like Brandeis, even though Brandeis represented a different principal, namely Glavis. He then advised Gifford to engage George Wharton Pepper of Philadelphia. We sent for George and unfortunately did employ him, with the result that, to all intents and purposes, Gifford had no counsel; that is to say, no one that would stand against the Taft and Ballinger forces, Taft having become the central figure in the investigation because Brandeis had learned about the predating of the Wickersham brief report, and was making desperate efforts to prove it before the committee, to the consternation of the Republican administration.

When the committee got down to work, Harry's partner, Root, came forward as the main defender of the President and Ballinger, and chief opponent of Gifford, Glavis, and Brandeis. Pepper, while present in body, was absent in spirit, since he subsided whenever anything important was up, but, on the contrary, would do any amount of fine fighting over points of order and any sort of inconsequential matter. If it had not been for Louis' guts and skill, and Gifford's courage and character, the investigation, which ended in 1910, would, from our point of view, have collapsed.

Not long after the close of the Ballinger case, Taft, although hostile to almost all of Roosevelt's other friends, took Harry into his cabinet as Secretary of War, where Harry instituted several important reforms in the design of uniforms, puttee leggings, caps, cartridge belts, etc. He was as happy as possible under the shadow of Taft, just as he had been under Roosevelt and later became under Coolidge. King Theodore was dead. Long live King William! Always the same zealous public servant, with the best ideals and a simple faith in the party of Lincoln, Harry fitted equally well into any Republican administration that would take him, in exchange for his deserved reputation for respectability.

With the coming of Wilson, however, Harry went back to private life. But in 1915, with Root's protection, he became delegate at large to the New York Constitutional Convention, where Root, with

Harry's help, drafted a new charter of liberty for the people of their state, which was defeated by the largest vote ever polled up to that time in New York against any measure.

Harry, though I did not know it at the time, was mainly responsible for the budget section of the Root constitution, which a good many of us thought to be a pretty rotten section, in that it gave to the governor too much power to destroy the work of various bureaus and commissions by pinching out their budgets. Whether right or wrong in this, I organized a committee of fairly well-known men, including some outside of the state, such as Charley McCarthy of Wisconsin, and we hammered the constitution for all we were worth, to Harry's infinite exasperation. It was shortly after this that I met Harry in the washroom of the Downtown Club, and was chagrined by being practically cut dead by him. From which time on, he broke off all relations with me. Not realizing the obstinacy of his resentment, I, from time to time, made mild advances, but found that Harry, with heart of steel and face of flint, was opposed to me and all my works, despite the good old days of field and stream, and the mutual destruction of various unfortunate mammals of the North American continent. Meantime the European War mess came along, and my disbelief in the altruistic aims of our allies probably sank me still lower in Harry's esteem.

Now, back in '97, immediately upon my return from the West, where I had acquitted myself acceptably by Harry's standards, having slown [sic] the requisite number of dumb beasts by busting dumdum bullets into their interiors, Harry, as my guide, philosopher, and friend, put me up for membership in that splendid organization of America's foremost sportsmen and big-game shooters (of which Theodore Roosevelt, William Howard Taft, and other heroes of the Republican party were protagonists)—the Boone and Crockett Club. Under Harry's sponsorship, I was elected without a dissenting vote, despite the fact that, yielding to the pangs of hunger, the bacon having given out, Jack Monroe and I had bagged an elk and a mountain sheep in Idaho and Montana respectively (feeling rather lank on oatmeal) a day or so before the hunting season opened. The fact was that I didn't know the season was still shut, and also that under the circumstances I wouldn't, I fear, have given a damn anyhow.

Upon our entry into the Great War, I once more offended Henry

L. by forming a committee of ill-advised persons, including John P. White, president of the United Mine Workers of America, Professor Montagu of Columbia, Alexander McKelway, Harold Howland, Sidney Hillman, E. W. Scripps, and other undesirable citizens, for the purpose of suggesting to Congress that the war should be conducted as a pay-as-you-enter affair on the then incomprehensible English pattern, by heavy taxes on excess profits and large incomes, rather than by bond issues; and that the wealth of rich men should be conscripted as well as the persons of impecunious people unable to evade the draft.

It was just after the organization of this group that I received a communication from the executive committee of the Boone and Crockett Club, requesting me to resign on the ground that my views on the war and other matters were at variance from those of the rest of the members. This I refused to do, and was thereupon dropped from the club's rolls but not notified of this action. And when I accidentally learned of it later on, the secretary of the club, Mr. Kermit Roosevelt, informed me that I had been dropped for failure to pay my dues. Upon further inquiry, it was brought out, however, that no bills had been sent me because of the action of the committee in dropping me from the rolls.

Perhaps I am unjust in blaming the action of the Boone and Crockett Club on Harry, especially as the chairman of the executive committee at that period was Charles Stewart Davison (chairman as well of the American Defense Society), who had informally tried me for sedition, and who was then running around the city trying to get signatures on a petition to impeach Wilson on the ground of treason. Yet, as my sponsor and as an influential member of the inside ring of the club, which, like most clubs of its kind, was run by a clique, it would have been decent of Harry to have kept me in touch with what was going on and given me a chance to defend myself. However, upon my insisting that I should be either restored to membership or tried on formal charges, the executive committee chose the former course. And I am still a proud member of the organization, and pay my dues promptly out of spite.

In retrospect, Harry seems by no means a bad sort of person, but rather one of those not infrequent cases of a man who gets into machine business and machine politics before he has had much experience, and proceeds to accept current standards and make his way partly by ability, but also by a willingness to play, when necessary, a slightly off-color game—always in the interest of sweetness and light and good citizenship, be it clearly understood. Certainly he is himself sure that he is a highly scrupulous person and, in fact, is generally acknowledged to be so. And he would be awfully shocked at the suggestion that he had ever done an unfair or underhand or disloyal thing in his life—even to a bear. It must be remembered that, shortly after the age of puberty, Harry gave his mind and spirit into the keeping of Elihu Root, and learned from this expert the technique of always sticking close to the people who, whatever else may be said of them, are the possessors of money, influence, and power. The Root association, with all that grew from it, was therefore Harry's bad luck rather than his fault. Since 1906 Harry served every Republican president but Harding—Roosevelt, Taft, Coolidge, and Hoover, and served them pretty well, according to his lights. From 1906 to 1909, he adored Teddy, and got his job from him. When Theodore went out and broke with Taft, Harry switched to William, and loved him just as much as he had Theodore, and got a cabinet appointment. In 1915, there being neither a Teddy nor a Taft to hang on to, he went back home to the sheltering wing of Root, who set him up with his own furniture, so to speak, in New York State Republicanism. Then came the Democrats, and Harry was among the lean-outs all through Wilson's terms. So far as I know, he never fell for Harding and the Ohioans. Nor they for him. But he did not repudiate them either. Harding gone, he carried his sword to Coolidge's camp and secured two jobs there, one in Nicaragua and one in the Philippine Islands. And, having polished up the handle of the big front door for Cal, he next offered his services to Herbert, and has been a pillar of strength to him, as well as a very good friend to the Secretary of the Treasury. "Downtown," Harry has likewise followed the same successful but unprimrosed paths. After representing the railroads and traction companies, he saw the utility interests heaving in sight as the dominant industro-financial power—and promptly became a prominent utility lawyer, opposed the Walsh investigation, became counsel for the Georgia Power Company and other strong interests, and went around making speeches which were used as propaganda by the

National Electric Light Association. Now Harry seems to have edged into the protecting zone of Andy Mellon, and is earning favor, in an official capacity, by helping to secure the Colombian oil concession. On the whole, Harry's record has been consistent. He is a decent old-line Republican from New York, and he would be quite a decent man if he had had a little more nerve and enough sporting spirit to do something once in a while that he was not told to do by the rich, the good, and the great.

All of the foregoing is perhaps inconsequential. It is certainly so if it serves only to throw light on the progress, spiritual and temporal, of my erstwhile friend and companion, Henry L. Yet, in another way, it may have some importance. That is, if one looks at Harry not as Harry, but as a typical victim of that careerism which captures promising young college graduates and draws them, through their very virtues and abilities, into the dreary paths, where they gradually lose sense of those particular values which meant so much to them in an earlier, happier, and more hopeful phase. Harry, though a somewhat dull man, is a successful man, an able man, a rich man, and a fairly distinguished man, at least one holding a distinguished position. And yet he is the type of man that, with many good qualities and the best of intentions, has been effective in delivering this country to a materialism as sordid as any that exists in the world.

Amos Pinchot on Theodore Roosevelt*

I was never a friend of Roosevelt's. My association with him came about through his close friendship with my brother. My role was that of an admiring but relatively remote satellite, to whom he would occasionally entrust small commissions. . . . I talked with him frequently in those Progressive days, on political and economic matters. I do not flatter myself that he ever took my advice on any subject whatever, or was even in the slightest degree influenced by anything I ever said. But I certainly was always flattered by his notice of me. And a rare invitation to the White House or Sagamore Hill, a walk with his tennis cabinet through Rock Creek Park, or to the war college, was to me a great event.

Roosevelt was a kindly man. Lustily as he hated, his anger never lasted for long; and never did he harbor malice. He was always bubbling with the most infectious enthusiasms. The steam was always up, and the engine loudly chuffing. One's hopes were kindled by his certainty that he was doing big things. Even in his days of fading fame, ocean breezes seemed to sweep the stuffy *Outlook* office when the Colonel came in. And the "jolly" he royally dispensed to intimate friend and mere acquaintance indifferently, though overlavish and, eventually, largely mechanical, was enough to put heart in the most timorous of his followers.

I remember especially, as an example of the Colonel's methods in his later phase, a visit to his office in the early autumn of 1912. After a rather long talk on the subject of the switch some of us had made to him, after La Follette's breakdown at the Publishers Dinner at Philadelphia, I descended in the elevator, only to discover that it was pouring with rain, and that I had left my umbrella in the Colonel's room. Taking an upgoing car, and landing, I think, on the seventh floor, I proceeded along the hall, when the Colonel, doubling

* From the binder *Steel* (1930), pp. 122–24.

the corner at breakneck speed, spied me and seized me by the hand. The conversation we had just had, momentous as it had seemed to me, had evidently entirely faded from his memory under stress of more important matters, as had also the trifling fact that he had said good-by to me but three minutes before. He greeted me as a new-comer, wrung my hand, beat me on the shoulder with his clenched fist, and asked with great effusiveness what he could do for me. "Why nothing, thanks," I replied, a little dismayed. "I was just going back to your office to get my umbrella. It's raining."

"Bully!" cried the Colonel, "Bully! Splendid! Bully! Come in and see me again any time." And at every word he showed his powerful teeth, snapped his muscular jaws, and continued to thump me, until, wheeling suddenly, he hurtled off with a triumphant upward wave of the hand.

APPENDIX III

Amos Pinchot on Roosevelt and Price Regulation*

In 1912, like most of the men who fought and bled at Armageddon, my opinions on economic questions were far from clear or crystallized. In 1908, and again in 1911, Gary had voiced before congressional committees his hope that the government would step in and fix the price of steel. Gary had tutored Roosevelt into the belief that such a project was possible, and the fruit of his instruction, manifested first in his messages to Congress, was evidenced again in an article written by Roosevelt at the time when the Taft administration brought suit to dissolve the Steel Corporation, which was published in his autobiography as an appendix. Here Roosevelt, for the first time, I think, came out for federal control of prices, but he qualified it by adding obscurity by the phrase "just as in exceptional cases railway rates are now regulated,"† and further qualified it by the phrase‡ "although this is not a power to be used when it is possible to avoid it." At that time I had not studied the monopoly question. Indeed, with a very few exceptions, nobody had studied it in the light of the facts brought out by the congressional and state legislative hearings whose minutes, undisturbed by the college faculties of economics, were gathering dust on the least accessible shelves of our libraries. I did not realize the impossibility of arbitrarily fixing the price of products for a great industry like steel or oil production, nor did I understand that in the back of Gary's mind was the consideration that if the government were to fix the price of the steel rail, it would have to fix the same price for all companies in and out of the trust, and that a fair price for the independents would be several dollars more than a fair price for the trust, owing to the latter's advantages in ore supply and cheaper transportation. It seemed to me that there

* [AP's annotation]: Rough note for inclusion in *History of the Progressive Party.*
† Theodore Roosevelt, *An Autobiography*, 1916, p. 617.
‡ *Ibid.*, p. 619.

246

was something fundamentally wrong in a state of things in which a single group in an industry was able to destroy or browbeat its competitors and arbitrarily put prices at artificial levels. I realized that the Sherman law, applied as in the case of the Standard Oil dissolution, would not remedy the situation, but I did not realize then that the reason that dissolution was impotent was that it left the Rockefeller interests in control of the agencies of transportation. It did seem to me, however, that Roosevelt's price-fixing proposal had the same flaw that is contained in socialism, being founded on the hypothesis that in some way price regulators would be found, so honest, so wise, and so experienced, that they would fix prices with justice and profit to all parties. But at that time, it was not the absurdity of the Gary-Roosevelt conversion to the weakest point in the whole dogma of socialism, namely, arbitrary price-fixing by a commission, that made me apprehensive. It was two simple facts, (a) that he (Roosevelt) considered some monopolies good and others bad, and could not see that all monopoly was wrong; and (b) that he was willing to tolerate as leaders in our new party men who were on the record opposed to almost every tenet of social justice which the Colonel professed.

APPENDIX IV

Amos Pinchot on George Perkins

May 23rd, 1914.

To Senator Joseph M. Dixon and the Members of the Progressive National Committee.

Gentlemen:

A situation exists within the Progressive Party which must be terminated before it can command general popular support.

The situation I refer to is this: (1) An element in our party leadership, headed by Mr. George W. Perkins, the present Chairman of the National Executive Committee, favors the protection of private monopoly in American industry, and, since the party's formation, has been taking active steps to commit the party to that policy. (2) The Chairman of our Executive Committee is actively opposed to the recognition of labor's right to organize and deal with capital through labor unions, and has frequently gone on record to this effect. Our party is therefore subject to the charge that it is lukewarm, or even antagonistic, to the interests of organized wage earners.

On both these subjects the Progressive Party has placed itself positively and definitely on record in opposition to Mr. Perkins. But the fact that the executive leader and recognized spokesman of the party is an active member of the governing committees of the Steel Corporation and International Harvester Company, the two great monopolies which have succeeded most completely in exploiting the public and crushing organized labor, has led to a natural and unfortunate confusion in the public mind.

Through the Progressive Party's official bulletin, through public speeches and interviews, and in pamphlets, printed as Progressive Party literature and distributed from the party's headquarters in New York and Washington, Mr. Perkins has conducted an extensive pro-trust propaganda calculated to convince the party and the public that the trusts are useful and sacred institutions; that those who attack them are bent upon the destruction of all healthy industry on a large scale, and finally, that the Progressive Party fully agrees with him in these views. The result is that we have been placed in a false and fatal position. Our sincerity has been attacked. Our energy is largely expended in defending ourselves. And we are constantly under the embarrassing necessity of explaining that the party stands for something directly contrary to that which the spokesman and executive leader says it stands for.

Mr. Perkins' pro-trust activity within the Progressive Party began soon after the party's formation. It has continued until the present time.

During the Progressive Convention at Chicago in 1912, Mr. Perkins vigorously opposed putting any endorsement or approval of the Sherman Law in the Progressive Platform. The Resolutions Committee, however, took the opposite view and inserted a clause in the trust plank endorsing the Sherman Law and recommending that it should be strengthened.

It is true that the Sherman Law, as now interpreted, is by no means a perfect agency for solving the trust problem. It is true that it has generally been used to attack the results instead of the causes of monopoly. But however imperfect the Sherman Law may be considered, it is at present the only law on the statute books which offers the slightest check to the power of great monopolies in American industry. Without it, both the consuming public and the independent business concern would be far more at the mercy of our great industrial combinations than they are to-day. Our party cannot afford to repudiate this law.

If the clause referred to above had been left out of the trust plank and the Progressives had won in 1912, no matter what stand our individual candidates might have taken, we would not have been committed, as a party, either to the enforcement of the Sherman Law, or to an anti-monopoly policy.

Monopolists all over the country are claiming that the trusts, with their huge concentration and enormous power, are necessary for economy and efficiency in production. Those opposed to monopoly, on the other hand, believe that enormous companies, such as the United States Steel Corporation and the International Harvester Company, which are combinations of already large consolidations, are neither economical nor efficient. We believe that these great combinations were formed, not at all in order to attain economy and efficiency, but simply to prevent competition, fix prices and make exorbitant profits out of the consuming public. We are not opposed to production on a large scale, but we are utterly opposed to monopoly and extortion. We hold that the size of industrial corporations should be determined by efficiency; and the only way to determine what size produces efficiency is by competition. This, I believe, is the position of the public and of the vast majority of the Progressive Party.

Mr. Perkins, in his fight against the endorsement of the Sherman Law in our platform, represented the demand of America's monopoly group. The Resolutions Committee, on the other hand, took the position of the party and the public.

A trust plank, including a clause relating to the Sherman Law, was accordingly passed by the Resolutions Committee. It was read to and adopted by the convention. Mr. Perkins and myself were both in the convention hall when it was read and adopted. But this clause was cut from the version of the platform furnished to the press associations and omitted from the copies of the platform which were printed and issued in large quantities, during the campaign, from Progressive Headquarters.

I am assured on the best authority that those responsible for cutting the clause referring to the Sherman Law from the platform did so under the impression that it had never been adopted by the Resolutions Committee, and that it was read to the convention by mistake. I do not question this statement. I do not say that Mr. Perkins had anything to do with this expurgation, or with giving the gentlemen who directed it the impression that the clause was read to the convention by mistake. But I do say that, if it had not been for Mr. Perkins' fight against the Sherman Law, while the platform was being drawn, there would have been no misunderstanding, and the party would never have been led into a false and indefensible position.

Later on, at my insistence, and after considerable controversy, the missing clause was restored to the platform. This was done in December, 1912, and January, 1913. It is all a matter of party history.

250

Shortly after the Progressive Party was formed, in August, 1912, the National Committee began to publish a party organ called "The Progressive Bulletin." Mr. Perkins has been in direct control of the Bulletin and has personally directed its publication and policy. It has been consistently and, I think, unwisely used as Mr. Perkins' personal organ: to defend the trusts, to attack the Sherman Law, and to glorify the two great monopolies of which Mr. Perkins is respectively a director and a member of the finance, or governing, committee. And finally, it has been regularly employed to ram home the conception that our party did not endorse the Sherman Law, and is hostile to it.

The first issue of the Bulletin was on September 1, 1912. It contained a full-page editorial, reprinted from a daily paper which had offered us the use of its columns, entitled: "George W. Perkins and the Roosevelt Progressive Party." This editorial was also printed in leaflet form and distributed from headquarters as Progressive campaign literature. It read in part as follows:

The country needs the work of such men as E. H. Harriman, powerful enough and strong enough to build thousands upon thousands of miles of railroad in a life that ended too soon. The country needs the imagination and power of such men as J. Pierpont Morgan, wasting his energies now in the accumulation of money that does him no good, and spending the money in the accumulation of collections that will do him no good—although they may be useful to the country in the future. . . . One such man as George Perkins, giving to the business of the people the energy and capacity that he has given to private business undertakings, would be a good, new thing in politics and a useful man in government. . . . Mr. Perkins directs the financial and practical management of the Roosevelt Party—luckily for the party.

This issue of the Bulletin also contains a voluminous digest of the Progressive platform, which omits all reference to the clause endorsing the Sherman Law and gives regulation as our sole policy in regard to the trusts.

In the next issue, September 16th, there appeared another similar digest of the Progressive Platform omitting reference to the missing clause.

In the issue of September 23rd was printed an editorial condemning the Sherman Law. It is entitled "The Only Honest Plank on Trusts," and is in part as follows:

The new party is the only one that has a single intelligent and honest word to say upon the trust problem. . . . The plank that Mr. Bryan wrote goes back of even the Sherman Law, and rests on the naive faith that the way out of the difficulty lies in "busting" everything of size. . . . Both these platforms (the old parties' platforms) rely upon compelling competition; and no policy which relies upon that will bring us one step nearer to an actual grapple with the trust problem. . . . The Progressive Party begins with the sane belief—backed by the economic experience of the whole world for a full generation—that competition may be harmful and combination salutary. It is only from this point of view that any solution of the trust problem will ever be found.

On September 30th an editorial appeared entitled: "Equal Justice vs. 'Rats.' The Difference Between the Progressive Attitude Toward Trust Control and that of Governor Wilson. . . . The following is the Progressive Party's plank on trust control." (There is then quoted the incomplete trust plank.) The editorial concludes, "If Governor Wilson has anything of a constructive nature to suggest, now is the time for him to do it. This is no time for evasion."

In the same issue there is published a reprint of Mr. Perkins' article in the *Saturday Evening Post,* in which he scores the Sherman Law, and ends with the following:

If anybody wants to know why the country is torn asunder politically let him contemplate what has happened, and he will no longer be filled with wonderment, but he will be filled with amazement that such colossal blundering can take place in such an enlightened country as ours is supposed to be.

Somebody in this country is making a colossal mistake. Somebody is woefully wrong. Is it the theoretical politician, or the practical business man? Did our Federal Government make a mistake in adopting a policy of federal regulation with our banks and railroads, or is it making a mistake in not adopting a similar policy with our interstate industries? Did it make a mistake in eliminating ruthless competition among railroads, or is it making a mistake in enforcing ruthless competition among industrials?

The third page of the Bulletin of October 3rd contains a full-page article by Mr. Perkins, entitled "Where Does Mr. Wilson Stand on Trusts?" Mr. Perkins printed this article first in the *New York Evening Journal*. It is a discussion of the comparative merits of the Democratic and Progressive trust programs. It adroitly leads the reader to suppose that the Progressive Party is hostile to the Sherman Law, and that its only policy toward the trusts is one of protection and control.

The Bulletin of October 14th contains a double-page article quoting professors and political economists against attacking the trusts, and in favor of preserving and regulating them.

In the same issue appears a half-page article entitled, "Perkins to Bryan," being a reprint of a letter written by Mr. Perkins to Mr. Bryan, scoring the Sherman Law and holding up to scorn the attempts of the last administration to enforce it.

At about this time a very vigorous protest was made against Mr. Perkins' pro-trust activities, and a halt was called. Then came the election, after which the Bulletin devoted itself for a while to matters of party organization and to criticisms of the administration in power. But in June, 1913, the pro-trust propaganda was resumed. And a column article appeared entitled: "Putting Social and Industrial Justice into Practice."

At least half a dozen of the important "human welfare" planks of the Progressive national platform appear as accomplished actualities in the annual report of the International Harvester Company. . . .

The fact lends unusual human interest to the dry-looking, drab-covered pamphlet which set forth in serried array the statistics and accomplishments for 1912, of the one American "trust" which lays fair claim to the name of the most decent of them all.

Not that the Harvester Company tries to exploit its "social welfare" advances. The story of these reforms is set down in the general summary as matter-of-factly as any conservative director could desire.

It then goes on to quote the Harvester Company's report in regard to its humane treatment of its employees, its anti-tuberculosis work, etc.

253

Here we have almost half a million dollars spent for purposes that would have been considered, in not so ancient a past, as quite outside the province of the hard-headed, individualistic business man, who was "not in business for his health"—or that of his employees.

The report marks a distinct social advance. It must win for the International Harvester Company a large measure of that respect which the American public is always ready to bestow on that class of "big business" which has the enlightenment to keep step with the march of the times.

In the July number there followed an article showing what a blessing the Standard Oil Company has been to the people of Missouri.

Missouri's experience with the trust problem. . . . "Busted" Standard Oil instead of regulating it and now seeks to undo the work. Finds she used wrong remedy. Ousting the trust punished her own people, so now she wants the Standard back under regulation and control. . . . The proposition of regulating or "busting" the trusts has been put squarely up to the people of Missouri in the litigation growing out of the Standard Oil ouster suit. The verdict of the people was "regulate." . . . Sentiment even among the farmers is strong for the company to remain.

The article explains how the application of the Sherman Law worked a hardship on the Missourians.

These are some instances in which Mr. Perkins has used the Progressive Bulletin in pro-trust propaganda work, but I find that at the same time he is distributing very widely from party headquarters, and under the party's emblem, a large number of pamphlets designed to accomplish the same end, as well as to defend his personal reputation. For instance, a pamphlet entitled: "A Constructive Suggestion. Address by George W. Perkins, Chamber of Commerce, Youngstown, Ohio." In this pamphlet Mr. Perkins says that the Sherman Law was conceived in a spirit of oppression, that it is prohibitive, and that it lends itself to destruction. He points out that there is little use in attacking trusts, and recommends, as the true trust remedy, merely Federal incorporation and commission supervision. If the Government should adopt a policy in consonance with Mr. Perkins' Youngstown address, our trusts would receive governmental authority to continue in their present course of oppressing industry, fixing prices and over-charging the public.

During the presidential campaign, Mr. Perkins had printed and distributed in large quantities a remarkable pamphlet entitled: "Is Perkins Honest?" I am informed by a Progressive leader in Colorado that when Colorado headquarters wired Mr. Perkins for Progressive literature, he responded by sending large crates containing this pamphlet. It is in part as follows:

It was the night before Albert J. Beveridge delivered his keynote speech of the new political crusade. He asked Col. Roosevelt, George W. Perkins and a few other leaders to come to his room and hear him read the manuscript. The reading proceeded in tense silence. Beveridge was evidently laboring under emotion, and Col. Roosevelt was himself visibly moved. But on George W. Perkins' cheeks the tears were coursing—and when Beveridge came to those passages in which he outlined the course of justice for the men who make the nation, Perkins, with a sob he could not stifle, hastily left the room and paced the corridors to gain his self-control. . . . He saw that the world of business was built on what he calls the three M's—Men, Money, and Machinery. . . . His gospel was that justice promotes peace, and peace promotes prosperity, and that the workman's prosperity was necessary to the business men's prosperity. He put loyalty on the books as a commodity no concern could continue without. He went to the Morgans, and the Garys, and the Rockefellers, and the McCormicks and showed them that any great business was a partnership between directors and workmen, and that the denial of that partnership was what caused all the industrial trouble of the times. He tried to demonstrate to them that the fostering of the spirit of partnership in a substantial way, by making it a partnership in profits as well as work, was one of the foremost parts of any business. In time, he convinced them, and now his schemes are all at work, but only in those few factories where he was personally interested. . . . So he left the banking firm of J. Pierpont Morgan. It was said at the time there was some difference between him and Mr. Morgan. Undoubtedly there was. This able younger man, always planning something for the first M of business, was sometimes uncomfortable to have about. When Perkins left he gave out a statement to the effect that his next job would be the solution of industrial problems, the bringing in of a better understanding and a more equitable distribution of the good things produced equally by labor and capital. . . . Mr. Perkins wants the American business man to do the

255

square thing without having it forced upon him. He wants him to see that the square deal is not business loss but business gain. He wants, in his own phrase, "to peopleize" industry. It is brotherhood brought down to the pay envelope. . . . Perkins is, therefore, a prophet to the rich. Other men are able to tell the masses what they ought to have. But Perkins, with his proved business ability, his immense practical experience, his complete knowledge of the situation from the rich man's point of view, is able to tell the captains of industry what they ought to do to be saved. . . . These are the facts of his life, as interpreted by himself, and as verified by his acts. They may serve to answer the question, "Is Perkins Honest?"

Apropos of this pamphlet Mr. Perkins has frequently assured the public that the Steel Corporation has not crushed labor organizations. He says it has merely persuaded the men that it is better for them not to organize, inasmuch as it is the policy of the company to make each employee a partner and "bring down brotherhood to the pay envelope." In spite of this we find that, in 1902, the Corporation organized a supply store's company to provide its employees with various necessities of life. I do not know how much actual money was put into this company, but it was capitalized at $500,000. I also do not know how much, if anything, the company put back in the business after paying dividends. The first year, 1903, it did not pay anything at all. In 1904, it paid in dividends $250,000; in 1905, $405,000; in 1906, $805,000; in 1907, $500,000; in 1908, $320,000; in 1909, $440,000; and in 1910, $520,000, or 104 per cent on its capitalization. These earnings taken out of the wages of the employees of the corporation seem a little excessive and suggest inconsistency with the co-operative brotherhood theory.

Speaking of labor conditions in the Steel Corporation, Mr. Louis D. Brandeis (at about the same time that Mr. Perkins circulated the pamphlet above quoted) gave the following testimony before the Stanley Committee:

I say these are conditions which have driven out American labor, and the most important thing I want to impress upon you in regard to that is not merely the long hours and the low wages, but it is that it has been and is attended with conditions of repression, the like of which you cannot find, I believe, this side of Russia.

Mr. Brandeis might have included the Harvester Trust in this statement, for, according to the report of the New York Factory Commission, conditions of employment in its plant have been very similar to those in the Steel Corporation.

Mr. John Fitch, who is a man of moderate expression, as well as America's foremost authority on labor conditions in the steel industry, goes further than Mr. Brandeis.

I wish (said Mr. Fitch in his sworn testimony) to reiterate my statement that the Steel Corporation wields a power such as to make it a menace to the well being and peace of the people. I have talked with many of their employees, and I know that their attitude toward labor is creating bitterness in all parts of the country. . . . They have carried the matter beyond the limits of justice. When the employee tries to protest, he is discharged for protesting. After awhile, the resentment will grow so keen and so bitter that something will happen. I do not know just what that will be. But it is holding men down; it is a denial to men of the right to express themselves, and to have something to say about the conditions under which they live and work, that creates the greatest sort of resentment in the community.

In fact, Mr. Fitch describes a condition similar to that which has recently prevailed in the properties of the Colorado Fuel and Iron Company.

Mr. Fitch also refers to the elaborate system of espionage by which the Steel Corporation effectively discourages complaints and even free conversation in regard to the labor conditions under which its employees live. He gives cases where men have been discharged on the mere suspicion of attempting organization. And he explains how the system of pensions and bonuses, conditioned upon many years of service without protest, is used to prevent the employees from protesting against injustice. The last annual report of the Steel Corporation shows that it works over fifty thousand of its men twelve hours a day.

During the campaign Mr. Perkins also issued, as Progressive Party literature, a pamphlet explaining the contribution of $48,500 which he made to the Republican National Committee in 1904, out of funds of the New York Life Insurance Company. In fact, the number of pamphlets written by Mr. Perkins and his associates, largely in defense of Mr. Perkins and of big business, and issued as Progressive

Party literature, seems to have been almost as great as those containing the utterances of Col. Roosevelt and Governor Johnson combined.

From time to time, since he has been Chairman of the Executive Committee, Mr. Perkins has had occasion to make speeches and give out newspaper statements on various industrial questions. On Lincoln's birthday of last year, Mr. Perkins was the principal speaker at a dinner of five hundred given by the Los Angeles Chamber of Commerce. The subject of his address was, "Our Commercial Future." In that speech, he declared that the only way to prevent the existence of trusts was to prohibit modern inventions; that competition in American industry was unnecessary; that the meagre wages and long hours of women and the prevalence of sweat shop conditions were all due to the evil principle of competition, and that the only remedy for these things was to do away with competition. He urged that the Chamber of Commerce of Los Angeles should organize, mix in politics, and use pressure on Congress to further the interests of big business.

In Chicago, on June 25th, during the hearings of the Government suit against the International Harvester Company, Mr. Perkins expressed his indignation at the attitude of the Federal authorities toward the Harvester Trust. He said that the company was being "persecuted," and that, in Canada, people were being knighted by the King of England for doing the same thing that he, Mr. Perkins, had done in building up the Harvester Company.

"One would think," he declared, "from the way we have been persecuted by the Government, that wherever we went blight followed, but the fact is that just the contrary has happened. Wherever we have gone the land has bloomed."

On Lincoln's birthday of this year, Mr. Perkins spoke at the Progressive Party banquet in this city. His speech has been published in pamphlet form together with those of Miss Jane Addams, Mr. John M. Parker and Mr. Everett Colby, and sent out in large quantities from Progressive Headquarters, Forty-second Street Building, New York. On this occasion his address was largely glorification of big business, a reproof to those who criticize the trusts and an appeal to the people of the United States to lend a deaf ear to such criticism.

Under date of March 7th, 1914, there is being issued from the

Progressive Headquarters in New York and Washington, a five-column reprint of Mr. Perkins' recent controversy with Senator Borah on the monopoly question. In this document, Mr. Perkins defends the Harvester Trust and says that the farmers all love it; that it is not a monopoly; that to attack the Steel Corporation successfully would be a national calamity; that the Steel Corporation is a model employer of labor, etc.

The above may furnish some idea of how Mr. Perkins has made use of his position in the party, and his control of party machinery, in furthering the interest of private industrial monopoly.

It is only fair to Mr. Perkins to say that, while he has carried on his pro-trust propaganda from headquarters, he has, at the same time, positively assured the public that he is firmly opposed to monopoly. He says that trusts such as he is interested in are good trusts and not monopolies. He asserts that while such trusts have fortunately succeeded in preventing competition they have nevertheless gained no monopoly power. That the era of competition is happily past and that monopoly has not taken its place is Mr. Perkins' reassuring statement to the consumer. But what Mr. Perkins or Judge Gary would say if asked how the steel industry, or any other industry, can proceed without the presence of either competition or monopoly, it is difficult to imagine.

Mr. Perkins denies that the Steel Corporation is an industrial monopoly. He is fond of saying that the Steel Corporation is a monopoly in nothing but brains. Let us examine the facts.

The Steel Corporation, through its unscrupulous and illegal practices, its control of iron ore and coal, its powerful influence over the railroads which are steel industry's customers, and, above all, through its immense profits in hauling the ore of so-called independent companies over its own railroads, has been able to crush competition and to fix prices for practically the whole industry. Under such conditions and with these enormous railroad profits rolling into the Steel Corporation's treasury, no independent producer dares to attempt real competition. Every steel man knows this and Mr. Gary himself and Mr. Temple have virtually admitted it in their sworn testimony.

According to the very able report of Mr. Farquhar J. McRae, the Steel Corporation has paid over one hundred and sixty million dollars in commissions to insiders since its organization, or not far from fifty per cent. of the total value of its assets. In spite of this, it has earned and paid dividends on its one thousand millions of watered stock. In 1908, Mr. Gary admitted on the stand that a thousand millions of the then value of the United States Steel Corporation consisted in capitalized profits. Mr. McRae informs us that the net earnings of the Steel Corporation for nine years, January 1st, 1902, to December 31st, 1910, were $1,029,685,389.28, or an average of $13 a ton upon sales to outside customers, or a net profit of forty per cent. on the actual cost of production on sales to outside customers. In 1908, Mr. Jesse F. Orton, Secretary of the Tariff Reform Committee of the Reform Club of New York, put the figure at fifty-four per cent. This has not been done by efficiency. Its great size has prevented high efficiency in the Steel Corporation. It has been done by killing competition, controlling prices and rigging the market.

The lowest official estimate of the Corporation's earnings I have ever heard was that of Herbert Knox Smith. He said it netted a little over twelve per cent. on its assets. But this estimate was founded on figures voluntarily offered by the Steel Corporation itself, before the lid was removed by the Congressional Investigation of 1912. It cost the Steel Corporation an immense sum to collect and furnish the Government with these figures. This was done in order to ward off a Government suit.

I understand that the International Harvester Company's earnings are at least as large as those of the Steel Corporation. Both corporations are monopolies. Both use their monopoly power mercilessly for purposes of oppression and extortion. If these corporations are not monopolies, there are not and never have been monopolies in the United States.

I do not for a moment question Mr. Perkins' sincerity in defending the trusts. I do not in the least doubt that Mr. Perkins believes it his sacred duty to swing the nation into accord with the trusts, and the Progressive Party into the monopoly camp, or the "efficient business" camp, as he would call it. I do not say that I am right and Mr. Perkins is wrong about monopoly, or that the future may not show that the Steel Trust, with its destruction of competition, its gigantic monopoly of profits and its denial of the rights and liberties of its army of dependents, may not be a good thing for this country. But I do say, that even if an angel with a fiery sword should descend from Heaven at this time, and try to persuade the people of the United States to love the trusts and vote for those who protect them, he would make very little headway before election day—even with the assistance of Mr. Perkins' pamphlets.

When, a year and a half ago, a few of us talked of making a public protest against Mr. Perkins' remaining Chairman of the Executive Committee of the party, we were prevented by the consideration that to accept Mr. Perkins' money and industry during the campaign, and then turn upon him as soon as we were defeated, would be ungrateful and unfair. But to wait until after the fall election now—until after Mr. Perkins has once more given us the benefit of his efforts and his financial support, and then to make this protest—would be still more unfair. It would be as unfair to Mr. Perkins as to the Progressive Party. If we are ever to protest against trust leadership in the Progressive Party, we must do it now.

To-day a crisis has been reached in the affairs of the Progressive Party. We are approaching an election which will, in a large measure, decide whether we are to exist as a separate political organization. We must prepare our party for action and rid ourselves of all unnecesssary handicaps.

In spite of anything Mr. Perkins may say, and in spite of the Steel Corporation's extensive whitewashing campaign, carried on in newspapers and magazines which it owns or influences, America's industrial monopolies are very cordially hated by the general public. No person or party that stands for the perpetuation of these monopolies can reasonably hope for wide public support. No party ought to succeed which is not willing to take the public's side in the fight against monopoly exploitation.

Moreover, practically all the wage-earners working in the industrial plants in the United States know the labor records of the Steel and Harvester trusts as well as Mr. Brandeis and Mr. Fitch know them. They know that Mr. Perkins' name has been repeatedly signed to resolutions of the Steel Corporation declaring against organization within its plants. They are aware that Mr. Perkins' views on the most critical issues between capital and organized labor coincide closely with those of Mr. John D. Rockefeller, Jr.

When the Progressive Party was organized, it was joined by thousands of earnest men and women who had never taken an active interest in politics before. They believed that, in the Progressive Party, they had at last found a home for their hopes and efforts. They believed that they had finally discovered a party which was uninfluenced by organized wealth and free to fight for the rights of the average citizen. They saw in the Progressive Party an instrument to accomplish a more equal distribution of the things of the world—a force which, in the eternal struggle between privilege and the people, would stand frankly on the people's side.

In a party organized on such a plane, in a party which owes its existence to a revolt against the domination of money in the old parties, in a party pledged to social and industrial justice and claiming to be the party of the under-dog, leadership borrowed from the directorates of America's most sordid and hated trusts, and financial support derived from the same sources, is more than unfortunate. To talk against monopoly, to place the words "Social and Industrial Justice" upon our banner, and then to hand over this banner to a man who has been monopoly's ardent supporter and one of the most distinguished opponents of social and industrial justice that our generation has produced, is, in my opinion, a handicap to the party, and a fraud on the public. It is also highly and destructively ridiculous.

If we do not immediately take steps to remedy this situation—if we do not free the party from trust leadership and trust support, one of two things will inevitably happen: either the Progressive Party will dwindle rapidly and die for lack of popular support, or else our politicians will mellifluously declare that the Republican Party has been purged of all iniquity; that it has now accepted progressivism; that, after all, not names but principles count; that patriotism is above partisanship, etc., etc., etc. We will be informed, in short, that our first duty to the nation is to oust the Democrats and get in power ourselves, and that the only way to do this is to amalgamate with the "purged" Republicans, i.e., go out of business as a separate party, and become a part of the organization which we have recently denounced so bitterly.

Either of these alternatives will equally mark the extinction of the Progressive Party. Either of them will mean that the great body of earnest and enthusiastic men and women, who joined our party with high hopes, will be dispersed, discouraged, and forever rendered cynical of any political movement which purports to stand for democracy and economic justice.

Our party cannot exist as a party of balanced phrases and equivocations. It cannot stand on the one hand with the people, and on the other hand with the forces that oppress the people. It cannot shout for industrial justice in one breath, and tolerate monopoly exploitation in the next. There is little room to-day in American politics for parties, or individuals, who attempt to be all things to all men. Our party must take sides in the struggle between democracy and privilege—and we must make it clear as sunlight which side we have taken.

Only by repudiating trust leadership and trust support can we gain the confidence of the public, or put the party in a position where it will be possible for us to stand on the public's side in the great economic questions, which are more and more becoming the only political questions that people are equally interested in. However our personal regard for Mr. Perkins may make such a step regrettable, we must, nevertheless, place the party's strength and usefulness above all personal considerations.

I think I am warranted in saying to you gentlemen of the National Committee that, in view of these facts and in view of the approaching elections, the rank and file and a large majority of the leaders of the party feel that Mr. Perkins' resignation as Chairman of the Executive Committee is necessary. I am sure that, upon reflection, you will agree, as will Mr. Perkins himself, that the success of the party demands such action immediately.

Very sincerely yours,

Amos Pinchot

Section IV

N O T E S

BIOGRAPHICAL INTRODUCTION*

[1] AP, Note, "Progressive Party," [p. 1].

[2] AP, *What's the Matter with America,* [1912], p. 28.

[3] Gifford Pinchot, *Breaking New Ground* (1947), p. 2.

[4] GP, "James Pinchot," July 10, 1936. Gifford Pinchot Papers.

[5] Gifford Pinchot, *op. cit.,* p. 90. Also, Mrs. A. R. E. Pinchot to the author.

[6] Edith Wharton, *A Backward Glance* (1934), pp. 54–55. See also Oswald Garrison Villard, *Fighting Years* (1939), pp. 24–25.

[7] "Notes on a talk with Mr. [E. T.] Riviere" [about Gifford Pinchot, 1914].

[8] AP, Notebook, "Words and Phrases"; hereafter called "Words and Phrases."

[9] This is a random selection from "Words and Phrases" and includes only a few of the lot.

[10] See Appendix I.

[11] St. Louis *Globe-Democrat,* December 13, 1919.

[12] *What's the Matter with America,* p. 28.

[13] AP to GP, February 15, [19]08.

[14] AP, unpublished fragment, probably part of an early draft of "A Letter to the County Chairman . . . Amos Pinchot's Explanation of the Failure of Good Government," [1913].

[15] See Appendix I.

[16] Gifford Pinchot, *op. cit.,* pp. 442, 470.

[17] "Words and Phrases."

[18] George Rublee to the author; Roger Baldwin to the author; Fola La Follette to the author; John Haynes Holmes to the author.

[19] AP to George Wharton Pepper, May 3, 1910.

[20] *Ibid.* For Senator Pepper's attitude toward the case, see his autobiography, *Philadelphia Lawyer,* pp. 82–89.

* Where manuscripts are cited, I have used AP for Amos Pinchot and GP for Gifford Pinchot. Where I have not listed the collection, the source is the Amos Pinchot Papers.

[21] *Brief on the Cunningham Coal Entries in Alaska* [,] *Submitted to the President in Behalf of Mr. Gifford Pinchot*, [p. 1].

[22] AP to Hiram Johnson, October 5, 1912.

[23] Louis D. Brandeis to Amos Pinchot, September 5, 1911. Cited in Alpheus Mason, *Brandeis: A Free Man's Life* (1946), pp. 287–88.

[24] George Rublee became one of the first commissioners of the Federal Trade Commission and a member of the War Shipping Board in World War I.

[25] George Rublee to the author.

[26] A highly selective list includes James Garfield, Walter Fisher, E. W. Scripps, Gilson Gardner, Harold L. Ickes, Medill McCormick, Ben Lindsey, Edward P. Costigan, Hiram Johnson, William Kent, and Francis J. Heney.

[27] For Pinchot's own comments on La Follette, see *History*, Chapter IV.

[28] AP to W. Kirkpatrick Brice, September 1, 1910.

[29] *Ibid.*

[30] *Ibid.*

[31] AP to George E. Thompson, August 31, 1910.

[32] AP to W. Kirkpatrick Brice, September 1, 1910.

[33] AP to GP, September 1, 1910.

[34] AP to Mrs. James W. Pinchot, September 1, 1910.

[35] AP to GP, September 1, 1910.

[36] AP to Mrs. James W. Pinchot, September 1, 1910.

[37] AP to GP, January 2, 1911.

[38] AP to W. Kirkpatrick Brice, September 1, 1910.

[39] Robert Marion La Follette, *La Follette's Autobiography* (1911, 1913), p. 494; hereafter called *Autobiography*.

[40] AP to W. Kirkpatrick Brice, September 1, 1910.

[41] *McClure's Magazine*, XXXV (September 1910), 581–90.

[42] W. B. Colver to AP, September 3, 1910.

[43] J. M. Nelles to AP, April 1, 1911; see also J. M. Nelles to Medill McCormick, August 23, 1911.

[44] Albert J. Beveridge to AP, September 28, 1910.

[45] GP to Mrs. James W. Pinchot, September 6, 1910.

[46] Miss Augusta T. Daniel to AP, August 27, 1912.

[47] Binder *Steel*, chap. i, p. 50.

[48] AP to GP, September 1, 1910.

[49] La Follette, *Autobiography*, p. 494.

[50] *Ibid.*, p. 522. Italics mine.

[51] AP to GP, March 21, 1911.

[52] AP to Charles R. Crane, March 19, 1911.

[53] AP to E. A. Van Valkenburg, October 24, 1924.

[54] AP to GP, March 21, 1911.

[55] AP to R. M. La Follette, March 29, 1911.

[56] AP to John J. Hannan, July 13, 1911.

[57] La Follette, *Autobiography*, p. 596.

[58] *Ibid.*, pp. 516–21.

[59] *Ibid.*, p. 530.

[60] *Ibid.*, pp. 530–32.

[61] AP to George P. Hampton, September 25, 1911.

[62] AP to James R. Garfield, October 3, 1911.

[63] AP to William Kent, October 19, 1911.

[64] Ray Stannard Baker, Notebook L (Notebooks A-L, 1892–1909, Series 2, Box 43), p. 68. Ray Stannard Baker Papers, hereafter called Baker Papers.

[65] AP to John R. Drexel, October 30, 1911.

[66] Baker, Notebook L, pp. 66–67, Baker Papers.

[67] *Ibid.*

[68] *Ibid.*, pp. 69–73.

[69] *History*, pp. 131–32.

[70] *Autobiography*, p. 542.

[71] Fola La Follette to the author. Senator La Follette's *Autobiography*, p. 543, states that Walter Houser was in favor of sending a letter that would force Theodore Roosevelt's hand, and that two or three versions were drafted. But there is no evidence that La Follette composed such a letter, or that he considered getting out of the campaign.

[72] R. M. La Follette to AP, January 27, 1912.

[73] *History*, pp. 132–34.

[74] Early draft, "Progressive Party," No. 4, May 25, 1928.

[75] Undated fragment ["Progressive Party," p. 4].

[76] AP to R. M. La Follette, February 1, 1912.

[77] AP to W. B. Colver, February 2, 1912.

[78] GP to AP, February 26, 1912.

[79] AP to Philip B. Stewart, April 13, 1912.

[80] John Haynes Holmes to the author.

[81] AP, Note, "Decay of the Progressive Party," October 9, 1930, p. 14.

[82] Norman Hapgood to AP, May 14, 1912.

[83] AP to Henry L. Stoddard, April 9, 1912; AP to E. A. Van Valkenburg, April 9, 1912; AP to Hiram Johnson, April 9, 1912.

[84] See *History*, p. 134.

[85] AP to Arthur W. Little, undated and unsent letter.

[86] P. S. Stahlnecker [GP's secretary] to AP, April 24, 1912; see also Lawrence F. Abbott to AP, April 23, 1912.

[87] See Appendix II.

[88] Note dated October 31, 1930.

[89] Note, October 31, 1930, 24b.

[90] *Ibid.*, 24a.

[91] Julia Lathrop remarked that the Colonel's way of reaching a conclusion reminded her of the line in the hymn, "Between the saddle and the ground, he mercy sought and mercy found." James Linn, *Jane Addams* (1935).

[92] AP to Fola La Follette, January 5, 1938.

[93] AP to Amos Eno, May 29, 1912.

[94] AP to W. J. McGee, June 25, 1912.

[95] AP to T. Redmond St. John, June 29, 1912.

[96] *Ibid.*

[97] AP to Ernest Cawcroft, July 12, 1912.

[98] AP to Hiram Johnson, July 18, 1912.

[99] AP to Medill McCormick, July 3, 1912.

[100] *Ibid.*

[101] AP to Hiram Johnson, July 18, 1912.

[102] AP to Norman Hapgood, July 20, 1912.

[103] AP to Walter Hines Page, October 8, 1912.

[104] AP to Overton Price, October 8, 1912.

[105] AP to Helen Keller, October 8, 1912.

[106] AP to George Record, October 8, 1912.

[107] AP to Helen Keller, October 8, 1912. See also AP to Medill McCormick, October 8, 1912.

[108] New York *World,* June 11, 1916.

[109] Note ["The Progressive Party"], [n.d.], pp. 4–5.

[110] *History,* Chap. VII; see also typescript "T.R.," pp. 23–24.

[111] *History,* Chapters VI–VII.

[112] See *History,* Chapter IV, note 18.

[113] AP to George Perkins, October 17, 1912.

[114] George Mowry, *Theodore Roosevelt and the Progressive Movement* (1946), p. 270.

[115] From proofs of an article by AP, "Government Ownership of Railroads," intended for the *Metropolitan Magazine,* May 1915. The article did not appear; there is no indication that it was published here or elsewhere.

[116] AP, Binder "1936," p. 34.

[117] AP to Gilson Gardner, December 9, 1913.

[118] AP, "The Cause of Industrial Unrest" (1915), p. 24.

[119] AP to GP, February 25, 1914.

[120] George Haydock to AP, 1912.

[121] AP to Albert J. Beveridge, October 8, 1912.

[122] AP to Louis D. Brandeis, October 8, 1912.

[123] See *History,* p. 180. The 18th District consisted of parts of the then 15th, 17th, 20th, 22d, 24th, and 29th Assembly Districts.

[124] AP to Hiram Johnson, October 5, 1912.

[125] Article for the *Evening Mail* (typescript), October 9, 1912.

[126] AP to Hiram Johnson, October 5, 1912.

[127] Thomas G. Patten, Democrat, 13,704; Amos R. E. Pinchot, 6,644; S. Walter Kaufman, Republican, 4,942; Algernon Lee, Socialist, 2,085; Elzey E. Meachen, 21.

[128] GP to Theodore Roosevelt, December 17, 1912. Theodore Roosevelt Papers.

[129] GP to Theodore Roosevelt. *Ibid.*

[130] See *History,* pp. 183–212.

[131] GP to Theodore Roosevelt, May 6, 1913. Theodore Roosevelt Papers.

[132] John A. Kingsbury to Jane Addams, January 17, 1913.

[133] AP to GP, January 23, 1913.

[134] See correspondence in Beveridge Papers, 1913.

[135] Rough draft for AP, "A Letter to the County Chairman . . . Amos Pinchot's Explanation of the Failure of Good Government," [1913].

[136] AP to Gilson Gardner, December 9, 1913.

[137] *Ibid.*

[138] *Ibid.*

[139] New York *Evening Post.* (Clipping in Pinchot's 1914 file. The date has been removed.)

[140] AP to Francis J. Heney, January 20, 1914.

[141] AP to Francis J. Heney, January 20, 1914; AP to E. A. Van Valkenburg, April 2, 1914.

[142] GP, *Diary,* January 21, 1914. Gifford Pinchot Papers.

[143] *Ibid.,* January 23, 1914.

[144] *Ibid.,* March 30, 1914.

[145] *Ibid.,* April 1, 1914.

[146] AP to E. A. Van Valkenburg, April 2, 1914.

[147] E. A. Van Valkenburg to AP, April 9, 1914.

[148] GP to AP, April 20 and 27, 1914.

[149] A. Nevin Dietrich to AP, April 24, 1914.

[150] AP to Gilson Gardner, April 24, 1914.

[151] AP to Theodore Roosevelt, May 22, 1914.

[152] Letter to Senator Joseph M. Dixon. See Appendix IV.

[153] Albert J. Beveridge to GP, June 1914. Gifford Pinchot Papers.

[154] William T. Coe to AP, June 15, 1914.

[155] AP to Herbert Knox Smith, June 4, 1914. See also AP to Col. Henry N. Osborne, June 16, 1914.

[156] New York *Evening Post,* June 10, 1914.

[157] *New York Times,* June 11, 1914; New York *World,* June 11, 1914.

[158] *New York Times,* June 11, 1914.

[159] New York *Evening Post,* June 25, 1914.

[160] George Record to AP, August 6, 1914.

[161] AP to E. W. Scripps, November 12, 1914.

[162] George Mowry, *op. cit.,* p. 299.

[163] David Hinshaw to William Allen White, Nov. 7, 1914. William Allen White Papers.

[164] Walter Lippmann, "Publicist and Radical," in *Walter Weyl, An Appreciation* (1922), p. 103.

[165] Max Eastman, *Enjoyment of Living* (1948), p. 456.

[166] AP to Henry Lane Eno, July 20, 1914.

[167] *Ibid.*

[168] *Ibid.* Italics mine.

[169] "Cost of Private Monopoly to Public and Wage Earner," in *Annals* of the American Academy of Political and Social Sciences (1913), p. 182.

[170] John Haynes Holmes to the author.

[171] AP, testimony, "The Cause of Industrial Unrest," p. 2. See also AP to John L. Stevens, June 5, 1914, and AP to Harold L. Ickes, September 3, 1938.

[172] Other members of the Council included Frank P. Walsh, chairman; Clarence Darrow; Charles Erskine Scott Wood; and Edward P. Costigan. (This list is not complete.)

[173] John Haynes Holmes to the author.

[174] Eastman, *op. cit.,* p. 456. This description is supported by friends, including Roger Baldwin, Margaret De Silver, and John Haynes Holmes.

[175] Charles T. Hallinan to AP, undated letter [April 1916.]

[176] At this time *The Masses* became *The Liberator* (owned and controlled by Max and Crystal Eastman) and continued for six years.

[177] Arturo Giovanitti, "What I think of *The Masses,*" *The Masses* (July 1916), p. 5.

[178] Eastman, *op. cit.,* p. 455.

[179] *New York Times,* March 6, 1913.

[180] Eastman, *op. cit.,* p. 470.

[181] *Ibid.,* pp. 470–73.

[182] AP to George Bernard Shaw, October 29, 1914.

[183] AP to Francis J. Heney, February 4, 1916.

[184] AP to Sidney Norman, July 25, 1916.

[185] AP to E. W. Scripps, November 3, 1915.

[186] *Woodrow Wilson and the Progressive Era*, pp. 239–40.

[187] Olean *Evening Herald*, October 24, 1916.

[188] Dante Barton, "The Wilson Volunteers in New York State" (typescript); Rochester *Herald*, October 23, 1916.

[189] Quoted in Edward A. Fitzpatrick, *McCarthy of Wisconsin* (1944), p. 166.

[190] Theodore Roosevelt to AP, November 3, 1916. Theodore Roosevelt Papers.

[191] Typescript, "Beware of Peace. A Letter to the Senate Committee on Foreign Affairs." See also "This Orgy of Hysteria and Hate [;] A Letter by Amos Pinchot Revealing the Truth About a War Which the American People Do Not Want" [n.d.]; AP to Robert M. La Follette, December 11, 1917.

[192] AP to Francis J. Heney, February 28, 1916.

[193] AP to the Executive Committee of the Boone and Crockett Club, April 26, 1921.

[194] *New York Times*, March 14, 1917.

[195] See Appendix I.

[196] *New York Times*, January 25, 1919. Archibald Stevenson made this statement to a Senate committee. He gave 62 names; besides Pinchot, the list included Jane Addams, Roger Baldwin, Charles A. Beard, Eugene Debs, Elizabeth Gurley Flynn, Frederic C. Howe, David Starr Jordan, Vida Scudder, Norman Thomas, Oswald Garrison Villard, and Harry F. Ward.

[197] St. Louis *Post-Dispatch*, December 10, 1919. For an extended discussion of the Committee of 48 see Belle Case La Follette and Fola La Follette, *Robert M. La Follette* (1953), II, 998–1010. See also *Platform of the Committee of 48* [1920?]; Amos Pinchot, "Mr. Pinchot Cites the Wrongs That the '48-ers Would Right," *Reconstruction*, II (1919); *Facts* (issued by the Committee of 48 . . . New York City); current newspaper accounts; and the extensive and pertinent material in the Amos Pinchot Papers. I am particularly indebted to Dr. John Haynes Holmes, Miss Fola La Follette, and Mrs. Gilbert Roe for information and insights I could not have got otherwise.

[198] Chicago *Daily News*, July 13, 1920.

[199] AP to J. A. H. Hopkins, November 26, 1920.

[200] *New York Times*, November 27, 1919. The *Times* described the

signers of the call to the conference as "two hundred prominent 'intellectuals' including Amos Pinchot, Dudley Field Malone . . . twenty-nine ministers, and a score of well known college professors." (*New York Times,* November 26, 1919.)

[201] AP to R. M. La Follette, June 25, 1920.

[202] Chicago *Herald and Examiner,* July 14, 1920.

[203] Why Pinchot and his group were not more fully prepared for the consequences of this "family row," as he called it, is a point that cannot be ignored; for he knew all about it and anticipated trouble. See AP to James H. Maurer, March 23, 1920; AP to Robert M. La Follette, June 25, 1920.

[204] Chicago *Tribune,* July 13, 1920.

[205] *New York Times,* July 14, 1920.

[206] Gilson Gardner to R. P. Scripps, July 19, 1920.

[207] AP to Mrs. Laurence Todd, January 13, 1925.

[208] He defined plutocracy as "a government in which political power is monopolized by rich men, and employed in furthering their selfish interests without regard to the general welfare." Binder *Steel,* Introduction, p. 11. Cf. AP to Glenn Frank, October 28, 1930: "I have been writing something on the means by which power is created in modern industrial civilization. In one chapter of the book, which doesn't seem to go very well, I have questioned the wisdom and fitness for leadership of the men who, through their surplus wealth, which amounts to surplus power, control the destinies of this country."

[209] AP to the Editor, *New York Times,* February 29, 1924.

[210] *Steel,* Introduction, p. 13.

[211] Ibid., p. 14.

[212] Ibid., p. 16.

[213] *Wealth Against Commonwealth* (1936), p. 364.

[214] AP to R. M. La Follette, June 25, 1920.

[215] See AP, Introduction to George L. Record's *How to Abolish Poverty* (1936), pp. 11, 12. Pinchot reports that he first met Record in 1912, but there is evidence that the two men knew each other in October, 1911.

[216] *Ibid.,* p. 20.

[217] Note on William Howard Taft, October 25, 1930.

[218] *History,* p. 91.

[219] See Editorial Note.

[220] AP to David K. Niles, September 23, 1932. Pinchot was not with-

out his reservations, however; see his letter to Charles Hallinan, September 20, 1932.

[221] AP to David K. Niles, September 23, 1932. For a different point of view on Amos Pinchot's generally optimistic outlook, see the remarks of his old friend, Albert Jay Nock, *A Journal of These Days, June 1932-December, 1933* (1934), pp. 57–58.

[222] AP, Introduction to George L. Record's *How to Abolish Poverty* (1936), pp. 18–19.

[223] AP to Louis D. Brandeis, January 28, 1936.

[224] AP, "Letter in Support of Senator Borah's Candidacy," May 8, 1936.

[225] AP, "Open Letter to John L. Lewis," September 3, 1938.

[226] *Ibid.*

[227] AP, "Open Letter to Harold L. Ickes," October 14, 1936.

[228] AP to Hiram W. Johnson, August 31, 1940.

[229] *New York Times,* August 7, 8, and 9, 1942.

[230] Eastman, *op. cit.,* p. 456.

CHAPTER I

---

[1] [Robert Marion La Follette, *La Follette's Autobiography*, Madison, 1911, 1913.]

[2] [Claude G. Bowers, *Beveridge and the Progressive Era*, Boston, 1932.]

[3] [Herbert S. Duffy, *William Howard Taft*, New York, 1930.]

[4] [Archie Butt, *Taft and Roosevelt: The Intimate Letters of Archie Butt*, 2 vols., Garden City, 1930.]

[5] [Lord Charnwood, *Theodore Roosevelt*, Boston, 1923.]

[6] [Joseph Bucklin Bishop, *Theodore Roosevelt and His Time*, 2 vols., New York, 1920.]

[7] [Mark Sullivan, *Our Times*, Vol. IV: *The War Begins* (1904–14), New York, 1932.]

[8] [*Ibid.*, p. 394. Usually known as the Ballinger-Pinchot controversy, this celebrated case has been described as a "bitter contention over the conservation of natural resources. Early in the Taft administration an order of former President Roosevelt withdrawing from sale certain public land containing water power sites in Montana and Wyoming was cancelled. Chief Forester Gifford Pinchot protested and publicly charged Secretary of the Interior Richard A. Ballinger with favoritism toward corporations seeking water power sites. Pinchot defended L. R. Glavis, Land Office investigator, dismissed for accusing Ballinger of favoring the Cunningham syndicate's claims to valuable Alaskan mineral lands. Pinchot likewise was dismissed. A joint congressional investigating committee exonerated Ballinger. But failing to regain public confidence, Ballinger resigned. The incident widened the cleavage in the Republican party." (F. A. Ogg, *National Progress*, quoted in *Dictionary of American History*, ed. James Truslow Adams, New York, 1940, I, 149.) On De-

---

*Footnotes without brackets are Pinchot's; bracketed footnotes have been supplied by the Editor.

cember 27, 1911, Gifford Pinchot wrote to Albert J. Beveridge, "The essential reason of the trouble between Ballinger and me was this— that Ballinger had attacked the Conservation policies, especially as to water power and the proper care of forests on Indian Reservations, in addition to his efforts to give away the fraudulent Cunningham claims. I was never able to get people to understand that my fight was a defensive one—to preserve policies already in effect—and not an attack on Ballinger out of a clear sky, but that is the fact nevertheless." (Beveridge Papers, Box 277.) Amos Pinchot's own account of the controversy can be found in the binder *Steel* (1930), chap. ii, "The Taft Administration," pp. 1–51. The literature dealing with this case is sizable; the reader is referred to Alpheus T. Mason, *Bureaucracy Convicts Itself*, Princeton, 1941, for an opposing point of view to Harold L. Ickes, "Not Guilty!" *Saturday Evening Post* (May 25, 1940), and to Ickes' book, *The Autobiography of a Curmudgeon* (New York, 1943), pp. 153–54.]

[9] [Sullivan, *op. cit.*]

[10] [George Woodward Wickersham, 1858–1936: Attorney-General of the United States in the Taft administration. In the binder *Steel* (1930), chap. ii, [p. 1], Pinchot says that Taft's appointment of Wickersham was in many ways both admirable and natural: "he was born a law partner of Mr. Taft's brother, and a man of high standing at the bar. . . . "]

[11] [Sullivan, *op. cit.*, p. 394. Pinchot is mistaken here. Sullivan says the memorandum "contained 50,000 words."]

[12] [*Ibid.*, p. 392.]

[13] [*Ibid.*, p. 396.]

[14] [Roosevelt and Pinchot met at Porto Maurizio, Italy.]

[15] [Gilson Gardner, 1869–1935: Newspaperman; Washington correspondent for Newspaper Enterprise Association for many years; member of editorial board, Scripps newspapers.]

[16] [Jonathan Prentiss Dolliver, 1858–1910. Member of House of Representatives, 1889–1901; United States senator from Iowa, 1900–10.]

[17] [Pinchot has *not* already said this in the *History of the Progressive Party*, but the chapters in the binder *Steel* take this point as a basic assumption.]

[18] [Elbert Henry Gary, 1846–1927: Corporation lawyer and financier. Best known as the dominating influence in the United States Steel Corporation.]

[19] *Taft's administration indictments, compared with Roosevelt's:* Some have attributed the activity of the Department of Justice under Mr. Taft

solely to the President's desire to correct the bad impression made by the Ballinger disclosures. It is my belief that such a view does injustice to both Mr. Taft and Mr. Wickersham. However this may be, the fact remains that Mr. Taft's administration was much more active in enforcing the Sherman law than was Mr. Roosevelt's. During the seven and a half years in which Roosevelt held office, there were brought under the Sherman law 18 bills in equity, 25 indictments, and 1 forfeiture proceeding. The oil trust, the tobacco trust, and the power trust were attacked; the Northern Securities and other railroad combinations were broken up, nominally at least; lesser combinations in meat packing, salt, paper, liquors, elevators, naval stores, furniture, and other industries, were proceeded against.

In the four years that Mr. Taft was president, there were 46 bills in equity, 43 indictments, and one contempt proceeding, a total of ninety, as against Mr. Roosevelt's total of forty-four. The suits filed by Attorney-General Wickersham included powerful combinations overlooked by the Roosevelt regime. Among these were the United States Steel Corporation, American Sugar Refining Company, United States Shoe and Machinery Company, International Harvester Company, National Cash Register Company, the General Electric Company, Corn Products Refining Company, American Thread Company, etc. Attorney-General Wickersham was, in fact, so active in preventing combinations in restraint of trade that he earned from American monopolists an enmity that has, in some cases, lasted to the present day.

[20] [Ida M. Tarbell, *The Life of Elbert H. Gary,* New York, 1925.]

[21] Taft's first letter after the election returns were in was to President Roosevelt: ". . . The first letter that I wish to write is to you, because you have always been the chief agent in working out the present state of affairs and my selection and election are chiefly your work. . . . The great comfort that I have in being under such a heavy obligation to you is that I know that the easiest way for me to discharge it is to make a success of my administration and to justify you in your wish and effort to make me your successor. . . ." (Duffy, *William Howard Taft,* p. 219.)

[22] [George Walbridge Perkins, 1862–1920: Banker. Official chairman, National Executive Committee, Progressive party, 1912–16.]

[23] [Herbert Knox Smith, 1869–1931: Lawyer; Commissioner of Corporations, 1907–12; Progressive candidate for governor of Connecticut, 1912.

[Concerning the suppressed Steel Report, Pinchot says that by 1905 the public feeling against trusts had grown to such a degree that Congress passed a resolution requiring an investigation of the Steel Corporation:

["Accordingly, in January, 1905, Mr. James R. Garfield, the commissioner of the Bureau of Corporations, called on Judge Gary at his office in New York, and informed the latter that the President desired him, Garfield, to commence an investigation. Whereupon Judge Gary went to Washington, and at a conference with the President, Secretary of Commerce Metcalf, and Commissioner Garfield, it was arranged that an investigation should take place, but that no matters deemed confidential by Mr. Gary should be published, until after they had been referred to the Secretary of Commerce, 'and, if necessary, to the President for a decision.' (This last quotation is from Tarbell, *Life of Elbert H. Gary,* pp. 185, 186.)

["Appeased by the fact that an inquiry had at least been put on the calendar, the wrath of the public simmered down, and, as is the rule in such cases, the investigation dragged on indefinitely. In fact, it was not heard of again until some three years after Colonel Roosevelt left the White House, when the Stanley Investigating Committee, in 1911, put Mr. Garfield's successor on the stand, and learned that the report itself had never been finished, and that the only thing available was a partial summary, not intended for publication, of which but two copies were in existence.

["Nevertheless, this summary, prepared by Mr. Herbert Knox Smith, who succeeded Mr. Garfield as commissioner of corporations, is, as far as it goes, a frank and able analysis of the Steel Corporation. . . .

["Garfield, though a public servant of high character and ability, was handicapped in his dealings with the Steel Corporation by his overtrustfulness and overwillingness to accept information furnished him by them. . . .

["But with the advent of the new commissioner, the situation was altered. Smith was a born investigator and at least normally suspicious, and, though he never finished this work, what he did produce was of a nature that Mr. Gary could ill afford to have disseminated. Obviously, the only thing to do was to give Mr. Smith his head, and delay the publication of his findings as long as humanly possible.

["But, though Mr. Gary, in 1905, succeeded in shunting the threatened investigation to a siding, where it remained with, metaphorically speaking, grass growing around its wheels, until 1911, the Sherman Law was still on the statute books, and constituted a danger that required his continued effort." Binder *Steel* (1930), chap. i, pp. 13–17.]

[24] [Augustus Owsley Stanley, 1867–   : Member of House of Representatives, 1903–15; governor of Kentucky, 1915–19; United States senator, 1919–25.]

[25] [Farquhar McRae: Statistician of the Stanley Committee. In the

History (p. 95) and in his letter to Senator Joseph Dixon (p. 248 ff.), Pinchot spoke admiringly of McRae's "able report" and used his figures relating to the Steel Corporation. But McRae's figures were not accepted with unanimity. Shortly after the "Letter" was first circulated, Herbert Knox Smith, who had received a copy, wrote a long letter to Pinchot in which he compared the findings of the Bureau of Corporations and of the Stanley Committee. Smith understandably had no use for the Democratic investigators. He disdainfully mentioned "that absurd 'expert'" who was connected with "that still more absurd Stanley Committee." McRae had tried to do his best, he conceded, but he had been considerably hampered by lack of money, men, and native intelligence. Smith ridiculed McRae's figures, suggesting that the statistician had used divination rather than accurate information. As for the Stanley Committee, Smith wrote, it was partisan, slipshod, and "perfectly incompetent," unable to assess even the very small amount of material its staff had managed to collect. (Herbert Knox Smith to Amos Pinchot, May 29, 1914).]

[26] [George L. Record, 1895–1933: Lawyer and reformer. Although he was never elected to a public office, Record was an outstanding figure in the New Jersey Progressive movement. His influence on Governor Wilson was considerable. For Amos Pinchot's attitude toward Record, see Biographical Introduction, p. 78.]

[27] [*The New Freedom,* 1913. This book, as Wilson states in the preface, "is the result of the editorial skill of Mr. William Bayard Hale, who has put together . . . in their right sequences the more suggestive portions of my campaign speeches."]

CHAPTER II

[1] [Frank A. Munsey, 1854–1925: Publisher of magazines, including *Munsey's Weekly,* 1889, which became *Munsey's Magazine;* publisher of newspapers, including the New York *Mail, Sun and Globe,* and *Evening Telegram.*]

[2] [There is no such footnote.]

[3] [Elihu Root, 1854–1937: Corporation lawyer and jurist; Secretary of War, 1899–1904; Secretary of State, 1905–9; United States senator from New York, 1909–15.]

[4] [Henry Cabot Lodge, 1850–1925: Representative from Massachusetts, 1887–93; United States senator from Massachusetts, 1893–1924.]

[5] [I have been unable to find this article.]

[6] [Senator Nelson W. Aldrich, 1841–1915: Member of House of Representatives, 1879–83; United States senator from Rhode Island, 1881–1911.]

[7] [Albert J. Beveridge, 1862–1927: Lawyer, biographer, United States senator from Indiana, 1899–1911.]

[8] [Dr. Harvey Wiley, 1844–1930: Chief chemist, United States Department of Agriculture, 1883–1912; author of 60 government bulletins and a number of papers and books attacking food adulteration.]

[9] [Winthrop Murray Crane, 1853–1920: Paper manufacturer; governor of Massachusetts, 1900–2; United States senator from Massachusetts, 1904–13.]

[10] Kane: a misspelling for John Kean, 1852–1914: Member of House of Representatives, 1883–85, 1887–89; active in New Jersey politics; United States senator from New Jersey, 1899–1905, 1905–11.]

[11] [Boies Penrose, 1860–1921: Lawyer; United States senator from Pennsylvania, 1897–1921.]

[12] [Joseph G. Cannon, 1836–1921: Member of House of Representatives, 1873–91, 1903–13, 1915–21; Speaker, House of Representatives, 1903–11.]

[13] [The reference is not to a previous chapter in the *History,* but to the chapter on the Ballinger-Pinchot case, Binder *Steel* (1930).]

[14] [Overton W. Price, 1873–1914: Associate Forester of Bureau of Forestry, 1901–10; active in National Conservation Commission.]

[15] [Albert Baird Cummins, 1850–1926: Lawyer; governor of Iowa, 1902–4, 1904–6; United States senator, 1908–27.]

[16] [Joseph L. Bristow, 1861–1944: Newspaper owner, politician, and farmer; United States senator from Kansas, 1909–15.]

[17] [Charles Taft, 1843–1929: Cincinnati lawyer; newspaper owner and editor.]

[1] [At this point I have deleted nine and a half lines that in substance repeat the descriptions of Herbert S. Duffy, *William Howard Taft,* New York, 1930; Archie Butt, *Taft and Roosevelt: The Intimate Letters of Archie Butt,* 2 vols., Garden City, 1930; and Lord Charnwood, *Theodore Roosevelt,* Boston, 1923.]

[2] See Cabot Lodge notes attached. [These notes are included in Pinchot's text, pp. 107–11.]

[3] [Reed Smoot, 1862–1941: United States senator from Utah, 1903–33.]

[4] [George von Lengerke Meyer, 1858–1918: Ambassador Extraordinary and Plenipotentiary to Italy, 1900–5, to Russia, 1905–7; Postmaster-General in cabinet of President Roosevelt, 1907–9; Secretary of the Navy in the cabinet of President Taft, 1909–13.]

[5] [See note 14, p. 277.]

[6] [James Wilson, 1835–1920: Secretary of Agriculture, 1897–1913, in the cabinets of Presidents McKinley, Roosevelt, and Taft.]

[7] [Herbert Croly, 1869–1930: Founder and editor of *The New Republic;* author of *The Promise of American Life,* 1909, *Progressive Democracy,* 1914, and other books.]

[8] *Works of Theodore Roosevelt,* 1923–26, XIX, pp. 14, 20, 21.]

[9] [Probably John Morley's *On Compromise,* London, 1874.]

[10] From *Theodore Roosevelt, An Autobiography,* 1916, p. 429. "But Gifford Pinchot is the man to whom the nation owes most for what has been accomplished as regards the preservation of the natural resources of our country. He led, and indeed during its most vital period embodied, the fight for the preservation through use of our forests. He played one of the leading parts in the effort to make the National Government the chief instrument in developing the irrigation of the arid West. He was the foremost leader in the great struggle to coordinate all our social and governmental forces in the effort to secure the adoption of a rational and farseeing policy for securing the conservation of all our national resources.

He was already in the Government service as head of the Forestry Bureau when I became President; he continued throughout my term, not only as head of the Forest Service, but as the moving and directing spirit in most of the conservation work, and as counsellor and assistant on most of the work connected with the internal affairs of the country. Taking into account the varied nature of the work he did, its vital importance to the nation and the fact that as regards much of it he was practically breaking new ground, and taking into account also his tireless energy and activity, his fearlessness, his complete disinterestedness, his single-minded devotion to the interests of the plain people, and his extraordinary efficiency, I believe it is but just to say that among the many, many public officials who under my administration rendered literally invaluable service to the people of the United States, he, on the whole, stood first. A few months after I left the Presidency he was removed from office by President Taft."

[11] Charles G. Washburn, *Theodore Roosevelt, The Logic of His Career*, 1916, p. 170.

[12] *Ibid.*, p. 168.

[13] *Ibid.*, p. 172.

[14] [William Kent, 1864–1928: Member of House of Representatives, 1911–17; member of United States Tariff Commission, 1917–20.]

[15] [E. W. Scripps, 1854–1926: Newspaper editor; controlling director of the Newspaper Enterprise Association; publisher of the Scripps-Howard Newspapers.]

[16] *The Intimate Letters of Archie Butt*, II, 516–17. [Henry White, 1850–1927: Sometimes called the first American "career diplomat." Entered Foreign Service, 1883; ambassador at Rome, 1905–7, at Paris, 1907–9.]

[17] *The Intimate Letters of Archie Butt*, II, 520.

[18] *Ibid.*, II, 518.

[19] [This statement is erroneous. Scripps threw his newspapers to La Follette early in the game, but he did not make the first move.]

[20] Scripps often spoke to me of his affectionate admiration for Gardner. Once I asked him why, if he felt so keen about Gardner, he did not double his salary. "I find," he said, "that men in my organization become conservative and lose their eye as soon as they save up a couple of dollars. I intend to keep Gilson poor so as to be able to trust his judgment."

As Scripps grew older, he kept Gardner near him more and more, trusting increasingly in his point of view, and distrusting his own, or pretending to. One day, while at lunch in his room at the Biltmore Hotel, he said to me, jokingly: "My decency on almost every question, especially public ones, has always been shamefully exaggerated. That's why I keep Gilson around as my conscience, and even so go wrong about half the time." To make up for his lifelong policy of preserving Gardner from the corrupting touch of money and ease, he left him a legacy in his will, and named him, together with Roy Howard and Thomas Sidlo, as trustee of his newspaper properties.

21 [Joseph Medill McCormick, 1877–1925: Publisher, Chicago *Daily Tribune;* vice-chairman, Progressive National Committee, 1912–14; member of House of Representatives, 1917–19; United States senator from Illinois, 1919–25.]

22 James Kerney's *The Political Education of Woodrow Wilson,* New York and London, 1926, *passim.*

23 [Frederic Clemson Howe, 1867–1940: Lawyer; Cleveland reformer and authority on municipal administration; director of The People's Institute, New York, 1911–14; Commissioner of Immigration, Port of New York, 1914–19; author of many books, including *The City, The Hope of Democracy,* and *Confessions of a Reformer.*]

24 [Charles R. Crane, 1858–1939: Manufacturer; member of President's Special Diplomatic Commission to Russia, 1917; American minister to China, 1920–21.]

25 [Francis J. Heney, 1858–1937: Lawyer, graft prosecutor, and prominent California Progressive.]

26 Robert Marion La Follette, *La Follette's Autobiography,* 1911, 1913, p. 697.

27 [Pinchot is referring to the magazine articles, in which form part of the *Autobiography* first appeared.]

28 [Chap. ix.]

29 Matthew Josephson, *Zola and His Time,* New York, 1928, p. 253.

30 *Ibid.,* p. 339.

31 [John Sharp Williams, 1854–1932: Member of House of Representatives, 1893–1909; Minority Leader of the House, 1903–9; United States senator from Mississippi, 1911–23; member of Foreign Relations Committee and Finance Committee of the Senate; author of *The Permanent Influence of Thomas Jefferson on American Institutions.*]

32 [Cong. Record, 65 Cong., 1 Session, p. 234.]

33 Paul Oscar Husting, 1866–1917: Lawyer; author of *Wisconsin Waterpower Law*; advocate of income tax, workmen's compensation, and Corrupt Practices Act; United States senator from Wisconsin, 1915–21.]

34 [Cong. Record, 65 Cong., 1 Session, p. 238.]

---

[1] Robert Marion La Follette, *La Follette's Autobiography*, 1911, 1913, p. 537.

[2] [Moses E. Clapp, 1851–1929: Attorney-General of Minnesota, 1887–93; United States senator from Minnesota 1901–17.]

[3] [See Biographical Introduction, pp. 25–26.]

[4] [Walter Rogers: 1877–   : At this time Charles R. Crane's assistant.]

[5] [P. 593.]

[6] ["President Taft—Candidate for Re-election," *Pearson's Magazine*, XXVII (1912), 533–44.]

[7] [Independent mayor of Philadelphia.]

[8] [Gilbert E. Roe, 1865–1929: Lawyer, associated with Robert M. La Follette 1890–99 and thereafter often his legal adviser and counsel; counsel to the United States Senate Committee on Manufacturers investigating the high cost of gasoline and other petroleum products, 1922–23; Eastern regional director, La Follette-Wheeler Progressive Campaign Committee, 1924; author of *Our Judicial Oligarchy*.]

[9] *Autobiography*, pp. 608–9.

[10] On the evening of February 5, Record said at the Hudson County Progressive dinner: "I have just been called to the telephone by W. L. Houser, one of the managers of Senator La Follette, who is in Washington, and tells me the Senator has withdrawn in favor of any other candidate that may be named by the Progressive Republican party."

Shortly after this, Record told me that Houser read the whole statement to him, which appeared the next morning, over the long-distance telephone, and said that it was drawn by La Follette.

[11] From the *New York Times*, February 6, 1912, p. 1, col. 7. [I have deleted the long newspaper story that Pinchot quotes.]

[12] [A letter from Gilbert Roe to Senator La Follette, written immediately after the conference, fixes the date as February 8, 1912.]

¹³ *Autobiography,* p. 612.

¹⁴ New York *Tribune,* April 9, 1912.

¹⁵ Charles G. Washburn, *Theodore Roosevelt, The Logic of His Career,* 1916, p. 177.

¹⁶ [Charles McCarthy, 1873–1921: Librarian for Wisconsin, 1901; set up legislative reference departments in many state libraries; author of *The Wisconsin Idea,* 1912.]

¹⁷ [Charles Richard Van Hise, 1875–1918: President, University of Wisconsin, 1903–18; author of *The Conservation of the Natural Resources of the United States* and *Concentration and Control—a Solution of the Trust Problem in the United States.*]

¹⁸ [Harold L. Ickes, *op. cit.,* pp. 306–37.]

¹⁹ [Thomas C. Platt, 1833–1910: United States senator from New York, 1897–1909. Leader in New York Republican politics for many years.]

CHAPTER V

¹ [James Watson, 1863–1948: Member of House of Representatives, 1895–97 and 1899–1909; United States senator from Indiana, 1916–33.]

² Senator Borah threw a bombshell into the Committee by opposing this rule and offering one providing that a roll call could be requested by ten members. "I cannot believe this Committee is going to seat men who manifestly have no right to a seat, but if you are going to do so, for the sake of your party do it openly, and above board, and put your individuality and your courage, though in a bad cause, behind your vote. . . . What are you men afraid of? What is it that you are going to do? If these delegates are entitled to seats, why should you conceal your record? Have you lost your courage? Are you ashamed of what is going to happen? Mr. Borah's motion was quickly voted down." (George Henry Payne's account of the Progressive Convention, pp. 136, 137.)

3 [Joseph M. Dixon, 1867–1934: Member of House of Representatives from Montana, 1903–7; United States senator, 1907–13; chairman, Roosevelt Progressive National Committee, 1912; governor of Montana, 1921–25.]

4 [Henry J. Allen, 1868–1950: Newspaperman, writer and publisher; United States senator from Kansas, 1929–30.]

5 [J. Franklin Fort, 1852–1920: Well-known New Jersey prosecutor and judge; governor of New Jersey, 1908–11.]

6 [Robert Perkins Bass, 1873–   : Expert on industrial relations; governor of New Hampshire, 1911–13.]

7 [John Foster Bass, 1866–1931.]

8 [Herbert Spencer Hadley, 1872–1921: Prosecuting attorney; governor of Missouri, 1909–13; author of *The Standard Oil Trust, What the Railroads Owe the People,* and other books.]

9 [Walter Roscoe Stubbs, 1858–1929: Kansas Republican; governor of Kansas, 1909–15.]

10 [Bainbridge Colby, 1869–1951: Lawyer; delegate to the Progressive National Convention, 1912; Progressive party nominee for United States senator from New York, 1914; Secretary of State in the cabinet of President Wilson, 1920–21.]

11 [John M. Parker, 1863–1939: New Orleans businessman; Progressive party nominee for vice-president of the United States, 1916; governor of Louisiana, 1920–24.]

12 [Hiram W. Johnson, 1866–1945: Lawyer; governor of California, 1911–17; United States senator, 1917–45.]

13 "Had the southern delegates, chiefly colored, controlled by office holders, been taken out of the Taft column, Roosevelt would have had almost two to one of the convention." Henry L. Stoddard, *As I Knew Them [Presidents and Politics from Grant to Coolidge* (New York, 1927)] p. 400.

[1] [Pinchot's data are incomplete. Suit against the International Harvester Company was filed in the Federal District Court in Minnesota on April 12, 1912. On August 15, 1914, the lower court entered a judgment that the International Harvester Company was illegal (see 214 Fed. 987). The defendants appealed to the Supreme Court and then dismissed their own appeal. The final decree was entered on November 2, 1918. In 1923 the government proceeded again and asked for further relief against the International Harvester Company. The District Court refused to grant it and the Supreme Court affirmed (see 274 US 693). The International Harvester Company was sued under both sections of the Sherman Act.]

[2] [*Preliminary Report of the Factory Investigating Commission*, 1912. Transmitted to the Legislature March 1, 1912.]

[3] ["The United States Steel Corporation," *Munsey's Magazine*, XXXIX (June 1908), 363–69.]

[4] [*Ibid.*, p. 364.]

[5] [*Hearings Before the Committee on Investigation of the United States Steel Corporation*, 8 vols. (1912), p. 2841.]

[6] *Ibid.*

[7] *Ibid.*, p. 2859.

[8] *Ibid.*, p. 2860.

[9] *Ibid.*, p. 2861. The writer made a trip through the steel towns of Pennsylvania in 1914 when Penrose was running for the Senate. He saw five thousand men discharged, on but a day's notice, from a mill on the Thursday before election. They were notified at the gate that the mill would remain closed indefinitely unless Penrose were elected.

[10] Robert Bacon, Newberry, and Satterlee.

[11] Standard Oil Company of New Jersey *v.* the United States, Decision, May 15, 1911, p. 11.

[12] [Abraham Berglund, *The United States Steel Corporation; A Study*

288

of the Growth and Influence of Combination in the Iron and Steel Industry, New York, 1907.]

[13] Woodrow Wilson, *The New Freedom,* 1913, pp. 189, 205, 196, 201. [I have deleted Pinchot's rather extensive quotations from the text.]

[14] [Edward Prentice Costigan, 1874–1939: Lawyer; Colorado Progressive; United States senator, 1931–37.]

[15] [George Bruce Cortelyou, 1862–1940: Chairman, Republican National Committee, 1904–7; Postmaster-General, 1905–7; Secretary of the Treasury, 1907–9.]

[16] *Democratic Campaign Book* (1912), p. 240.

[17] *Ibid.,* p. 232.

[18] *Ibid.,* p. 229.

[19] "George Perkins and Frank Munsey influenced the politics of this country in 1912 more than any other men with whose activities at that time I am familiar. . . . Perkins managed the battle, but Munsey agreed to share the deficit." (Henry L. Stoddard, *As I Knew Them* [*Presidents and Politics from Grant to Coolidge,* New York, 1927], pp. 421, 424.) [At this point I have deleted, because of restrictions on quotations stipulated in Mr. Ickes' will, a quotation from a letter from Harold L. Ickes to Amos Pinchot. The letter, written on December 2, 1912, deals with the dangerous influence of George Perkins on the Progressive party.]

[20] [Raymond Robins, 1873–1955: Writer, social economist, lecturer; chairman of the State Committee of the Progressive party in Illinois and Progressive party candidate for United States senator, 1914; temporary and permanent chairman, Progressive National Convention, 1916.]

[21] Letter from Amos Pinchot to Perkins:

October 17, 1912.

George W. Perkins, Esq.,
National Progressive Headquarters,
Manhattan Hotel, City.

My dear Mr. Perkins:
    Apropos of our conversation the other night, here is a plan that I want to lay before you. I believe it will triple our efficiency in the last dash of the campaign. It is substantially what Colby and I suggested to you the other night. In view of the Colonel's present disability, I think it is not less necessary, and perhaps more feasible, than ever, as it makes more natural the bringing together of the Progressive forces in New York for consultation.
    Have a number of well known Progressive leaders come to New York, some of them to remain here until the end of the campaign, others to drift in and out again for purposes of consultation and publicity.
    Have say Johnson, Beveridge, Van Valkenberg, William Allen White, Raymond Robins, Gifford, Heney and Van Hise come to New York now, and others come later, as many and as often as the situation warrants. They will visit the Colonel at Oyster Bay, give out interviews, make speeches, attack and answer attacks. Each,

along his own line, whether it be conservation, child labor, the trust question, popular government, the tariff, or industrial conditions, will step forward and, not only answer the arguments of Wilson, Hillis, Root, *Collier's Weekly*, Taft, McAdoo, Brandeis, etc., but carry the war into the enemy's country. Each man with a national reputation as a Progressive and as a specialist upon the particular subject in question will speak with authority and force. Our attacks and defenses coming, as they will, from different men representing different sections of the country will be interesting and fresh to the public. As the work will be divided up between a number of men, each familiar with his own subject, there will be time to seize every strategic position and to take advantage promptly of every blunder of the enemy.

We will thus create a great fighting center of Progressive energy and the vibrations of its continuous activity will be felt all over the country.

This group of men, some of them remaining permanently and others staying for a few days and going back to their own states, will make the last two weeks of this campaign an insistent, driving attack. They will deliver broadside after broadside and break down Wilson's vulnerable position on big national questions, the platforms, etc.

Colby and I spoke to you the other night about a matter which I believe touches the success or failure of this campaign more deeply than anything else. This opinion of mine, however, is not a personal one, I get it from almost every man with whom I talk who has at heart the cause that you and I have at heart.

Brandeis, Wilson, Bryan, La Follette, Norman Hapgood, and a lot of other people have concentrated their energy upon trying to make the public believe that our party is the friend of the trusts and the exponent of the exploitation of the average man. Of course this charge is utterly unfair and must be shown to be so. We must drive it home to every fair-minded man that we furnish the only solution of the industrial question in which there is any real hope for the people. If I did not believe this was true I would not be in the party and neither would you. Now, as a matter of fact, the people are fighting mad on this trust and big business question. The average man wants to get after big business with a club for he believes, and we all believe with him, that he has not had a fair share of the prosperity that recent years have developed in the United States. We have got to make it plain, plain beyond any possible shadow of a doubt, that we do not stand for legalized monopoly; that, as Roosevelt says, the anti-trust law should be strengthened in order to make it effective against combinations tending toward monopoly, and that our proposed commission is not a commission to say this is a bad trust or that is a good one, but to investigate the affairs of great corporations and make them obey the law, just as the Interstate Commerce Commission does.

Owing to the fact that you have been for many years a financier and a business man of national reputation, and owing to the fact that the people are not in a mood to discriminate between one leader in the business world and another, it is, in my opinion, bad policy for you to take the lead in this campaign of public education. The appearance of a financier outlining the industrial policy of a movement which the people are told is primarily designed to strike against abuses in an industrial system which has generally failed to give the average man his fair share of prosperity and opportunity puzzles and distresses the average man. It makes him feel that he does not fully understand what the Progressives are driving at. It makes the situation composite instead of simple. It creates a demand for explanation which has to be met everywhere.

I know that you understand all of this quite as well, or better, than I do, and I know that you are entirely willing to take your share of the misunderstanding which is the lot of every man in your position who goes into a cause like ours. I believe, also, that you must be aware of the appreciation that we all have of your generosity and your effective and constant work. But what we all want is to do everything that is humanly possible to make the last dash of this campaign successful. And I believe that this plan of having our attitude toward the industrial situation published to the people from the National Headquarters, not only by yourself but by a group of Progressive leaders unidentified with the financial world, will do more than anything else to bring about victory.

Every man who cares for this Progressive cause has got to look things square in the face, and take account of the weak points as well as the strong points of our position. We must do all that is in our power to strengthen the weak places and make still stronger the strong ones.

Sincerely yours,

(A. P.)

²² [See p. 282, note 9.]

CHAPTER VII

¹ Joseph Bucklin Bishop, *Theodore Roosevelt and His Time* (2 vols.; New York, 1920), II, 348.

² [April 28, 1730. *The Correspondence of Jonathan Swift, D.D.*, ed. F. Elrington Ball (London, 1913), IV, 147.]

³ [Chester H. Rowell, 1867–1948: California journalist; an organizer of the Lincoln-Roosevelt League; active in the Progressive party, 1912–16.]

⁴ [T. R. has confused his authors. He is referring to John A. Hobson, "Causes of the Rise of Prices," *Contemporary Review*, CII (October 1912), 483–92.]

⁵ [Edwin T. Earl, d. 1919; Publisher, Los Angeles *Tribune* and Los Angeles *Herald*.]

⁶ [Charles E. Thompson, 1870–1933: Industrialist and steel manufacturer.]

⁷ [Oscar S. Straus, 1850–1926: Lawyer; businessman; Member of Permanent Court of Arbitration at The Hague, 1902, reappointed by Presidents Roosevelt, Taft, Wilson; Secretary, Department of Commerce and

291

Labor, 1906–9; Ambassador Extraordinary and Plenipotentiary to Turkey, 1909–10. Author of many books.]

8 [Christopher P. Connolly, "Big Business and the Bench," *Everybody's*, XXVI: 146–60, 291–306, 439–53, 659–72, 827–41; XXVII: 116–28 (February-July, 1912).]

9 Bishop, *op. cit.*, II, 358. Letter dated January [27], 1915.

10 [See Biographical Introduction, pp. 37–59.]

11 [John J. Leary, Jr., *Talks with T.R.* (1920), pp. 47–48.]

12 *New York Times,* December 19, 1915.

13 Gary was chairman of the Finance Committee of the Harvester Trust. Four out of six members of the Finance Committee of the International Harvester were also members of the Finance Committee of U.S. Steel. *Stanley Report,* p. 800.

14 For an account of Hughes' services to the Rockefeller interests while Secretary of State, see Ludwell Denny, *America Conquers Britain* (1930), pp. 20, 157, 227, 245, 276, 288, 291, 424. [I have cut Pinchot's lengthy quotations in connection with these citations.]

15 *Democratic Campaign Book* (1912), p. 224.

16 *Ibid.,* p. 229.

17 Henry Stoddard and many apologists for Roosevelt have argued that the latter's motive in permitting the Progressives to hold a convention in 1916, and in allowing them to believe that he would run if nominated by them alone, was not so much to effect his own nomination by the Republican party as to compel that party to name someone who would be aggressive on preparedness and favorable to our entry into the war. There may be a good deal in this, yet its force is weakened by the facts, first, that Roosevelt at a time when he did not expect to run himself favored the choice of Knox,* who was far from sharing his aggressive views on these two subjects; and, second: he later endorsed Hughes without reservations, although Hughes, as Roosevelt admitted in various letters, including one to Sir Edward Grey, was notably backward on the preparedness issue, lukewarm toward war, and had spared no pains in placating German-American sentiment.

* ". . . I told him I would do my best to get the Progressives to support Knox, if he were the man available [Note by T.R.: "But Knox has been defending hyphenated-Americanism lately in a way which if persisted in will make him as undesirable as Burton."]; that I did not think Knox had the proper understanding of our foreign questions; but that if he would put Root into the Secretaryship of State, I believe we would get a first-class administration, for while I am fairly certain the Progressives would under no circumstances support Root for President, I did not believe they would object (and I am certain they would have no right to object) to his being made Secretary of State." (*Letters of Roosevelt and Lodge,* II, 464, November 27, 1915.)

[18] It has been said by friends of Perkins that his activities in the Progressive party had no ulterior motive other than a desire to play a distinguished part and in case of a Roosevelt victory receive a place in the cabinet or an ambassadorship. Knowing Perkins as I did, I think too well of him to believe this was his object. His ideas, though not all liberal in essentials, were most earnestly held. He believed fanatically in the great mission of big business and was convinced, as I believe Gary was, of the necessity of protecting it from "mob attack" by bringing a party into power that would sympathize with its aims. He was not a selfish man and was in a sense a big man and an exceedingly able one, as evidenced by his meteoric rise from an insurance agent to president of a great insurance company, to partnership in the Morgan firm, to chairman of the Finance Committee of the Steel Corporation and successful organizer of the Harvester combination. Perkins was working, under Gary's less ingenuous leadership, for one aim, the safeguarding of the system of production and distribution which in his opinion had made America great, and to him the system was embodied in the Steel and Harvester corporations. That it was built on unfair privileges, and that it exploited the consumer, struck down independent initiative, concentrated power in a few hands, were, in his eyes, mere details, to be taken care of when the system itself, which was monopoly, had been made safe from attack.

[19] Bishop, *op. cit.,* II, 419.

[20] "Colonel Theodore Roosevelt formally entered the race for the nomination as president by the Republican and Progressive conventions at Chicago on June 7th, in a letter which he sent to Guy Emerson, secretary of the Roosevelt Non-Partisan League.

"Stripped of superfluous words, the Roosevelt letter means just that. The league was organized with the object of obtaining his nomination by a recognized party. Colonel Roosevelt says in so many words that he 'approves' of what the league is doing. . . . One sentence was considered especially significant as it was generally believed to refer to Justice Hughes, whom, according to many inspired stories, Roosevelt and the Progressive Party were ready to support. The sentence reads:—'I do not have to improvise my convictions on either Americanism or Preparedness. . . .' " (*New York Times,* May 12, 1916.)

[21] "Chicago . . . It is Roosevelt himself who is conducting this campaign. It will be his voice that is heard in the convention. He is not here in person, but Perkins, John W. McGrath and Oscar King Davis are in constant touch with him. . . . The Roosevelt leaders feel well satisfied with the effect their 'drive' has had so far. It has not brought the Old Guard one whit nearer to accepting Roosevelt as the presidential candi-

date, but it has had a notable effect in chastening the Old Guard's spirit and making it anxious to do almost anything that Roosevelt wants. At present the Old Guard is of the opinion that Hughes must be its candidate whether he will or not, but it would be useless to nominate Hughes if Roosevelt is not going to support him. Roosevelt will support him, however, and the Progressives will nominate him if the Republicans do. . . . It is the prettiest game of politics that has been played at any convention since that of 1888." (*New York Times,* June 3, 1916, p. 1.)

[22] [Henry L. Stoddard, *As I Knew Them* [,] *Presidents and Politics from Grant to Coolidge.* New York, 1927, p. 435.]

[33] Roosevelt frequently spoke to Gilson Gardner of the Scripps newspapers and John Leary of the *World* of his distrust of Hughes. At the end of the 1916 campaign, he referred in a conversation with Leary to the "self-respect I lost supporting Hughes." (Leary, *op. cit.,* p. 62.)

During the campaign he told Leary that the people looked upon Hughes as a "man without a policy. . . . It is his own fault. I told you he would have won even the German votes by preaching straight Americanism." *Ibid.,* [pp. 59–]60.)

Shortly after Hughes' nomination, says Leary, Roosevelt said to him: "Close contact with him (Hughes) doesn't make him more attractive for he is a very selfish, very self-centered man. . . . What these men (the newspaper correspondents) hate is his cowardice—his refusal to say anything, however right, that might jeopardize his chances." (*Ibid.,* pp. 53, [54].)

In a letter to James Bryce of the same period, Roosevelt speaks of Hughes as both un-American and pro-German. Hughes was "nominated largely in consequence of the German-Americans who were against me.[. . .]

"A nomination," continues Roosevelt, "made for such a cause is in my own judgment evidence of profound political immorality on the part of those making it." (Bishop, *op. cit.,* II, 413.)

[24] "Mr. Wilson and his party have in actual practice lamentably failed to safeguard the interest and honor of the United States. . . . They have dulled the moral sense of the people. They have taught us that peace, the peace of cowardice and dishonor and indifference to the welfare of others, is to be put above righteousness, above the stern and unflinching performance of duty, whether the duty is pleasant or unpleasant." (*Works of Theodore Roosevelt,* 1923–26, XIX, 575.)

[25] [Leary, *op. cit.,* pp. 2–3.]

CHAPTER VIII

¹ [See Appendix III.]

² [Conceivably Byron Webber Holt, 1857–1933: Not a Harvard professor but a financial writer and tariff expert. Editor of *Moody's Magazine* (financial), 1905–8. Author of *Export Prices to Date* (1906), pp. 1–16; compiler of *The Gold Supply and Prosperity* (1907); see particularly pp. v-xv, 193–257.]

³ [See Binder *Steel,* chap. "United States Steel."]

⁴ [See Binder *Steel,* chap. "United States Steel," pp. 1–108 and section "Roosevelt," pp. 135–42.]

INDEX

Addams, Jane, 33, 46, 182, 195, 258
Aldrich, N., 90, 100, 106, 107

Baker, R. S., 20, 24, 25
Ballinger, R. A., 52, 90, 100, 239
Ballinger-Pinchot case, 14–16, 30, 39, 90, 96, 102, 134, 149, 180, 237, 276–77
Bates, L., 43–44
Beveridge, A. J., 16, 19, 24, 29, 43, 45, 55, 58, 100–1, 107, 113, 115, 166, 179, 182, 194–96, 255
Big Business in America, 4, 76, 80
Boone and Crockett Club, 13, 240, 241
Booth, E., 8, 11
Borah, W., 160, 178, 212, 216, 227
Bourne, J., 24
Brandeis, L. D., 5, 16–17, 20, 22, 24, 40, 43, 60, 64, 78, 90, 92, 94–95, 103, 113, 121–22, 124, 131, 137, 156, 168, 175–77, 187, 193, 216, 238, 256–57, 261
Bristow, J. L., 43, 101, 107, 190
Bryan, W. J., 186, 187
Bryant, W. C., 8
Bryce, Lord, 76–77, 78

Cannon, J., 90
Carnegie Hall Meeting, Jan. 22, 1912, 26, 132

Glavis, L., 16, 101, 103, 238, 239
Godwin, P., 8

Hamilton, A., 40, 76, 120, 139
Hanna, D., 132
Hapgood, N., 5, 22, 29, 34, 35, 66, 68, 122, 238
Harding, W. G., 181, 242
Heney, F. J., 5, 21, 35, 43, 45–46, 49, 51, 57, 81, 123, 132, 179, 182, 187, 211
History of the Progressive Party, 3–5, 21, 27, 32, 37, 76, 79–80
Holmes, J. H., 64, 66, 72
Hopkins, J. A. H., 72
House, E., 59, 106, 121
Houser, W., 24–25, 122, 132, 134, 136–38, 151, 285
Howe, F. C., 68–69, 121
Hughes, C. E., 69, 216–17, 218, 220–25, 294

Ickes, H., 5, 44, 45, 81, 83
International Harvester Company, 33, 94, 167, 174, 178, 186, 188, 190, 194, 205–6, 211, 216–18, 250, 253, 257–59, 260–61

Jefferson, T., 40, 78, 120, 126, 172
Johnson, E., 8
Johnson, H., 29, 30, 35, 43, 45, 49, 51, 57, 83, 134–38, 141, 144, 145, 151, 154, 161, 164, 179, 182, 187, 221, 222, 258

Kent, W., 5, 21, 22, 24, 32, 66, 119, 122 131, 149, 155
Kirchwey, G., 46
Knox, Philander, 175, 218

La Follette, Fola, 32
La Follette, R. M., 4, 16, 19, 20–29, 40, 60, 64, 66, 70, 71, 73–75, 78, 79, 89, 98, 101, 105, 107, 113, 115, 121–30, 131–39, 148–57, 176, 200, 222, 244
Leary, J., 214, 225
Lenroot, I., 122, 131, 136, 138
Lewis, W. D., 52, 123, 177, 188, 197
Lincoln, A., 78, 116, 120, 145, 166, 184, 191, 198, 212

Perkins, G. W., 6, 33, 36–37, 39–40, 42–47, 49–57, 60, 69, 93, 95, 97–98, 117, 122, 133, 140, 146, 149, 155, 159, 162, 165–66, 169, 173–74, 177–79, 183, 184–221, 224, 249–63, 289–91, 293

Pinchot, Amos: education, 11–12; supports La Follette, 21–28; supports Theodore Roosevelt, 28–37; opposes George Perkins, 38–59; supports labor, 62–63; *The Masses,* 65–68; supports Wilson, 68–70; Committee of 48, 72–76; support of and break with F. D. Roosevelt, 80–83; Committee on Constitutional Government, 83; America First Committee, 84; death, 84; *History of the Progressive Party,* 89–231

Pinchot, Antoinette, 10, 13, 59

Pinchot, C. D. C., 10

Pinchot, G., 6, 10–15, 19, 21, 24–30, 35, 36, 45–56, 78–80, 90, 91, 100, 101, 108, 109, 113–15, 117, 119–21, 131, 140, 141, 144, 153, 161, 182, 187, 195, 198, 199, 203, 209, 211, 235–39

Pinchot, J. W., 8, 11

Pinchot, Mrs. J. W. (Mary Eno), 9, 11, 53

Pinchot-Ballinger controversy, *see* Ballinger-Pinchot case

"President Taft—Candidate for Re-election," 30

Price, O. W., 52, 101, 237

Progressive Conference, La Salle Hotel, Oct. 1911, 23, 24, 122

Pueblo Iron and Fuel Company, 194

Record, G. L., 5, 17, 24, 41, 45–47, 52, 57, 64, 72, 74–75, 78, 81, 95, 121–22, 135–36, 138 161

Reed J., 65–66

Republican National Convention, 1912, 31, 32, 98, 159–63

Robins, R., 45, 54, 55, 179, 219–20

Roe, G., 21, 66, 134, 136, 138

Rogers, W., 132, 136, 138

Roosevelt, F. D., 3, 80, 81–83, 84

Roosevelt, T., 4, 6, 7, 13–15, 17, 20, 21, 23–35, 39, 40, 42–47, 49, 51, 54–57, 69, 79, 89–91, 93, 94, 96, 98–100, 102–3, 105, 107, 109–21, 123–26, 131, 138–57, 159, 160–62, 164–66, 169–231, 235, 237, 239, 240, 244–46, 255, 258, 278

Root, E., 18, 98, 103, 107, 108, 117, 146, 153, 156, 161, 163, 164, 167, 175, 217, 218, 237, 238, 242

Rowell, C., 24, 36, 190

Rublee, G., 16, 273

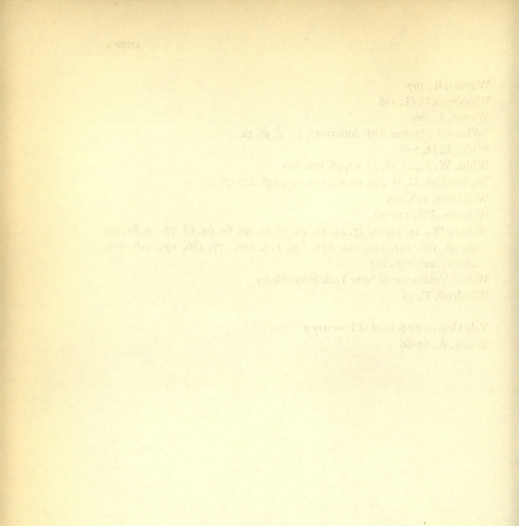